Comparative Perspectives on the Psalms

Comparative Perspectives on the *Psalms*

Essays on the Psalms—Volume 3

Erhard S. Gerstenberger

EDITED BY

K. C. Hanson

CASCADE Books • Eugene, Oregon

COMPARATIVE PERSPECTIVES ON THE PSALMS
Essays on the Psalms, Volume 3

Copyright © 2025 Erhard S. Gerstenberger. All rights reserved. Except for brief quotations in critical publications or reviews, no part of this book may be reproduced in any manner without prior written permission from the publisher. Write: Permissions, Wipf and Stock Publishers, 199 W. 8th Ave., Suite 3, Eugene, OR 97401.

Cascade Books
An Imprint of Wipf and Stock Publishers
199 W. 8th Ave., Suite 3
Eugene, OR 97401

www.wipfandstock.com

PAPERBACK ISBN: 978-1-6667-4084-4
HARDCOVER ISBN: 978-1-6667-4085-1
EBOOK ISBN: 978-1-6667-4086-8

Cataloguing-in-Publication data:

Names: Gerstenberger, Erhard S. (2023–1932) author. | Hanson, K. C. (Kenneth Charles), 1951–, editor.

Title: Comparative perspectives on the Psalms : essays on the Psalms, volume 3 / Erhard S. Gerstenberger ; edited by K. C. Hanson.

Description: Eugene, OR: Cascade Books, 2025. | Includes bibliographical references and indexes.

Identifiers: ISBN 978-1-6667-4084-4 (paperback). | ISBN 978-1-6667-4085-1 (hardcover). | ISBN 978-1-6667-4086-8 (ebook).

Subjects: LCSH: Bible. O.T. Psalms—Criticism, interpretation, etc. | Bible. O.T.—Criticism, interpretation, etc. | Prayer—Biblical teaching. | Bible—Prayers. | Sumerian rites and ceremonies. | Navajo Indians—Arizona—Music. | Assyro-Babylonian prayers.

Classification: BS1430.2 G47 2025 (print). | BS1430.2 (epub).

10/17/25

Unless otherwise noted, Scripture quotations are from the New Revised Standard Version of the Bible, copyright 1989 by the Division of Christian Education of the National Council of Churches of Christ in the USA and used by permission.

Contents

Editor's Foreword by K. C. Hanson | vii

Acknowledgments | ix

List of Abbreviations | xi

1 The Dynamics of Praise in the Ancient Near East, or Poetry and Politics | 1

2 The Power of Praise in the Psalter: Human–Divine Synergies in the Ancient Near East and the Hebrew Scriptures | 11

3 Praise in the Realm of Death: The Dynamics of Hymn-Singing in Ancient Near Eastern Lament Ceremony | 28

4 "World Dominion" in Yahweh Kinship Psalms: Down to the Roots of Globalizing Concepts and Strategies | 39

5 Psalms and Sumerian Hymns | 56

6 Navajo Chants, Babylonian Incantations, Old Testament Psalms: A Comparative Study of Healing Rituals | 66

7 Singing a New Song: On Old Testament and Latin American Psalmody | 93

8 Enemies and Evildoers in the Psalms: A Challenge to Christian Preaching | 109

9 Delight in the Torah: The Book of Psalms | 123

10 Psalms in the Book of the Twelve: How Misplaced Are They? | 150

Bibliography | 169

Index of Authors | 183

Index of Ancient Documents | 187

Editor's Foreword

THIS VOLUME IS THE third and final collection of essays on the book of Psalms and related lyric literature by Erhard S. Gerstenberger. Volume 1 is titled *Charting the Course of Psalms Research* (2022). Volume 2 is titled *Praise and Petition in the Old Testament* (2024).

In this volume, Gerstenberger demonstrates not only his great exegetical skills but also the importance of comparative perspectives. Early in his career, he went to Navajo reservations in the Southwest to learn about their prayers, healing, and song traditions. He also first studied Akkadian and Sumerian both in graduate school and while he was teaching at Yale University. Engaging the Mesopotamian literature shows up in his published *Habilitationsschrift* in 1980, *Der bittende Mensch: Bittritual und Klagelied des Einzelnen im Alten Testament* (The Petitioning Person: Petition Rituals and Complaint Songs of the Individual in the Old Testament). But after retirement, he completed another PhD in Sumerian at the University of Marburg, publishing his dissertation in 2018: *Theologie des Lobens in Sumerischen Hymnen* (Theology of Praise in Sumerian Hymns). Gerstenberger's various studies demonstrate the importance of paying attention not only to texts, but also to traditions of ritual and music.

I appreciated getting to know Prof. Gerstenberger, first through his publications, but, beginning in 1999, personally through our meetings both in Germany and in the US.

He died on April 15, 2023. I miss both his depth of knowledge, but also his kindness and friendship.

Lastly, I am very grateful to Dr. Björn Gerstenberger for his willingness to correct the proofs.

K. C. Hanson

July 31, 2025

Acknowledgments

THE AUTHOR AND PUBLISHER gratefully acknowledge the earlier publications of these essays and permission from the original publishers.

Chapter 1: "The Dynamics of Praise in the Ancient Near East: Or, Poetry and Politics" was first published in *The Shape and Shaping of the Book of Psalms: The Current State of Scholarship*, edited by Nancy L. deClaissé-Walford, 27–39. Ancient Israel and Its Literature 20. Atlanta: SBL Press, 2014.

Chapter 2: "The Power of Praise in the Psalter: Human–Divine Synergies in the Ancient Near East and the Hebrew Scriptures" was first published in *Between Israelite Religion and Old Testament Theology: Essays on Archaeology, History, and Hermeneutics*, edited by Robert D. Miller II, 31–48. Contributions to Biblical Exegesis and Theology 80. Leuven: Peeters, 2016.

Chapter 3: "Praise in the Realm of Death: The Dynamics of Hymn-Singing in Ancient Near Eastern Lament Ceremony" was first published in *Lamentations in Ancient and Contemporary Cultural Contexts*, edited by Nancy C. Lee and Carleen Mandolfo, 115–24. SBL Symposium Series 43. Atlanta: SBL Press, 2008.

Chapter 4: "'World Dominion' in Yahweh Kingship Psalms: Down to the Roots of Globalizing Concepts and Strategies" was first published in *Horizons in Biblical Theology* 23 (2001) 192–210.

Chapter 5: "The Psalms and Sumerian Hymns" was first published in *Jewish and Christian Approaches to the Psalms: Conflict and Convergence*, edited by Susan Gillingham, 229–39. Oxford: Oxford University Press, 2013.

Chapter 6: "Navajo Chants, Babylonian Incantations, Old Testament Psalms: A Comparative Study of Healing Rituals" was first published in *Intégrité* 17 (2018) 16–36.

Chapter 7: "Singing a New Song: On Old Testament and Latin American Psalmody" was first published in *Word & World* 5 (1985) 155–67.

Chapter 8: "Enemies and Evildoers in the Psalms: A Challenge to Christian Preaching" was first published in *Horizons in Biblical Theology* 4 (1983) 61–77.

Chapter 9: "Delight in Torah: The Book of Psalms" was first published in *Biblische Notizen* 191 (2021) 3–29.

Chapter 10: "Psalms in the Book of the Twelve: How Misplaced Are They?" was first published in *Thematic Threads in the Book of the Twelve*, edited by Paul L. Redditt and Aaron Schart, 90–103. BZAW 325. Berlin: de Gruyter, 2003.

Abbreviations

AOAT	Alter Orient und Altes Testament
BH	Biblia Hebraica
BZAW	Beihefte zur Zeitschrift für die Alttestamentliche Wissenschaft
ED	editor's note
ET	English translation
ETCSL	The Electronic Text Corpus of Sumerian Literature. Edited by Jeremy Black. Oxford, 1996–2007
FOTL	The Forms of the Old Testament Literature
FRLANT	Forschungen zur Religion und Literatur des Alten und Neuen Testaments
JSOTSup	Journal for the Study of the Old Testament Supplement Series
l./ll.	line/s
LXX	Septuagint
MT	Masoretic text
NRSV	New Revised Standard Version
OBO	Orbis Biblicus et Orientalis
OT	Old Testament
RIMA	Royal Inscriptions of Mesopotamia: Assyrian Periods

TDOT	*Theological Dictionary of the Old Testament.* Edited by G. Johannes Botterweck, Helmer Ringgren, and Heinz-Josef Fabray. 17 vols. Translated by David E. Green et al. Grand Rapids: Eerdmans, 1974–2021
THAT	*Theologisches* Handwörterbuch *zum Alten Testament.* Edited by Ernst Jenni and Claus Westermann. 2 vols. Munich: Kaiser, 1971–1976
trans.	translated
TWAT	*Theologisches Wörterbuch zum Alten Testament.* Edited by G. Johannes Botterweck, Helmer Ringgren, and Heinz-Josef Fabray. 10 vols. Stuttgart: Kohlhammer, 1973–2015
WMANT	Wissenschaftliche Monographien zum Alten und Neuen Testament
ZAW	*Zeitschrift für die alttestamentliche Wissenschaft*

1

The Dynamics of Praise in the Ancient Near East, or Poetry and Politics

Just as general anthropologists have a hard time intelligently defining the nature of human beings, various specialists in human speech have been challenged by an intrinsic exigency to understand and describe the essence of human vocal or verbal articulation and communication. Should we regard language as the unique divine gift that elevates humans above all other creatures? Can it be seen as the prime vehicle of interpersonal or intergroup communication? Is it perhaps only one type of countless systems of participation, be it in the physical, chemical, or organic world, a functional array of sounds, melodies, signifiers transporting information from sender to recipient, whatever they may be? The answers greatly depend on basic assumptions such as whether or not we consider human beings a supreme species *sui generis*, separated from the rest of being by power and glory. But are they really the "crown" or climax of creation? Does language *per se* belong to the metaphysical realm rather than to real and earthly existence?[1]

Poetic language certainly occupies a rank of its own among modes of verbal expression. Form, style, structure, and contents of cultivated verbal articulation do indicate "higher" levels of organization and meaning. Solemnity and emotion permeate pieces of poetry. Is the distinction of "low" day-to-day speech and "high" poetic articulation sufficient? Ought we to consider the contexts and functions of communication as well? Where are

---

1. "What or who are human beings?" is a central question that has been agitating thinking minds from the very beginning of reasoning, probably some hundreds of thousands of years ago. This innate quest for meaning also produced whole libraries in the past centuries; see only Wendt and Loacker, eds., *Kindlers Enzyklopädie: Der Mensch*.

the dividing lines between those ways of expression, and how do we adequately define each of them?[2]

Archaic Utterances of Praise

Just to remind ourselves of our prehistoric roots: Primitive exclamations in archaic guise, shouts of jubilation, outbreaks of joy and awe may be surmised to head the continuous tradition in all cultures of human praise expressions.[3] Short formulas, probably a heritage of preliterate epochs, abound even in much later literature; they appear like ancient rocks in the stream of eulogies directed to divine forces: Sumerian[4] *zà-mí ᵈNN*, "praise [noun!] to the God NN," *zà-mí-zu dùg-ga*, "your praise is splendid" are the earliest extant examples. Hebrew[5] *halĕlûyāh*, "extol [imperative!] Yahweh" *mĕhullāl yhwh*, "to be praised is Yahweh," *bārûk yhwh*, "blessed be Yahweh," follow at the end of the line. In between we may find similar formulas in Akkadian, Egyptian, Hittite, Ugaritic, and other ancient Near Eastern literature. Arabic "Allah is the greatest" (*allāhu akbar*) and other shouts are still used today in Islamic rituals. All these exclamations really are hymns in a nutshell, often condensed expressions of power. They already may tell us about the complex texture of praise in terms of its psychology, ritual fiber, and social setting. Furthermore, archaic shouts of praise, awe, glorification, enhancement, etc., still virulent in various contexts, may definitely alert us to the fact that praise is not only an aesthetic or stylistic speech form, with possible theological implications, but a real primordial force not to be tamed by modern interpretations.[6]

In historic times praise to the gods was couched in intricate oral and literary poetry (lyrical rhetoric). These artful compositions could appear and be handed down only after the invention of adequate writing systems

---

2. Poetic Hebrew language has always been a choice object of Old Testament scholars. See Berlin, "Poetry, Hebrew Bible." The express reference point of the SBL working group session in which this paper was presented was P. D. Miller's probe into "The Theological Significance of Poetry."

3. See Gunkel and Begrich, *Einleitung*, 37–38 [ET *Introduction*, 26]; Bowra, *Primitive Song*, 57–64 ("emotive sounds" precede poetic songs).

4. Sumerian is the oldest written language known thus far. The largest collection of Sumerian literary texts is ETCSL (Electronic Text Corpus of Sumerian Literature), encompassing about four hundred individual texts. They are freely available in transliteration and English translation at http://etcsl.orinst.ox.ac.uk.

5. See Ringgren, "*hll* I und II."

6. See Bowra, *Primitive Song*; Elliott, "Toward a Grammar of Exclamatives"; Rosengren, "Zur Grammatik und Pragmatik der Exklamation."

(ca. 2600 BCE). Cuneiform tablets found in Mesopotamia and other neighboring regions covering a period of more than two millennia constitute the first human written literature and demonstrate the level of literary achievement.[7] A special rhetoric of praise is already in full swing including a wide range of characteristics: terminology, metaphors, style, structure, and so on. We can probe only into very limited sections of this spectrum. And we have to keep in mind that verbal articulations are only vehicles of that internal or concomitant dynamic of theological rhetoric we are really looking for. The main questions are, why religious communication uses such special or "high" forms of linguistic expressions, and what makes poetic language suitable for dialogue with gods.

Motivations, Affects, Linguistic Form

Hymnic speech-forms in the Hebrew Scriptures first were investigated by Robert Lowth (1753) and Johann Gottfried Herder (1782), among others. Later, Hermann Gunkel and Sigmund Mowinckel took up their heritage.[8] Disciples of these scholars have enlarged and modified their research over the decades. Other literary and ritual experts have joined in and there have been harvested during the past century good amounts of insights.

There is a considerable range of verbal and nominal expressions connoting "praise" in all the ancient oriental languages. Starting with Sumerian, that millenary liturgical language, and moving to Akkadian and Hebrew (a glance at Hittite, Egyptian, and others, would be useful but is left aside at this point), we may marvel at the rich heritage of meaning. We list some main verbs and nouns: **Hebrew**—*hll* [piel]; *ydh*; *brk* [qal; piel]; *gdl* [piel]; *rûm* [pil]; *šbḥ* [piel]; *yd* [hiphil]; *ngd* [hiphil]; *šir*; *zmr* [piel]; *šlm* [piel]; *'dr* [hiphil]; *p'r* [hiphil]; *rnn*; *pṣḥ*; *shl*; **Sumerian**—*zà-mí* ("praise"), *ar* ("to praise"), *meteš* ("eulogy"), *šir* ("to sing; song"); **Akkadian**—*dalalu* ("venerate"); *nâdu* and *elû* D ("extol"); *karābu* ("greet reverently"); *alālu* ("sing joyfully"); *zakāru* ("mention with praise"); *šurbû* ("enlarge"); *šurruḫu* ("praise"). Ugaritic, Syriac, and Arabic, to name only a few more Semitic languages, all show a similar vocabulary of praise. The examples adduced above betray a wide variety of connotations and emotive involvements. Noteworthy are ties to music, singing, instruments, to the tensions and grades of power between adorer and adored, and to the intention to lift up, enhance, and magnify the deities.

---

7. See Black, *Reading Sumerian Poetry*; Vogelzang and Vanstiphout, eds., *Mesopotamian Poetic Language*.

8. Gunkel and Begrich, *Einleitung* [ET *Introduction*]; Mowinckel, *Psalmenstudien* [ET *Psalm Studies*]; Mowinckel, *The Psalms in Israel's Worship*.

Attributions of power, majesty, and sovereignty to higher beings are so natural in praise language that we need not actually specify them.[9] But it is noteworthy that metaphors, similes, and comparisons abound in this rhetoric. The addressed ones are likened to, identified with, or brought into close contact with the animal kingdom (lions, bulls, dragons), weather phenomena (storms, floods, thunder), celestial potencies (light, radiance, beauty), war and battle insignias (weapons, prowess, revenge), universal order (justice, equity, castigation), and life-generative forces (fertility, wholesomeness, prosperity). Throughout the history of tradition there have occurred modulations of the praise attributes. What counts more, however, is the basic continuity of this "spiritual iconography" so that we may give examples from the Old Testament which is, in a sense, the last receiving link in the age-old Near Eastern chain of eulogy.

Yahweh in particular is eulogized by images of glory, majesty, and power, which are "perhaps the essence of poetry," but also in very anthropomorphic ways.[10] Human occupations symbolically serve to describe God: He is "King," "Sovereign," "Warrior," "Craftsman," "Judge," "Avenger," "Shepherd," and "Farmer,"[11] and possibly "Midwife," "Spouse," "Mother," and "Wailing Woman." Animal metaphors for Yahweh in the Bible include "Eagle," "Lion," "Bird," "Bear," and "Moth."[12] Gunkel paints a euphoric picture of Old Israel's praise in the Psalms.[13] He dares to affirm "that the hymns let transpire the objective side of religion, namely Yahweh himself, his qualities and actions."[14] Here we actually meet a deep theological appreciation of Old Testament praise rhetoric.

Structural and stylistic means constituting ancient poetic languages, especially praise rhetoric, are manifold and by no means translucent as yet.[15]

---

9. See Gunkel and Begrich, *Einleitung*, 42–71 [ET *Introduction*, 29–49]. Some basic forms of direct praise may have been: "God is great (majestic; powerful)," with the response "you are great" (e.g., Pss 24:8; 48:2; 62:12; 77:14; 104:1; 138:5–6), and "God has performed marvelous deeds" or, with direct address, "You have...": (Pss 40:6; 74:13–15; 77:15; 92:6; 126:2–3). As Gunkel and Begrich (*Einleitung/Introduction*) prove, there is a rich variety of formulations in the Psalter. See also, e.g., Westermann, *Praise and Lament in the Psalms*; P. D. Miller, *They Cried to the Lord*, 178–232; and Brueggemann, *Israel's Praise: Doxology against Idolatry and Ideology*.

10. Alonso Schökel, *A Manual of Hebrew Poetics*, 95, 128–29: Human qualities are also named, such as faithfulness, justice, etc.

11. Alonso Schökel, *A Manual of Hebrew Poetics*, 137–38.

12. Alonso Schökel, *A Manual of Hebrew Poetics*, 138.

13. See Gunkel and Begrich, *Einleitung*, 71–83 [ET *Introduction*, 49–57].

14. Gunkel and Begrich, *Einleitung*, 71 [ET *Introduction*, 49].

15. Poetological studies in the different literatures of the Ancient Near East are not numerous. See Groneberg, *Syntax, Morphologie, und Stil der jungbabylonischen*

The technical details of poetic language will not lead us much further individually, but in aggregate they reveal the possibilities of human mind and art to approach borderlines of existence in terms of space and time. Praise language in particular stretches out into the past, wrestles with reality by acknowledging accomplishments, grasping actuality and probing into the future, and in all these regards also tries to mold reality according to desired well-being, peace, and justice.

The specific problems, for example, of the oldest poetic literature in Mesopotamia, the "verbal art of these long lost civilizations"[16] are only beginning to be discussed by experts.[17] Some facts, however, are obvious: Poetic language, used in various settings, in its written form is line-bound (i.e., is normally fixed in cuneiform lines). It possesses a wide range of vocabulary and structural forms, is highly figurative, and sometimes creates its own grammatical rules or even a complete (artificial?) language, like Emesal ("light/high [women's] language") in Sumerian.[18] Still, according to some Sumerologists and biblical exegetes, the borderline between prose and poetry is in constant flux. There is an "alternating movement of descent and ascent" in discourse, and "purism is a symptom of decadence" according to Luis Alonso Schökel.[19] Furthermore, many scholars stress the intimate yet little researched liaison of poetic literary speech forms with oral performance of the texts. "The rhythm and patterns of the poetry went hand in glove with musical expression," states Michalowski.[20] Language, as it were, is embedded in action, behavior, ritual, music. It is neither self-sustainable nor self-sustaining.

"hymnischen" Literatur; Alonso Schökel, *A Manual of Hebrew Poetics*.

16. Michalowski, "Ancient Poetics," 141. This is a clear warning *to overestimate* the texts that were written down for "vocal expression." "The voice was an integral part of the text" (144). See also Jeremy Black, "Poesie/Poetry," 196. According to him, all poetry "was performed aloud," some with musical accompaniment, some in ceremonial contexts.

17. See Black, *Reading Sumerian Poetry*; Black, "Poesie/Poetry"; Michalowski, "Ancient Poetics"; Groneberg, *Syntax, Morphologie*; Vogelzang and Vanstiphout, eds., *Mesopotamian Poetic Language*; Wilcke, "Formale Gesichtspunkte in der sumerischen Literatur."

18. See Black, "Poesie/Poetry"; Michalowski, "Ancient Poetics."

19. Alonso Schökel, *A Manual of Hebrew Poetics*, 19.

20. Michalowski, "Ancient Poetics."

The Power of Praise

A close reading of any ancient Near Eastern hymnic text, including Old Testament praise poetry, will invariably reveal that our present day conceptions of "eulogy," "praise," "hymn," "laudation," and so on, do not completely coincide with the related ancient notions, a fact that should be considered normal in every cross-cultural comparison. What is more significant is a possible basic divergence in theological ideas ancient and modern. Such a chasm would place the Bible into the realm of antique views in contrast to our present so-called "modern" perspectives. The other way around might indicate that "archaic" notions of power transfer are still clandestinely present even today, against our dogmatic convictions, in real performances of collective praise.

Looking at Old Testament hymns, we sometimes are struck by a solidly "materialistic" and "dynamistic" understanding of praise. Psalm 29:1–2 summons the "divine beings" to "give, deliver"[21] "glory and power" to Yahweh (just as "clans of the nations" are supposed to do in Ps 96:7), a phrase reminiscent also of Ps 19:2, where "the heavens tell the glory of God and the firmament announces his handiwork." The result of a laborious attribution of "glory and power" is, among other aspects, the construction of a firm throne that Yahweh needs for his universal government (Ps 22:4).[22] Enigmatic Ps 8:3, asserting something like the establishment of "power" by the "mouth of babes," may belong in this context.[23] Significantly, in a universal perspective, the supreme heavenly deity does insist on eulogies from the whole of creation (cf. Ps 148). Especially the primeval forces, overcome by the creator, have to extol the victorious God by clapping their hands (cf. Pss 93:3–4; 98:8; the empowering function of "applause" in contemporary societies comes to mind); thus they possibly lend their strength to him. Human praise in some texts apparently acquires an automatic dynamic when, for instance, the levitical singers defeat the enemies by their hymns alone (2 Chr 20:22) or faithful Yahweh-believers are saved by their sacred songs (Dan 3 with LXX additions). The spectrum of verbs, already mentioned, which instill praising affirmations with the sense of "enhancing, enlarging, empowering" the name or majesty of God supports this notion, notably *gdl*,

---

21. The word *hābû*, imperative of an unattested verb *yhb*, "to give" is neglected by two important theological dictionaries (*THAT* and *TWAT*).

22. The grammatical construction *yôšēb těhillôt*, "the sitter of praise songs" is not quite clear; however, see Gunkel and Begrich, *Einleitung*, 95 (emendation of text) [ET *Introduction*, 66]; Hossfeld and Zenger, *Die Psalmen 1–50*.

23. The interpretation of Ps 8 is difficult, especially as far as v. 3 is concerned (cf. Joel 2:16).

rum, and so on. Various other positive or negative expressions shed light on the dynamics of praise:

> I looked, but there was no helper;
>> I stared, but there was no one to sustain me;
>
> so my own arm brought me victory,
>> and my wrath sustained me. (Isa 63:5; cf. 59:16)

The absence of support for Yahweh is contrasted by numerous implicit assertions to keep up with his praise and thus contribute to God's will and ability to help:

> I will bless Yahweh at all times;
>> his praise shall continually be in my mouth...
>
> O magnify Yahweh with me,
>> and let us exalt his name together. (Ps 34:2, 4)

It seems that the worshippers of Yahweh, be they human or of other nature, by praising Yahweh not only motivate him to take action but also contribute to him essential power for his activity. Just as the human monarch gains strength by acknowledgment and veneration bestowed on him by his subjects, ancient gods thrive on the laudatory songs of their worshippers (cf. "Sing to Yahweh a new song," Pss 33:3; 96:1; 98:1; 144:9; 149:1; Isa 42:10; "blessed/praised"[24] be Yahweh," Pss 28:6; 31:22; 41:14; 66:20; 68:20, 36; 72:18, 19; 89:53, etc.). Praise of God is not only a grateful and overwhelming acknowledgment of majesty and graciousness but, even more, a creative act of generating those beneficial forces and transferring them to the deity, or offering them as due tribute.

This impression is strengthened by looking at Mesopotamian hymns and the functioning of their praise capacity. Most of all, Sumerian praise songs, dominating cultic ceremonies for more than a full millennium even after the language had given way in daily and worldly affairs to Akkadian idioms (around 2000 BCE), give us vivid pictures of gods *receiving* eulogies and they themselves *spending* good words, destinies, and blessings on each other and on terrestrial entities, human as well as natural, religious, or cultural phenomena. Along this vein we meet, for instance, in one of the most ancient hymns, Enlil speaking "in praise" (*zà-mí*) of Keš, thus

---

24. There is a fundamental discussion about an alleged "magic" force of the *bārûk*-formula. See Scharbert, *TWAT* 1:817; Aitken, *The Semantics of Blessing and Cursing in Ancient Hebrew*; Leuenberger, *Segen und Segenstheologien im alten Israel*.

attributing divine powers to the temple.[25] The high priestess of Inana, in a famous poem (ETCSL 4.07.2, ll. 60–65) recites a holy praise song which is tantamount to enumerating and fortifying the divine powers of the goddess (= ME). Šulgi, second king of the Ur III-dynasty, places great emphasis on hymn singing on his own behalf; he craftily indulges in the specific genre of "self-praise." One of his texts (Šulgi E, ETCSL 2.4.2.05) urges posterity not to forget those strengthening cultic performances in order to keep up the king's name and existence. In short, there is a very broad testimony in the corpus of Sumerian praise songs, as well as in later ancient Near Eastern specimens of praise texts, of the vital part they played in the upkeep of the good world order, natural as well as just societal processes, or let us say, life and history on earth. Hymn singing sustains all beings, conferring strength to everything and everybody in need of it. Small wonder that hymns in the Sumerian tradition are very much aligned with or directed to those divine powers (ME) that permeate the whole universe and which, strangely for us to acknowledge, are not identical with personalized divinities. The ME can work on their own, although they are also considered "properties" of deities, temples, and possibly kings. They may be conferred from one to other entities, and they even can be given away or stolen from their holders, as the mythical story of Inana and Enki (ETCSL 1.3.1) shows. But if we look closely at the Bible, we may discover traces of similar impersonal forces such as "Justice," "Truth," "Wisdom," and so on (Pss 36:6–7; 43:3; 85:11–12; 89:15; 117:2) in our scriptures.

Recognition of competing powers everywhere in the existing world, which may be influenced by strong and determined expressions of powerful praise after and beside the Sumerian example, can be followed through the history of Mesopotamian psalm singing.[26] Old Testament hymns take part in the Mesopotamian, Levantine, and Egyptian traditions, as past research has proven many times.[27] It may be affirmed also for the hymnic genres, therefore, what Aitken proposes for blessing and curse: "Words are power-laden," not *per se*, but because of the semantic conventions in which they are embedded.[28] The decisive difference which we may discover in the ancient

---

25. ETCSL 4.80.2 l. 9.

26. Groneberg, for example, has collected Neo-Babylonian materials (cf. Groneberg, *Syntax, Morphologie und Stil*). She distinguishes between "incantations," "sacral lyrics" (being of private, edifying nature), "cult hymns," and "narrative literature." Sacral lyrics are her field of investigation.

27. In a model kind of elaboration P. D. Miller (*They Cried to the Lord*), has demonstrated the close relationship of Israel's prayers to ancient Near Eastern supplication and praise. He cites many relevant studies pointing in exactly this direction.

28. Aitken, *The Semantics of Blessing and Cursing in Ancient Hebrew*, 21.

Near Eastern texts may be exactly the one hinted at before: hymnic language of old may not (as in our Western protestant theological perception) open up a binary rift between divine and human being—in fostering poetic, conceptual, theological, or intellectual juxtapositions—but rather may emphasize the unity of all existence and a common responsibility for order and justice by recognizing participation of all agents in the universal power play. Synergism, so much abhorred in Christian doctrine, was natural to old Mesopotamians and probably also to most Old Testament witnesses. Yahweh's words, deeds, bodily parts, and properties, after all, are in many texts of the Hebrew Bible agents in their own rights (see his "arms," "hands," "utterances," "love," "justice," "glory," "presence," "face," "wings," "angel (messenger)," "wrath," "dwelling," "authority," "strength," "plan," "foresight," "commandment," "aura," "house," etc.).

Conclusions

Poetic language in the ancient Mesopotamian world, as a refined means of articulation, is not content with descriptive and ordering speech; it always approaches borderlines of world interpretation penetrating into the mechanisms of all human and transhuman affairs. Praise rhetoric, in particular, visualizes the world in flux. It recognizes leading global players, known and unknown, personal or impersonal, which must be identified in their responsibilities. By enhancing the positive powers of the acting agents, the laudations presented to them in high moods of festive joy and awe, supported by music (and sacrifices?), praise oratory becomes a meaningful part of promoting world order and well-being of people and environments. It seems less the innate capacity of verbal expressions that makes poetic praise language a suitable receptacle for powerful action, but the creative, ceremonial enactment of laudation resounding in human religious history that forms and transforms the world.

In this fashion, cultic laudation is more than an aesthetic performance or an expression of theological exuberance, more also than a thanksgiving response to God's actions. Gerhard von Rad had a wonderful notion that Israel's hymnic praise was considered continually necessary for the upkeep of wholesome and blessed life.[29] What we may add and perhaps modify in

---

29. See von Rad, *Theologie des Alten Testaments*, 1:353–54 [ET *Old Testament Theology*, vol. 1]: "Unceasingly Israel gave praise to Yahweh. That late period which finally nominated the Psalter in Hebrew '*tehillim*,' even comprehended the whole supplicatory discourse of Israel including numerous complaints and laments and those didactically meditating psalms as one single, multi-voiced eulogy of Yahweh." And see 359: "Creation and sustenance of the world by Yahweh certainly was one of the noblest topics

this concept of "hymnic necessity" is on the one hand the fact that Israel was fully embedded in and taken along by the broad stream of ancient Near Eastern traditions of singing praises to the agents of power. The other insight may be that, together with other hymnologies, Old Testament praise rhetoric is based on what is, from our perspective, quite an unorthodox concept of God and humanity. Even the most high deity is deeply entangled with all the active forces in this world, including nature and human beings, rivers, earth, and beasts. They, too, it seems to be expected, should step in to articulate, implement, and promote the generative dominion of the benign forces for all beings. The adequacy of poetic communication with the Divine is neither questioned, nor analyzed, nor reflected upon. It is taken for granted and practiced in jubilant songs.

Letting go of idealistic bifurcations of being, we may say that poetry, especially of the hymnic types, propels history to the better. As Natan Sznaider, a sociologist in Tel Aviv, Israel, states, referring to a German expressionist writer: "Paul Celan called a poem once a 'bottled message, to be posted in perils of drowning, hopefully to be carried to the heart-soulland.' 'Poems,' continues Celan, 'are also on their way in this fashion: They are aiming at something. What are they aiming at? At something receptive, something to be occupied, maybe at an open minded You, or a sensitive reality.'"[30]

---

in Old Testament hymns, but surely not their last word. Singing praises included still another special knowledge about this world. Because it has been created by Yahweh so miraculously and is wondrously sustained by him, the world possesses such a glory, that it radiates all by itself praise and testimony; in other words: The world is not only an object of laudation but a performing subject as well."

30. Sznaider, "Das moralische Gefühl," 32. Translated by E. S. Gerstenberger.

2

The Power of Praise in the Psalter

*Human–Divine Synergies in the Ancient Near East
and the Hebrew Scriptures*

Hymns and Their Dynamics: Anthropology of Divine Works

GERHARD VON RAD, EMINENT Old Testament theologian of the past century, put hymnic praise as the first and foremost answer of Yahweh-believers over against the saving acts of their God.[1] His understanding of praise was wide and deep: Eulogies comprised unconditional acknowledgment of Yahweh's deeds in nature and history, recognition of cosmic agitation (cf. Ps 19A), absorption in theophanic beauty, articulation of potent human life.[2] The question to be asked in the light of Old Testament and Ancient Near Eastern evidence is this: Is that circumscription exhaustive or are there perhaps other ingredients visible in the old liturgical exaltations of the divine? Some OT observations should alert us to the possibility that praise may be a force all by itself emitted to build up or preserve the status of the addressed one.

There are, indeed, a number of passages and incidents in the Hebrew Scriptures which may point into that direction. Twice in the Psalter superhuman beings viz. all the nations are challenged to "bring to Yahweh glory and strength, bring to Yahweh the glory due to his name" (*kabod wa'oz / kebod šemo*, Pss 29:1–2; 96:7–8 = 1 Chr 16:28–29). Save for the entities called upon the wording is exactly the same in both psalms. The three-partite formula

---

1. Von Rad, *Theologie*, 1:353–67 [ET *Old Testament Theology*, vol. 1].

2. Von Rad, *Theologie*, 1:367. "To praise is the form of existence most appropriate of human beings. To praise and not to praise are opposing each other like Life and Death."

does sound like a liturgical shout. Its verb (*yahab*, "give," "bring") occurs mostly in imperative forms and has a strongly demanding tone (cf. Gen 29:21; 30:1; 47:15–16; Pss 60:13; 108:13; 1 Sam 14:41). Close parallels of the liturgical summons are Deut 32:3, "Give [*habu*, plural] greatness to our God!" and Ps 68:35, "Give [*tenu*, plural] power to God." The objects cited in all examples amount to veritable manifestations of the Divine: *kabod* is that majestic authority which may be clad in tremendous radiance of numinous energy deadly for human beings but on the other hand absolutely necessary for life and world-order (cf. Exod 19:9–22; 24:15–17; 33:18–23; 40:34–35; Ezek 1:26–28; 10:4; 43:2; Pss 19:2; 72:19; 113:4–5; 115:1; 145:11–12).[3] *'Oz*, on the other hand, signifies a broad spectrum of physical, political, mental strength and the protection these powers offer (cf. Pss 8:3; 28:8; 61:4; 62:8; 74:13; 89:11; 90:11).[4] The third gift to God, demanded from some adorer, is *godel*, "greatness" (Deut 32:3). This expression is rather unspecific for praise contexts occurring eight times in regard to God only (cf. Deut 3:24; 5:24; 9:26; 11:2; Ps 150:2). These designations of might and potency touched upon but briefly do not simply constitute qualities of the revered Lord but seem to have, at times, a certain autonomy. Yahweh acts "in his greatness" (Deut 9:26; Pss 79:11; 150:2) just as "according to his righteousness/lovingkindness/forgiveness/patience/love" etc. (cf. Pss 65:6; 143:11; 5:8; 6:5; 13:6; 21:8; 25:5–7; 103:11, 17; cf. also adjectival formulaic expressions: Exod 34:6; Pss 86:15; 103:8; 145:8; Joel 2:13). The prepositions used to denote such potencies include *ke, be, le,* and frequent possessive suffix of the 2nd person singular establishes a relationship with Yahweh. In some significant contexts, however, the impersonal numinous powers seem to move around and act on their own (cf. Ps 85:11–12), or appear as separate energies carrying out their own purposes in alliance with the divine person (**wrath and anger**: Pss 2:5; 21:10; 69:25; 90:7; 102:11; **vengeance**: Ps 94:1; Isa 59:18; Jer 50:28; Mic 5:14; **peace**: Pss 29:11; 34:15; Isa 26:12; 54:10; Mic 5:4).

The issue at stake, therefore, is wider than the functions or dimensions of eulogy. It does imply the very notions of the Divine in relation to the world and to humans as well as vice versa. Furthermore, we are confronted with the fact that our own theological thinking is taking place in determined cultural and religious patterns which western Christian tradition has formed through two thousand years of debate and indoctrination. In fact, Christian faith in western cultures is mainly based on doctrine rather than on spiritual practice. This difference alone makes for huge incongruences

---

3. Cf. Weinfeld, *kabod*.

4. Cf. Wagner, 6. Commenting on the admonition to "bring" or "give" potencies to God Wagner emphasizes that "nobody is able to give anything to Yahweh that he would not possess already."

between Scriptural and modern parameters of religion. One important consequence for Christian exegesis is this: Whoever reads the Old Testament without feeling here and there irritated in his or her coordinates of faith (determined by one's own denominational tradition) has not really understood the ancient texts.

Pre-Israelite Antecedents: Sumerian Praise-Concepts

We know full well today that Hebrew psalmody has been part of Ancient Near and Middle Eastern ways of celebrating the presence of divine beings and superhuman powers. Happily, written evidence for this broad and deep stream of liturgical traditions goes up into the second and third millenniums BCE as far as Mesopotamian and Egyptian hymnology is concerned. An astonishing number e.g., of Sumerian literary writings contain articulations of praise. The Oxford ETCSL edition[5] brings together nearly 400 literary texts, of which more or less 10% are too fragmentary to be useful for any investigation. Of the remaining 360 specimens at least 200 are showing some kind of expression connoting eulogies to divine entities.

To delve deeper into this treasure of praise affirmations it may be advisable to catch on to a special formulaic expression which occurs 64 times in Sumerian hymnic texts of ETCSL: "[Divine Name = DN; sum.: dDN zà-mí]! Hail!"[6] In its most simple form, in fact not a grammatical phrase but rather an elementary shout or exclamation, it impulsively puts side by side the name of the eulogized deity or object and the noun zà-mí. "Praise!" or "Hail!" would be a proper translation. To give a couple of examples:

> 34: O king, honeyed mouth of the gods!
> Praise be to Enki [den-ki zà-mí].
> 35: Ninĝišzida, son of Ninazu!
> 36: Praise be to Father Enki [a-a ᵈen-ki zà-mí].
> 37: A balbale of Ninĝišzida. [Colophon; ETCSL 4.19.1, ll. 34–36]

The context of the euphoric outburst is quite clear: Ningišzida (possibly: "Lord of the Good Tree") is being celebrated in l. 1–33 as a very powerful numen, both in mythological and political terms (l. 1–24), who once

---

5. The Electronic Text Corpus of Sumerian Literature = ETCSL (free accessible on the internet, see bibliography) is the most extensive body of Sumerian literature available in transcription and English translation; it has been accumulated until 2006 (and unfortunately left unfinished) in Oxford, England.
6. Cf. Gerstenberger, *Theologie des Lobens in sumerischen Hymnen*.

had received his extraordinary prowess from higher deities like Enki in the depths of Abzu (ll. 25–33). The double summons to the congregation or choir, then, to honor Enki, the power-font (ll. 34, 36) comes out of that very logic of praise: The source of strength is to be extolled in order to maintain the flow of energy to the beneficiary. The last line (l. 37) is a scribal colophon, marking the poem (for archival purposes?) as a special song for Ningišzida, not Enki.

Inana, the goddess of love and war, is well represented in Sumerian praise literature. One of the poems dedicated to her tells the story of Enheduana, the Accadian priest installed at the ancient city of Ur and her victory over local lords.[7] The final words are: "Praise be to the destroyer of foreign lands, endowed with divine powers by An, / to my lady enveloped in beauty, to Inana!" (ETCSL 4.07.2, ll. 153–154). The Sumerian text reveals the real impact of the final "hail," being the very last word of l. 154: ^{d}inana zà-mí. The epithets of the goddess ("destroyer of foreign lands, endowed . . . enveloped . . .") all precede the empowering shout. The zà-mí-cheer at the end seems to summarize what has been going on throughout the hymnic poem. The adorer, nominally Enheduana, "recites" the powers of Inana in order to give her strength for the political battle at hand (ll. 63–65, cf. l. 139–141; 150–152). All these passages do not use the expression zà-mí but specify clear enough synonyms like "holy song" (šir kug) and "divine power" (me).

There are, to be sure, some instances in the large corpus of hymnic texts that directly speak about "applying zà-mí" to a worthy recipient, corroborating the reading of the Inana hymn above. A most significant example is found in the ancient hymn for Keš, archaic city with a legendary sanctuary. Enlil, the most traditional and influential deity of Sumer, lord of Nippur and its temple Ekur ("Mountain House") is described in the Keš poem as the founder of sanctuary and city. "Enlil spoke in praise of Keš" (ETCSL 4.80.2, l. 9; cf. ll. 38–39). Unfortunately, the translation is hiding somewhat the original meaning of the phrase. The Sumerian wording is: ^{d}en-líl-le kèš^{ki} za-mi àm-ma-ab-bé "Enlil spoke a zà-mí to Keš," this means to say something like: "he endowed her with power." The widely used formula zà-mí dug-ga$_{4}$, "spoken/performed/delivered 'hail,'" furthermore, in its various shades of meaning supports the performative meaning of uttering praise.[8]

Zà-mí along this line becomes a synonym of other expressions denoting anonymous powers or energies, like e.g., "destiny" (nam-tar), "authoritative word" (inim), "divine potencies" (me), "holy rites" (ĝarza), "numinous

---

7. Cf. Zgoll, *Der Rechtsfall*.

8. Cf. Gerstenberger *Theologie des Lobens in sumerischen Hymnen*, 197–205. Pascal Attinger discusses the most relevant occurrences of that phrase, cf. Attinger, *Éléments de linguistique sumérienne*, 756–59.

auras" (*melem*), "law," "justice" (*si sá*), "order," "plan" (*ĝiš ḫur*) and others. All these forces, according to Sumerian understanding, did work in their own ways and settings. The "praise" element had its *Sitz im Leben* in liturgical ceremonies where groups of worshippers could voice their admiration and support. Interestingly, *zà-mí* and its companions never were employed in a technical sense designating genres of texts, postures, or actions. They all have been conceptualized in the Sumerian tradition as spiritual and impersonal powers wielded by gods and goddesses, but, in fact, semi-independent and silently influencing beings and courses of events.

How did *zà-mí* work, then? The addressees of eulogies be they personal entities, sacred objects like temples, musical instruments, or other cultic paraphernalia, were trusted to hold important positions of influence within the spiritual structure of world order and social order. They were considered champions of all the right and wholesome developments on earth or in certain locals of the world. The spiritual quality inherent in *zà-mí* is articulated in adjectival attributions: "Great Mountain, Father Enlil, your praise is sublime!" (ETCSL 4.05.1, l. 171: *kur gal a-a ᵈen-líl zà-mí-zu maḫ-àm*; cf. ETCSL 1.3.5, segm. D, l. 62; 2.6.9.2, l. 56). The lexeme *maḫ* signifies "greatness," "majesty," "power," paralleled by *gal* (ETCSL 2.4.2.03, segm. A, l. 20 etc. [refrain]; 2.5.4.01, l. 403). For the most part, however, the dynamics of praise in Sumerian hymnic texts is expressed by the adjective *dùg*, "good," "effective," "beautiful," "sweet" (43 occurrences in ETCSL).[9] Considering the dynamic character of "hail-shouts," and "hail-songs" (both: *zà-mí*) a mere emotive/aesthetic event or an exclusive description of static qualities we may read all adjectival attributions as indications of live manifestations of power. "Your praise is effective" (*zà-mí-zu dùg-ga-àm*; ETCSL translates: ". . . is sweet") is a standard affirmation (29 times in ETCSL) addressing various entities (ETCSL 1.3.4, segm. C, l. 37 [Inana]; 2.5.4.03, l. 13 [Nippur]; 2.5.6.2, l. 47 [Enki]; 4.12.1, l. 59 [Martu] etc.).

Further Old Testament Testimony

Israel's faith from the beginning has been embedded in the experiences of Ancient Near Eastern cultures and religions. We have to recognize and acknowledge this fact. With the appearance, at the latest, of the *Dictionary of Deities and Demons in the Bible* in 1995[10] it should have become clear that biblical theologies through the ages cannot be separated from contemporary theologies and rites of that pluralistic world Israel and beginning

---

9. Cf. Gerstenberger, *Theologie des Lobens in Sumerischen Hymnen*, 65–69, 177–85.
10. Cf. van der Toorn, ed., *Dictionary of Deities and Demons in the Bible*.

Christianity were living in. To focalize on the Old Testament: There are dozens or even hundreds of coincidences in theological and ethical conceptions making ancient Israel's faith a special variation of religious creed within a common stream of Ancient Near Eastern world views. So far, experts working in the field of Ancient Near Eastern religions (including Old Testament varieties of faith)[11] are pretty much in accordance when it comes to accept an intricate relationship of the relevant theological and ethical paradigms.

What has been largely neglected in academic theology, however, is the existence throughout the Ancient Near East of a good number of impersonal forces which hardly can be denominated as gods or spirits. They are incommunicable yet do constitute semi-autonomous beings. There are no odes addressing these bundled energies directly. But our own religious tradition in general postulates personality as an essential condition for all higher beings. Clear enough, because we want to communicate with the numina. Even the dictionary mentioned above concentrates on personalized deities and demons allowing little space for entries on anonymous i.e. impersonal forces or potencies.

As already indicated there are numerous examples of impersonal entities which participate in Yahweh's actions or do obeisance to Him. At this point we do not want to go into the countless cosmic beings which are summoned to praise him (cf. Ps 148) because they still pertain in some ways to the category of personalized superhuman authorities. We rather want to examine those faceless energies which nevertheless play such important roles in the world. To name but a few: "Justice/righteousness/order" (ṣedeq, ṣedaqah); "solidarity/care/truth" (ḥesed, 'emet); "word/saying/instruction" (dabar, torah). In some passages such potencies are nothing but direct actions of the Lord. Other affirmations allow for a certain distance between God and a self-enacting power. To look somewhat more closely at these texts:

The concept of "justice/righteousness/(world) order" was known and cherished throughout the Ancient Near East. Sumerian kings (e.g., Urnamma of Ur) try to comply with their divine obligation to establish equity, and famous Hammurabi of Babylon boasts in the epilogue of his "law code" of realizing God's will in this regard. The Old Testament has much to tell about this same intercultural phenomenon of justice and world order.[12] Ṣedeq, ṣedaqah, although frequently linked to Yahweh with possessive pronouns, have their own extension and being (cf. Ps 71:19; Isa 51:8 [NRSV

---

11. There is some justification in using the plural form of OT theologies, cf. Gerstenberger, *Theologies in the Old Testament*.

12. Cf. Botterweck, et al. *TWAT* 6:898–924.

ambiguously "my deliverance" for *ṣidqati*]). God maintains a relationship with "his just order" (Isa 45:24; Dan 9:7; Job 37:23) which seems less personal than his ties to wisdom in Prov 8 but nevertheless is a bipolar affair.

> [Yahweh] loves righteousness and justice [*ṣedaqah umišpaṭ*]
> the earth is full of [his] steadfast love [*ḥesed*]. (Ps 33:5 NRSV)

He even "puts *ṣedaqah* on his body "like a breastplate" (Isa 59:17). The passage enumerates neatly other powers in the vicinity of Yahweh to be used by him, maintaining his own identity:

> He put on righteousness [*ṣedaqah*] like a breastplate
> and a helmet of salvation [*yešu'ah*] on his head;
> He put on garments of vengeance [*naqam*] for clothing
> and wrapped himself in fury [*qin'ah*] as in a mantle.
> (Isa 59:17 NRSV)

The imagery seems profusely military (cf. Exod 15:3; Isa 63:1–6). It certainly does not present to us objective facts of a reconstructible spiritual world. But it reflects the way our forefathers and mothers conceptualized their encounter with the superhuman world. For them, Yahweh was the personal side of the world order. He carried with him or commanded over countless forces of edification and destruction which, for their part, emitted their inherent power, for better or for worse. In this context we remember the sad news of some Deuteronomists stating: "Still, Yahweh did not turn from the fierceness of his great wrath . . ." (2 Kgs 23:26), in spite of Josiah's perfect performance according the prescriptions of the Torah (2 Kgs 23:25). Wrath supersedes loving-kindness in this case. The positive forces acting in favor of the people of Yahweh need to be acknowledged and even praised and proclaimed by the community of believers (cf. Pss 22:32; 40:11; 51:16; 71:15–18; 88:13).

> The might of your awesome deeds [*nora'ot*] shall be proclaimed,
> and I will declare your greatness [*gedullah*].
> They shall celebrate the fame of your abundant goodness [*ṭub*],
> and shall sing aloud of your righteousness [*ṣedaqah*].
> (Ps 145:6–7 NRSV)

Hebrew possessive pronouns and genitive constructs are capable to signify a broad range of relationship between the "proprietor" and the "possessed." In our contexts they are likely not to denote personal qualities as may be expected in church dogmatics: The sovereign Lord in our mind acts solely on his own voluntary impetus. Obviously, in those ancient cultures of the Middle and Near East things looked different.

If this be true, the last quoted passage may be read as testifying to the solemn endorsement of divine powers by the individual singer and the congregation, culminating in "singing aloud your righteousness" (Ps 145:7; "singing ... of your righteousness" [NRSV] is an adaptation to current theological misconceptions).

The second couple of rather independent spiritual forces in the OT pointed out above is *ḥesed* and *'emet*.[13] There are a good number of antecedents, analogies and parallels in Ancient Near Eastern religious and ethical texts. The basic social level where the concept of solidarity in its wider sense is frequently alluded to is that of intimate human relations (cf. Pss 27:10; 35:13-14; 133; Gen 20:13; 21:23; 34; Exod 20:12; 23:1-13; Lev 19; 25:25-55; Deut 24:6-21; Josh 2:12; 2 Sam 9:7; 16:17; 1 Kgs 20:31-34; 2 Kgs 4:13; Isa 49:15; Jer 7:1-10; Mic 7:1-6; Zech 7:9-10; Prov 19:22). *Ḥesed* and related ideas of solidarity in most diverse situations are the glue of small social groups. Their presence is praised, their loss lamented in the Hebrew Scriptures. Quite understandably these energies have been lauded as special gifts and rather independent dynamic forces.

"Loving-kindness" and "fidelity," as the terms we focalize on are sometimes translated, truly are markers of good social relationship. To "do *ḥesed*" is tantamount to leave aside mere egoistic or economic motivations and help or support the less fortunate or weaker fellow being (cf. Gen 19:19; 20:13; 21:23; 24:49; 47:29 etc.). This does not preclude the expectation of a future reward for helpful behavior (cf. 2 Sam 2:5-6; 9:1-13). Quite often the solidarity concept is articulated by formulaic *ḥesed we'emet* to emphasize the trustworthy, solid, and lasting relationship.

Proverbial sayings recommend living by the two virtues: "Whoever pursues righteousness [*ṣedaqah*] and kindness [*ḥesed*] / will find life [*ḥayim*] and honor [*kabod*]" (Prov 21:21). "Do not let loyalty [*ḥesed*] and faithfulness [*'emet*] forsake you; / bind them around your neck, / write them on the tablet of your heart. / So you will find favor [*ḥen*] and good repute [*śekel ṭob*] / in the sight of God and of people" (Prov 3:3-4). Small wonder, that a basic note for all human life such as *ḥesed we'emet* becomes a living, imagined force in social affairs. As already indicated, they—together with other spiritual entities—gain a quasi-independent existence. The ruling king is being addressed in Ps 89:15:

---

13. Cf. Botterweck et al., *TWAT*, 3:48-71. Botterweck et al., *TWAT*, 1:313-48.

> Righteousness [*ṣedeq*] and justice [*mišpaṭ*] are the foundations of your throne;
> steadfast love [*ḥesed*] and faithfulness [*'emet*] go before you
> (NRSV)
>
> God will send forth his steadfast love [*ḥesed*] and his faithfulness [*'emet*]. (Ps 57:3 NRSV)
>
> [God] does not retain his anger [*'ap*] forever,
> because he delights in showing clemency [*ḥesed*].[14]
> (Mic 7:18 NRSV)

These and many more examples reveal a detached functioning of the cited spiritual powers. They are in a way serving the purposes of divine command, but they certainly also fulfill their tasks by essential drive or innate capacity. Being forces of social cohesion and well-being they are transferrable to the community of humans. A spirit of alliance between the people and God can be established by their work of common trust and help. Interestingly, Yahweh once is called an *'el 'emet* (Ps 31:6), apparently being classified according to known categories of deities. Trustworthiness may have been the renown of family or clan gods (cf. Gen 28:20–22).[15] Yahweh, along this line, adopted the prime capacity of those lower deities, or, more adequately to our subject, he affiliated with that spiritual force so characteristic of protective numina.

In the third place we opted for the concepts of "Word" (*dabar*) and "Torah" (*torah*) as further specimens of impersonal powers very influential in Old Testament theological thinking. Of course, the former has a long pre-history in ancient Near and Middle Eastern religions, while the latter seems to be unique in biblical faith and very characteristic of emerging Judaism during the Persian period.[16] The Word of high deities already was believed to be a means not only of communication with their clients but also an effective force of its own to create and maintain good living conditions as well as to destroy adverse potencies and check negative developments. Word and (loud) voice usually go together to connote the authority and might of God and his solemn announcements (cf. Exod 19:19; Deut 5:25–27; Amos 1:2). In the Hebrew Scriptures the topic of Yahweh's Word–Voice–Command–Orientation–Denouncement–Verdict apparently has

---

14. Literally: "because he regards kindness/solidarity highly."

15. Another type of deity in the Bible is the *'el gibbor* (Isa 9:5; 10:21), *'iš milḥamah* (Exod 15:3), *'el neqamot* (Ps 94:1), *'el qanna'* (Exod 20:5)—all pointing to the warrior God of clan and state contexts.

16. Cf. Gerstenberger, *Israel in the Persian Period*.

been greatly elaborated through Israel's history (cf. 2 Kgs 22–23; Jer 36). There are really countless references to his speaking which finally were crowned by due reverence to the Torah, that Pentateuchal and subsequent Prophetic collection of divine testimonies.

There are hardly any analogies for the genesis of sacred writings in Mesopotamian religions. But Old Persian Zoroastrianism seems to have developed in a similar fashion towards conceptions of revelation, mediation, and execution of divine commandments, admonitions, and promises.[17]

To give but a few examples of the extraordinary growth of Word- and Torah-theologies within the Old Testament.[18] The idea of God speaking through signs and chance constellations goes back to pre-biblical belief. The Babylonians e.g., cultivated an extensive system of watching and interpreting of *omina* of various types (natural phenomena; dreams; liver investigation; oil on water configurations etc.). Experts would observe and interpret such phenomena and give counsel as to what ritual was appropriate to contain and overcome the announced calamities.[19] Known mostly from the David story is solicitation of a divine decision (cf. 1 Sam 23:10–12). A priest apparently shakes a breast-bag containing two dice ("urim"; "tummim"), one signifying "yes" the other "no." The first one to jump out of the case is the answer of God. This means: Pure accident is made the medium of divine communication. First Samuel 28:6 mentions other ways of "asking" the Lord and receiving answers. All these avenues count on intermediate techniques of accessing the will of God. A side glance at more personal mediation helps to understand the pluriform conceptions of divine–human relations.[20]

The "Word of Yahweh" in later layers of the Old Testament ever more becomes an institution all by itself. God speaks as the creator, and there is the intended object as if made by magic (Gen 1:3–27):

> By the word of Yahweh [*debar yhwh*] the heavens were made,
> and all their host by the breath of his mouth [*ruaḥ piyo*].
> (Ps 33:6 NRSV)

"Word" and "breath/spirit" seem to function like inspired instruments in the creative act (cf. also Ps 33:4–5, 9 for more subsidiary implements in creation). The "Word of Yahweh" turns a preferred entity in late layers of the Pentateuch. Moses is the exclusive receptor of Yahweh's ordinances

---

17. Cf. Gerstenberger, *Israel in the Persian Period*, 68–76, 429–34.
18. Cf. Botterweck et al., *TWAT*, 2:89–133. Botterweck et al., *TWAT*, 8:597–637.
19. Cf. Heeßel, *Babylonisch-assyrische Diagnostik*.
20. Various ways of conceiving God as the president of a divine council are present in the Old Testament: 1 Kgs 22:19–28; Ps 82:1–4; Job 2:1–6.

and communicator to the people starting with Exod 19 through Num 36. Deuteronomy in its last redactions ostensibly poses as a repetition of Moses' singular mission. Yahweh speaks from Mount Sinai itself or from the Tent of Meeting to hand over that most precious divine "instruction" (torah) for the congregation. In some traditions it is immediately written down into a "book" or "scroll," thus assuming a visible, tangible, recitable treasure of tradition and symbol of divine presence. The Words of Yahweh assume a physical body and a spiritual force. They even fertilize the ground:

> For as the rain and the snow come down from heaven,
>
> > and do not return there until they have watered the earth,
>
> ... so shall my word be that goes out from my mouth;
>
> > it shall not return to me empty
>
> but it shall accomplish that which I purpose ...
>
> (Isa 55:10–11 NRSV).

And they may have a terrible destructive force:

> Is not my word like fire, says Yahweh,
>
> > and like a hammer that breaks a rock in pieces?
>
> (Jer 23:29 NRSV)

The last quoted saying comes from a context trying to clarify the difference between right and false prophecy (Jer 23:9–40). We may understand that legitimate prophecy has a convincing power of its own. It is self-fulfilling because of its divine strength. Many of the introductory and legitimizing introductions of prophetic words presuppose such potency in simply stating: "The word of Yahweh that came / happened to N.N." (cf. Jer 7:1; 11:1; 30:1; 34:1; 35:1, etc.). Prophets in this manner are put on an equal footing with Moses (cf. Deut 18:15–18, in contrast to Deut 34:10). They receive the mighty Words of Yahweh filled with divine strength and mysteriously identical with the original Mosaic Torah of which the later prophets are true interpreters (cf. Jer 26; 36). Small wonder that already in some traditions of the OT the written Torah receives some sort of veneration.

A key passage is the first reported reading of Torah by Ezra in the time of Nehemiah (Neh 8:1–8). The book of the "Law of Moses" is the central piece of worship. Ezra brought the scroll, "opened [it] in the sight of all the people ... ; and when he opened it, all the people stood up" (v. 5). We are witnessing the beginnings of synagogue worship revolving around the Torah. "the ears of all the people were attentive to the book of the law" (v. 3). The Levites present "helped the people to understand the law, . . . So they read from the book, from the Law of God, with interpretation. They gave the sense, so that the people understood the reading" (vv. 7–8). Holy Scripture becomes an agent of sorts in the cultic ceremonies of Judaism, Christianity, and Islam. In consequence, we find hymnic praises of the Torah in the Psalter:

> The law (*torah*) of Yahweh is perfect,
>   reviving the soul;
> the decrees (*'edut*) of Yahweh are sure,
>   making wise the simple;
> the precepts (*piqqudim*) of Yahweh are right,
>   rejoicing the heart;
> the commandment (*miṣwah*) of Yahweh is clear,
>   enlightening the eyes;
> the fear (*yir'ah*) of Yahweh is pure,
>   enduring forever;
> the ordinances (*mišpaṭim*) of Yahweh are true
>   and righteous altogether.
> More to be desired are they than gold;
>   sweeter also than honey,
> and drippings of the honeycomb. (Ps 19:8–11 NRSV)

The word *torah* and five synonyms open up the first six lines of this artful poem. (In Ps 119 with its blocks of eight lines beginning with the same letter of the alphabet we find seven synonyms in each block). Adjectives and participles of each line correspond with the nomen regens, that is with torah and its equivalents. They—the ordinances, decrees, precepts etc.—are the acting parts in the hymn. That is why they are so "desirable" and "sweet" (v. 11) which, really, must not be said of God. In short, the Word of Yahweh and the canonized collection of His sayings are to be acknowledged as spiritual forces *sui generis*.

God and Impersonal Energies

Exegetical work with ancient texts implies a consciousness of historical and mental differences. We cannot presuppose that our accustomed patterns of thinking and believing were operative already in the minds and hearts of biblical witnesses or any other people of the Ancient Near East in spite of a good number of anthropological constants. (Behavioral science discovers patterns of comportment going far beyond the human race into the animal kingdom.) But there have been so many ruptures and changes in societal and scientific development that basic axioms have shifted over the millennia.

This is particularly true for "reading" and understanding the world including all theological theories and doctrines. Whoever seeks in the Bible an endorsement of his or her modern world views and spiritual fixations certainly misses ancient outlooks, convictions, and sentiments. To say it more bluntly: Exegesis of biblical texts necessarily implies experiences of clashing civilizations and modes of believing. Some parameters of antiquity simply do not coincide with modern constructions of reality and values. The reason of such incongruence is bipolar: We are living in our "proven" intellectual shell just as our forbears had their "trusted" capsule of rules and insights. There is no such thing in human mental history as an absolute truth. Each society works out contemporary half-truths and tries to live in harmony with it. Therefore, it is the responsibility of exegetes to discover the proprieties of ancient thinking and believing and at the same time become aware of the fundamentals of one's own time and society. Otherwise there will be no way of dialoguing with biblical witnesses in order to learn from them.

As to our subject "God and impersonal energies" we are seriously blocked by our traditional conceptualization of the Divine to fully come to grips with biblical views of deities and powers that permeate the world. In particular, we are caught with Christian doctrines of the One and Only God who can be visualized only, e.g., under the mathematical figure of Unity and Exclusiveness (against a plurality of prime causes) and the psychological grid of personality (against impersonal energy). For us it is necessary to postulate God—against all Old Testament prohibitions of imagining Yahweh in the likeness of any earthly object or idea—as the sole source of all being, history, and religion. There must not be a second cause, influence, or goal in this world. And secondly, this One Deity must be a regular person like ourselves, endowed with care, perspicuity, and guidance. Truly, we want God to exist in our own image. Deviations from a basic module of the divine are not permissible. If biblical witnesses are able to open our eyes for their ancient perspectives on the numinous we may come back to evaluate "praise" as another form of impersonal power in this pluriform and wondrously mysterious world.

Oneness and Plurality of the Divine

The theological concept of one and only one divine will governing all affairs throughout the universe and the entire history is a logical construct which satisfies our desire for clarity and rationality. We cannot admit a plurality of causes because this would do away with other presuppositions of our tradition: The one and same Deity is thought of to be all-present, all-mighty, all-knowing, permeating macro- and micro-cosmos. Some Old Testament texts, notably the book of Isaiah laid the ground for this mode of thinking:

> Listen to me, O Jacob,
>   and Israel, whom I called:
> I am He; I am the first,
>   and I am the last.
> My hand laid the foundation of the earth,
>   and my right hand spread out the heavens;
> when I summon them,
>   they stand at attention. (Isa 48:12–13 NRSV; cf. Gen 1)

> Thus says Yahweh, the King of Israel,
>   and his Redeemer, Yahweh Zebaoth:
> I am the first and I am the last;
>   besides me there is no god.
> Who is like me? Let them proclaim it,
>   let them declare and set it forth before me. (Isa 44:6–7 NRSV)

> I am Yahweh and there is no other.
>   I form the light and create darkness,
> I make weal and create woe;
>   I, Yahweh, do all these things. (Isa 45:6–7 NRSV)

The "all but one" principle of world interpretation has been perfected in due course to exclude whatever other agents. In some (Protestant) churches it led to the extreme of a "doctrine of strict predestination" insisting in the all-encompassing authorship of all things by the one supreme deity. Splitting off the bad agents as satanic forces helped to maintain mono-causal thinking. Still, theologies of the one and exclusive deity always ran into great trouble with their own axioms. If there is a sole mover and decision-maker behind all things that happen, the discrepancies and inequalities of humankind and the natural habitat cannot be explained away by human free will nor by unpacified satanic opponents. The age old question of theodicy raises its head and irritates without end (cf. the book of Job).

Old Testament and Ancient Near Eastern faith is far removed from doctrinal narrowness of any kind. Sure, there are attempts to affirm the uniqueness and oneness of Yahweh (or other deities like El Elyon, El Šaddai). Nowhere in the Hebrew Scriptures do we find the notion of a mathematical oneness, not even in the famous Šemaʿ Yisrael of Deut 6:5: "Listen Israel, Yahweh is our God, Yahweh is one" (or: "Yahweh alone"; own translation). Many more witnesses, however, count on a plurality of divine figures and they include, as we have seen, impersonal forces attributing to them a certain range of effectiveness free of divine supervision. To reduce divine guidance, sustenance, restoration to an effort of one single "super-brain" (like an immense computer) to the ancients would have been an absurd idea. They rather acknowledged the impenetrable tangle of causes, side-causes, counter-causes, and, most of all, the strict prohibition of imagining God in human terms as the one brain of the universe. Therefore, they often left Him with the authorship of good and evil events, with a staff of heavenly assistants, and a good number of impersonal forces acting out divine purposes on their own account.

Personal and Impersonal Forces

We now have to focus on another feature of Christian doctrine which seriously narrows down biblical witness. The personification of God in the likeness of human personality (in the Bible mostly the masculine brand) is a common characteristic at least in Western thought. Jewish, Christian and Muslim Theologies, all of them, with the exception of any mystic currents throughout the ages and regions, adamantly cling to the concept of the Divine being a personal being. How else could we communicate with Him or Her? Humans have felt the dire need to speak to God and hear Him/Her talk to them. The Deuteronomist, fully aware of the prohibition of idols,[21] thought of Yahweh as a male speaker throughout. Wasn't this an act of idolizing God? Sure enough, humans want to talk to God (except for mystics who may find a higher way of communication in spiritual immersion). They need to do so. But they have to remain conscious of the fact, that such conceptualizations are products of our human brains which in no way can capture the full reality of God. Every theological affirmation is a highly risky and always an inadequate portrayal of the Supreme Being. All the *ipsissima verba* of God in the Bible at the same time are formulated in precarious human language be it Hebrew, Aramaic, Greek, Latin, English, or any other

---

21. Cf. Deut 4:15–16: "take care and watch yourselves closely, so that you do not act corruptly by making an idol for yourselves, in the form of any figure—the likeness of male or female . . ."

tongue. To force God into a personality-frame like we know it from our experiences with ourselves and other persons may be a dangerous fault of every theological discourse. Presumably, however, we cannot do without personifications of God. We should know, at the same time that the personal scheme is by far inadequate for a full description of the Ground of Being.

It is not needless to point to the fact that our life today is to a large part carried by impersonal thinking. Modern science and techniques are built on mechanical ways of thinking and constructing. Machines, electrical and electronic equipment, medical procedures, agriculture etc. cannot be directed by magic or prayers. Few people would try to do just that. What we want is to know and apply impersonal physical and chemical laws, causal chains without personal interferences. Unbelievable as it seems to be, our spiritual life appears to be untouched by the daily mechanisms. We mostly do not even try to live our faith within that ordinary world of science and techniques. Rather, Christians normally flee back into the realm of ancient myths and personality cults.

Ironically, it is the old biblical world which reminds us not to disdain impersonal manifestations of power. They do have their own potential of realizing the good and just society. They are effective, they are to be cherished and lauded, they deserve recognition side by side with God. Of course, our problem is what these impersonal assistants of the Unconditional Challenge are like in our present context. Justice and righteousness, mercy and love, forgiveness and solidarity are good companions also today. There may be newcomers among the impersonal powers which were less known in ancient times. Should Christians not officially welcome human dignity, democratic procedures, gender-, race-, religious equality among the divine energies?

Praise—The Power of Believers

A special mention is due to personal and communal praise as another example of spiritual strength in which each confessing congregation has a large stake. Traditionally, sacred eulogies have been understood as due offerings to the saving God who benignly governs the whole world putting the adorers on lower levels of existence. Ancient Near Eastern evidence, including Hebrew Scriptures, is different. Praise surely is an offering to deities and sacred beings. But it also constitutes energy on its own grounds, imbued with its own force. On the other hand, the addressees are in want of such support. Praise maintains and increases the potencies even of the highest God. Yahweh, at least, is demanding shares of might and glory from other heavenly beings (cf. Pss 29:1–2; 96:7–8). Psalm 148 implements this desire in grand style. It is a compact summons to praise Him issued to everything from the highest to the lowest beings.

> Praise Yahweh!
> Praise Yahweh from the heavens;
>   praise him in the heights!
> Praise him, all the angels;
>   praise him, all his host!
> Praise him, sun and moon;
>   praise him all you shining stars!
> Praise him, you highest heavens,
>   and you waters above the heavens!
> . . . . . .
> Praise Yahweh from the earth,
>   you sea monsters and all deeps,
> fire and hail, snow and frost,
>   stormy wind fulfilling his command!
> Mountains and all hills,
>   fruit trees and all cedars!
> Wild animals and all cattle,
>   creeping things and flying birds!
> Kings of the earth and all peoples,
>   princes and all rulers of the earth!
> Young men and women alike,
>   old and young together! (Ps 148:1–4, 7–12 NRSV)

Ongoing praise keeps up the Lordship of the creator. This is the meaning also of the liturgical formula "Blessed be Yahweh" (*baruk yhwh*; cf. Gen 9:26 [against NRSV, cf. Gen 14:20]; 24:27; Exod 18:10; 1 Sam 25:32, 39; 1 Kgs 1:48; 5:21; Ezek 3:12 [*kebod yhwh*!]; Pss 18:47; 28:6; 31:22 and 12 more times in the Psalter). Praise as well as blessings transmits power from the side of the eulogists to the side of the recipient of the homage. In this fashion Gerhard von Rad was quite right with his notion that praises had to be sung continuously to Yahweh the saving God who figuratively was "enthroned over the hymns of Israel" (Ps 22:4).

3

Praise in the Realm of Death

*The Dynamics of Hymn-Singing
in Ancient Near Eastern Lament Ceremony*

Introduction

QUITE OFTEN OUR APPROACH to complaint and laments in ancient Near Eastern traditions occurs via emotional and/or literary avenues. We sympathize with suffering individuals and communities because anguish and pain are universal phenomena. Or we vibrate with the ancient language of anxiety, grief, anger, contestation, as well as with expressions of trust, hope, and mental strength. Such linguistic articulations are like precious ornaments of psychic realities. Their structured beauty generalizes basic experiences making them accessible to listeners and readers. A third approach to psalmic texts of that kind is less representative in our Old Testament research: the cultic one (to which could be added a social-historical perspective), although there have been very notable efforts made to consequently place complaints and laments into a plausible setting. Sigmund Mowinckel's work looms large in this field of inquiry. I want to follow his paths again, using as a focusing point the elusive question of the occasional presence of praise elements inbetween dire outcries of agony. Neither the emotional nor the literary interpretation really can do justice to the phenomenon of "praise in the realm of death."

Evidence

To procure some evidence and thus illustrate the problem at hand, we could point to a late biblical text such as Dan 3:1-25: three steadfast Jews resist all orders to adore a Babylonian divine statue and are thrown into the "fire-oven." But the extreme heat kills only the police officers; it cannot harm one hair of Shadrach, Meshach, and Abednego. A fourth, divine figure inside the oven takes care of the victims (3:25). The Greek version elaborates the scene. The three condemned men, in liturgical procession, now sing a hymn to Yahweh, blessing his divine power (Dan 3:24 LXX). Further, Azariah, probably identical with Abednego, pronounces a solemn, hymnic prayer with confession of guilt and lament, while still in the oven (Dan 3:26-45 LXX), full of momentous eulogies to the saving deity. This is an explicit case of hymnic formulations being used in a complaint and lament situation; we are able to observe its (literary? cultic?) emergence in the Greek tradition. Somewhat similar in biblical contexts is, for example, the prayer of Hezekiah in Isa 38:10-20, showing anticipated, seemingly misplaced thanksgivings (38:17-20; see also Jonah 2). Is an inherent dimension of anticipation of divine intervention a sufficient explanation of this phenomenon?

In the same vein, some complaints of the Psalter do employ praise along with preeminent descriptions of suffering and petitions for help. Thus Pss 44 and 89 open their plea before Yahweh with extensive passages of praise. Psalm 44:2-9 [ET 1-8] is retrospective, just as Ps 89:2-38 [1-37] extols past deeds of God in favor of his people. But there are also lines that certainly are meant to express continuing experiences of divine power and loving care: "Righteousness and justice are the foundation of your throne" (Ps 89:13 [14]); "Happy are the people who know the festal shout they exult in your name all day long" (Ps 89:14-15 [15-16]); "through you we push down our foes in God we have boasted continually" (Ps 44:6, 9 [5, 8]). To what avail is hymnic discourse used under these circumstances? Are the transmitters of complaints, the experts of concomitant ritual, only referring to Yahweh's power for the sake of reminding him of better times and perhaps trying to entice him to action? The same question can be put to individual complaints. They also employ, here and there, laudatory language over against Yahweh. In fact, eulogies of the deity called upon in despair do constitute a standard form-element of individual complaints.[1]

For example, a little personal hymn, set into the context of complaint, petition, and imprecation of enemies (who are considered to have generated

---

1. See Gerstenberger, *Psalms, Part 1*, 12-13; Gerstenberger, *Der bittende Mensch*, 128-30.

the trouble at hand) frustrates our literary logic but falls in line with the liturgical agenda:

> O how abundant is your goodness
> > that you have laid up for those who fear you,
> and accomplished for those who take refuge in you,
> > in the sight of everyone.
> In the shelter of your presence you hide them
> > from human plots;
> you hold them safe under your shelter
> > from contentious tongues.
> Blessed be the Yahweh,
> > for he wondrously shows his steadfast love to me,
> > when I am beset as a city under siege. (Ps 31:20–22 [19–21]).[2]

In a living worship service, praise of God is a necessary part of that essential, enacted dialogue with the protective power at least partly responsible for the threatening situation of the supplicant. Praise in such a situation may encompass many things: acknowledgment of God's potency, reminder of former gracious help, activation of the deity's will to intervene, and so forth. The praise quoted is in direct-address form but clad in general terms, thus affirming validity for everyone. The culminating point, however, is the exemplification of God's glorious might in regard to the supplicant himself or herself (31:22 [21]): *baruk yhwh* "blessed be Yahweh," is a basic shout of exuberant joy, used frequently in liturgical events. A similar tiny inset hymn is Ps 35:9–10:

> My soul shall rejoice in the Yahweh,
> > exulting in his deliverance.
> All my bones shall say,
> > "O Yahweh, who is like you?
> You deliver the weak
> > from those too strong for them,
> the weak and needy from those who despoil them."

The last two verses of the same complaint psalm are a standard vow to give thanks and praise after deliverance; they do contain another formulaic

---

2. The last verse I put into the present tense, in order to avoid the wrong impression that salvation had already occurred.

liturgical expression of pure eulogy, parallel to the *baruk*-formula: "Great be the Lord, who delights in the welfare of his servant" (35:27b). On the whole, many psalms of individual complaint do employ expressions of praise in the immediate vicinity of complaining passages (see, e.g., Pss 5:5–7 [4–6]; 22:4 [3]; 28:6–7; 36:8 [7]; 40:17 [16]; 59:6 [5]; 92:6 [5]).[3]

Proleptic thanksgiving, on the other hand, with allusions to God's great capacities and enduring benevolence, is a feature of such prayers, too. The best example in question probably is Ps 107, which delineates four life-threatening situations that call for supplication to God. The stereotypical formula, however, does not call the prayer in any way petitionary but simply states, according to most translations: those who prayed in hopeless situations and were saved should give thanks. Apparently a clear time sequence is being envisioned: thanksgiving occurs after salvation. But quite possibly, the psalm is talking about proper supplication in distress that already includes anticipated thanks. The narrational contexts of the Hezekiah and the Jonah psalms do suggest such an interpretation. And some individual complaints such as Ps 22 (see Pss 22:23 [22]; 35:18; 59:10, 18 [9, 17]) talk about anticipated praise and thanksgiving quite explicitly and from various perspectives. Psalm 69:31–32 [30–31] calls it a very opportune gift to the Lord, who is being approached for emergency help: "I will praise the name of God with a song; I will magnify him with thanksgiving. This will please the LORD more than an ox or a bull with horns and hoofs."

Proleptic thanksgiving therefore must be seen as an integral part of complaint rituals in ancient Israel, and this particular kind of affirming gratitude is nothing else than one special form of praise to the deity concerned. At least it does function liturgically just like hymnic eulogies do. The negative statement that the "dead" are no longer able to offer thanks and praise (see 6:6 [5]; 88:11–13 [10–12]) illustrates the same fact: hymnic prayers are essential for the deity, too. They do have an authentic "setting" in lamenting rituals.

---

3. See the relevant passages in Gerstenberger, *Psalms, Part 1*. My comments on Ps 5 and its hymnic part at that point were the following: "Hymnic elements are by no means foreign to complaint psalms. God claims due reverence even in times of distress, and it is in the supplicant's own interest to acknowledge God's power and care" (58). My references as to earlier statements in the same vein go, among others, to Westermann, *The Praise of God in the Psalms*; and Crüsemann, *Studien zur Formgeschichte von Hymnus und Danklied in Israel*.

Sumerian Analogies

I now propose to look at a body of ancient Near Eastern literature that encompasses a great amount of hymnic materials of various forms and settings. What I have in mind is the Sumerian hymnic tradition, which originated in the third millennium BCE and continued, even in its native linguistic form, well into the first millennium BCE. Some people may object to drawing into our discussion such remote texts as the Sumerian ones. I am fully aware of the risks involved in this enterprise. Therefore, I do not even remotely think of "literary influences" of Sumerian hymns on Old Testament praise. But we certainly can count on some basic patterns of thinking and feasting common to the entire ancient Near East, because there has been a long-standing interchange across different cultures and religions of forms and features especially in the cultic realm. Further, the sociological rule probably also holds true for the area under consideration: similar recurring social or religious events create analogous actions and expressions. Thus, for example, some temple designs (house temples with statues of deities) have spread over practically all the Near, Middle, and Far (partially) East as well as Egypt.[4] If architecture as recovered by long-standing archaeological excavations and research betrays common traits, could not cultic rituals and ceremonial texts do the same?

Sumerian hymns are not uniform; terminology used in colophons as well as extant copies of real literary texts are greatly varied. For the most part, it seems, they were recited aloud, accompanied by musical instruments. Length of the text, literary structures, styles, and contents are highly diversified. Our interest is the use of hymnic affirmations in lament contexts, a wide field of investigation, to be sure. We focus on some exemplary cases of lament from different (ceremonial or life) settings, knowing quite well that all such distinctions are made from our own, modern perspective; they are not endemic to Sumerian literature.

City Laments

One group of lament literature, comparable to the Old Testament book of Lamentations, is concerned with catastrophes that overcame cities or regions. Devastation by enemies seems to be the prime background for these laments. Cities and temples have been destroyed and people massacred; the local deities have left in mourning; the people try to intervene with the

---

4. See Zwickel, *Der Tempelkult in Kanaan und Israel*; Zwickel, "Tempel"; Fritz, "Tempel II."

Sumerian highest divine authority, Enlil; starvation is threatening. While there are drastic depictions of the damage wrought and the sufferings inflicted by intruders, the origin of the genre certainly may be connected with historical events of this kind, such as at the end of the Akkad, Ur-III, and Old Babylonian Empires or similar occasions. But constant copying of the relevant texts over long periods and their use also in other than commemorative contexts (e.g., reconstruction work on decrepit temples) suggest a wider amplitude of meaning for those compositions.[5] What about hymnic components in the pertinent texts?

The picture certainly is not uniform, and the different literary traditions and textual conglomerates make it difficult to achieve a clear vision of the ceremonial implications. But there are sporadic hymnic elements in almost all the compositions, and the life setting at least to some extent is reflected in the writings. Thus the Lamentation over the Destruction of Ur, after ten wailing (liturgical) passages (*kirugus*) ends in a segment of prayer wishes (ll. 418–435), the last line calling for praise of the moon god Nanna/Asimbabbar, who will restore the destroyed city (*metes hé-i-i*, "may praise go forth").[6] A formally parallel lamentation about the destruction of Sumer and Ur ends in a fifth *kirugu* that notably deviates from the wailing tone of the preceding parts. The last piece is a "discourse . . . against the agent of destruction," "part incantation, part blessing,"[7] and also shows the form of prayer wish ("storm, retreat to your home!"). One surprising example of how much hymnic components are made part of dire lamentation in the face (or imagination) of calamity is the Nippur composition from the time of Isme Dagan,[8] fourth ruler of Isin (ca. 1953–1935 BCE), long after the downfall of the Ur-III Empire. The lamentation features twelve *kirugus* with a total of 322 lines. "With its first half rooted in lamentations, and its second half distinctly hymnic in character, NL forges a connection between these literatures."[9] The mighty and benevolent performances of the deity are enumerated in grand style from the sixth to the eleventh *kirugu*. The final line proclaims ongoing eulogies: "They will praise forever!" (*me-teš$_2$*

---

5. See Kramer, "Lamentation over the Destruction of Nipur"; Michalowski, *The Lamentation over the Destruction of Sumer and Ur*; Römer, *Hymnen und Klagelieder in sumerischer Sprache*; Römer, *Die Klage über die Zerstörung von Ur*; Tinney, *The Nippur Lament*.

6. Römer, *Die Klage über die Zerstörung von Ur*, LU l. 435.

7. Michalowski, *Lamentation over Sumer and Ur*, 15.

8. See above all Kramer, "Lamentation over the Destruction of Nipur"; Tinney, *The Nippur Lament*.

9. Michalowski, *Lamentation over Sumer and Ur*, 24.

àm₃-i-i-ne).¹⁰ The tradition of city laments has been continued in a generalized way by *balag*-compositions¹¹ without much reference to historical sites or events. *Balags* originally are musical instruments, harps or drums, used for the accompaniment of mourning rites. The players usually are gala-priests. The texts sung take on the same designation, as the colophons intimate. In addition, *balag*-compositions, in the wake of city laments, sometimes utilize regular praise, in contrast to large sections of wailing. To give but one example, the song Ana Elume (Honored One of Heaven)¹² has wonderful eulogies to the sun-god Utu.

> l. a+93 The hero, the great hero, he who decides the fates!
>
> a+100 The prince, emanating light! The great hero!
>
> a+101 From the ends of heaven and earth the great hero!
>
> a+103 You are the child, the respected one, of the pure heavens,
>
> a+104 you are the elevated child of Enlil.

Praises of the deities seem often to be connected to petitionary ritual, symbolized by the "journeying of the gods to Enlil to plead that he end the devastation.¹³

Descent into the Netherworld

A second realm in which people encountered death and deemed it necessary here and there to sound praises to the ones on high we may see reflected in that literature dealing with the descent into the netherworld,¹⁴ usually featuring Inanna as the main protagonist. Behind those mythological

---

10. See Tinney, *The Nippur Lament*, NL ll. 157–295. The twelfth *kirugu* is a jubilant celebration of the "beautiful day" Enlil has created, with l. 322 and its solicitation of praise from the saved ones.

11. See Volk, *Die Balag-Komposition Uru Am-ma-ir-ra-bi*; Cohen, *The Canonical Lamentations of Ancient Mesopotamia*.

12. Cohen, *Canonical Lamentations*, 208–21.

13. Cohen, *Canonical Lamentations*, 38; see also the numerous invocations with a praising intention, e.g., in the *balag Mutin Numuz Dima* (Fashioning Man and Woman; ibid., 222–52). The final hymn of *Elum Gusum* (Honored One, Wild Ox; ibid., 272–318) shows still another style: (e+281) "You are my lord. Light of the city, you are a warrior. (e+282) My shining one, Umungurusha, you are a warrior (e+284) Like the sun you whirl about (in) the clouds. (e+285) Like the moon you spread forth your light."

14. See Hallo and van Dijk, *The Exaltation of Inanna*; Black, "A-se-er Gi₆-ta, a Balag of Inana"; Farber-Flügge, *Der Mythos Inanna und Enki*; Sladek, *Inanna's Descent to the Netherworld*; Alster, "Inanna Repenting"; Alster, "The Mythology of Mourning"; Alster, "Edin-na ú-sag-gá."

dramatizations, the universal experiences of dying and being buried probably loom large. In singling out such a general sphere of human pain and frustration, and thus taking "life settings" or recurring events met by ritualized responses" as a guiding category, I am fully aware (to emphasize this again) that we are using modern conceptualizations. Yet we are forced to do so, because old Sumerian and Akkadian rubrics, so plentifully preserved in colophons, simply are not too meaningful for us. Modern categorization helps us to understand better what was going on in antiquity; we always have to be on the alert, however, that our categories and concepts are different from the ancient ones'.

The Inanna-Dumuzi cycle of texts reflecting ritualized ceremonies certainly is an important area to consider in this context. It may be seen in connection with seasonal feasts of the dying and rebirth of nature. At this point I should like to point to one literary example closer to individual death, although the demarcation line toward seasonal dying may be a little haphazard. The extended dirge for Urnamma, founder of the Ur-III dynasty,[15] after narrating his death and burial, elaborately reports about his journey into the netherworld. Lines 81–131 are dedicated to the sacrifices Urnamma offers down there to nine different deities, apparently to win their support. Right after this performance he is installed as a "judge for those abiding in the depth" (132–144). Then a large section of lament follows (145–196). After an intervention by Inanna herself on behalf of Urnamma (197–216), it is Ningeszida, an underworld deity, earlier having received sacrifices from the descended (and deceased) ruler (114–119), who freshly decrees Urnamma's fate, apparently in order to release him (217–233). Consequently, praise is issued for Ningeszida (234–240) as a kind of thanksgiving. The somewhat broken passage ends in the words $^{d}nin\text{-}geš\text{-}zi\text{-}da\ zà\text{-}mi$, "(to) lord Ningeszida be praise!"—a common formula to denote hymnic texts (l. 240).[16]

Illness and Other Threats

The third life situations confronting people with death in antiquity, as well as in our own time, are grave illness or other threatening conditions of extreme impact. The texts and concomitant rituals of healing, rescue, or rehabilitation are quite diverse.[17] They usually include descriptions of

---

15. Last edition by Flückiger-Hawker, *Urnamma of Ur in Sumerian Literary Tradition*, 92–182.

16. In terms of funeral dirges, there has been at least one more specimen published by S. N. Kramer, which was in fact found on a tablet together with Urnamma A; see his *Two Elegies on a Pushkin Museum Tablet*.

17. The list of pertinent publications is very long; see, e.g., Cohen, *Sumerian*

disease or ill-fate, entreaties, vows. Prominent are, even more so than in Old Testament complaints, expressions of praise, either tied to the invocation of the deities or brought to attention in separate passages of the song or prayer. A good number of Sumerian literary genres belong under the rubric of "healing" or "exorcising" songs, such as the *ergemma* ("wail of the *šem*-drum"), *ergašḫunga* ("wail to pacify the heart"), *šu-ila* ("lifting up of hands"), and *namburbi* ("its [ritual] release"). Obviously, hymnic elements in the concert of complaint, reproach, and entreaty make good sense, just as in the Old Testament psalms referred to above. They want to assuage the wrath of God, to say the least. Thus, the *ergemma* number 34.2 opens with a long praise section.[18] Line 17 is typical—"Jubilation! My praising! My praising!"—and ll. 20–27 consequently all end in the shout "my praising!" (*el-lu ár-re-mu*). Many *ergabunga*s amplify their invocation to include hymnic attributes.[19] The same phenomenon occurs in *gu-ilas*[20] and late *namburbi*s.[21]

The really important question after this quick review of three realms of life-threatening experiences is: How does praise function in face of death or in commemoration of such situations? What have been the sentiments and rational arguments of ancient people to place (besides reproachful complaints, etc.) adoring words of praise into their wailing and mournful prayers?

The Power of Praise

Theoretical considerations about what praise can or should do in mourning contexts are hardly to be expected within cultic literature. We therefore quite often ingeniously presuppose that the parameters of hymnic praise in antiquity correspond to our own modes of thinking. For us, eulogies belong to a set of interhuman exchange on a sociopsychological level. They are

---

Hymnology; Maul, *"Herzberuhigungsklagen"*; Maul, *Zukunftsbewältigung*; Cunningham, *"Deliver Me from Evil"*; Zgoll, *Die Kunst des Betens*.

18. Cohen, *Sumerian Hymnology*, 131–35.
19. Maul, *"Herzberuhigungsklagen,"* 18.
20. Zgoll, *Die Kunst des Betens*, passim.
21. Maul, *Zukunftsbewältigung*, 87; see also, e.g., 302, ll. 12–18: "Ihr, die großen Götter seid es doch, die / die Entscheidung über Himmel und Erde, über Grundwasser (und) Mee[re] recht leiten! / Euer Wort ist Leben, das, was aus eurem Munde kommt, ist H[ei]l, / euer Ausspruch ist doch Leben! Die das Innere des / fernen Himmels betreten, seid doch ihr, die das Unheil entfernen, / das [G]ute bereit[en], die lösen die unheilvollen, Kräfte' (und) Omenanzeiger, / die [schreck]lichen, unguten Träu[me], die den Faden des Unheils durchtrennen."

to flatter authorities, produce benevolence and assistance, enhance interpersonal and social well-being, and so forth. All this may be true also for ancient hymn-singing, but there may be more to those acts of laudation so plentifully expressed and performed in all kind of cultic poetry. The linguistic expressions used to indicate hymnic praise through ancient and partly well into modern languages may be suggestive of a basic intention. Praises to deities across ancient Near Eastern cultures and religions are meant to "exalt," "make great," "lift up," "glorify" the gods addressed. That means that a real transfer of power, from the hymn-singer to the deity, is taking place. Or, to put it differently, human adoration, materialized in sacrifices, accompanying cultic rites and not least in significance, hymnic praise, strengthens the deity. It is even essential for the deity himself or herself.[22] There are some passages within extant hymnic materials of old that seem explicitly to make a case for this interpretation. If this should be correct, we may find the key to understanding praise passages even in lamentations and complaints, those wailing texts confronting the threat of death.

The prayer of Enheduana, high priestess of Ur installed by her father Sargon of Akkad known under the Sumerian title *nin-me-šara*, "lady of thousands of *meš*," does offer conspicuous hints as to what praise can do.[23] To begin with, the closing line declares the whole poem, in spite of its plaintive and perhaps juridical air, a "hymn of praise": *nin-gú$_{10}$ hi-li gú è ^{d}Inana zà-mí* ("my mistress, clad in enchantment, [to you] Inanna, be praise!" l. 153).[24] In reciting praises for Inanna, the priestess in fact tells her *meš*, her divine powers (ll. 65–67, 123–132), thus helping to constitute the authority of the goddess. Thus Zgoll translates l. 134: "my mistress, this [recitation] has made you greater, you have become the greatest!" The author's overall comment is: "It is En-ḫe-du-Ana's task now, to make effective, in a maieutic (like a midwife's) way, the real potentiality of her Nin-me-šara, namely to help her goddess to give birth to the divine power, the fullness of her *mes*?"[25]

---

22. This seems to be a rather well-known fact in the science of religion and religious anthropology but a widely ignored one among theologians and philosophers who defend the omnipotence and omniscience of the exclusive and unique God.

23. See Zgoll, *Der Rechtsfall*. The text of 153 lines is given in transliteration and German translation on pp. 2–17 and as a text-critical edition with all available variants on pp. 205–94. The author discusses extensively not only philological and literary aspects but also the cultural and religious implications; see the chapter on "The Reality Represented by the *Meš*" (66–75).

24. The philological part notes that in most manuscripts the last words "to Inanna be praise" are somewhat set apart, but they nevertheless are not a colophon but an intrinsic part of the text (Zgoll, *Der Rechtsfall*, 494).

25. Zgoll, *Der Rechtsfall*, 147, with reference in n. 601 to Falkenstein, *Sumerische Götterlieder*, vol. 1, 21, a description of Enlil's *meš*.

One should perhaps modify the metaphor of "midwifing" to "creating" or "constituting" divine powers. In any case, the act of praising and making praise publicly known, often mentioned in Sumerian hymns, is part of the performative processes that are inherent in hymnic praise.

The Old Testament gives a comparable scenario in which the power and authority of Yahweh are strengthened or constituted by lesser divine beings, Ps 29:1–2:

> Ascribe to Yahweh, O heavenly beings
> > ascribe to Yahweh glory and strength.
> Ascribe to Yahweh the glory of his name;
> > worship Yahweh in holy splendor."

Ascription is really the act of "bringing to," of "furnishing" or "providing," the potentiality Yahweh needs and, of course, can legitimately ask for from his subordinates or vassals.

If there is some truth to these observations, a number of Old Testament passages could be understood along the line indicated. The thanksgiving of Jonah inside the big fish or that of Hezekiah in Isa 38 would not only be anticipated praises but could signify powerful motions to initiate the process of divine rescue. The same would be true for the late Greek version of Dan 2, when the victims in the fire-oven try to create or induce Yahweh's power so necessary for their salvation. Along the same vein, all other adduced Old Testament passages of praise, found in lamenting or complaining contexts, surely indicate an active participation of the supplicants to strengthen divine potentialities of saving the miserable from death.

4

"World Dominion" in Yahweh Kinship Psalms

Down to the Roots of Globalizing Concepts and Strategies

Yahweh's Kingship

Universal Reign

ALTHOUGH A GOOD NUMBER of literary and compositional problems remain unsolved,[1] the cluster of Pss 93 through 100 (plus Ps 47) does feature some remarkable and in a way unique theological concepts in comparison to many other layers of the Hebrew Scriptures. Among them, the idea of Yahweh's dominance over the whole world and all nations, no doubt, is the most prominent, comparable only to the preaching of Second Isaiah and some wisdom discourses in the book of Job.[2] What, in effect, is the exact meaning and location of such claims for a universal reign encompassing the entirety of earthly beings and all geographic regions? How did they come about in terms of cultural and religious history? Since we ourselves are—economically, politically, ideologically—very much involved in complicated issues of globalization, our interests in the beginnings of a unified world to

---

1. To name but a few: Why has Ps 47 been separated from the group, or has it not? What is the function of Ps 94 within the cluster of kingship texts? Can we really postulate a lucid scheme of composition in Pss 93 to 100? To what specific end has the compilation taken place? Cf. the most recent commentaries on the Psalms: Hossfeld and Zenger, *Psalmen 51–100*, 643–713 [ET *Psalms 2: 51–100*]; Gerstenberger, *Psalms, Part 2*, 173–206.

2. Cf., for example, Isa 44:6–8, 24–28; 49:1–6, 22–26; 52:7–12; Job 38–41.

be ruled by just one superior power is undeniable. Of course, such actual interest may cloud or distort recognition of ancient outlooks and evaluations. Be that as it may, we should venture a fresh look at the Psalter and at some evidence from the ancient Near East in order to get a fuller perspective on unified government over a unified world.

Yahweh the Supreme God

The psalms we are discussing focus on Israel's God, as a great many hymns in the ancient Near East customarily do in regard to determined central deities. Divine power and authority are being enhanced (cf. Ps 29). Singing and shouting to his or her honor in a very substantial, material way "brings about" that very glory, splendor, and strength demanded from adorants, be they celestial or human ones. Small wonder, therefore, that the Yahweh kingship songs instigate that glorification ("Sing to Yahweh . . . ," Ps 96:1-3) and at the same time heap on God honorific attributions: Yahweh, God of Israel, is the "awesome Most High" (*elyon kor*), the "Great king" (*melek gadol*), the "King of all the earth" (*melek kol ha-areṣ*).[3] He has taken up monarchic government—the famous phrase is, with slight variations (*melek elohim [yhwh]*).[4] Now he is executing his divine offices and responsibilities: as the creator of "heaven and earth" to provide good living conditions, to combat evil powers and sustain the just ones, to let shine forth his power to his own glorification. All these functions of a supreme deity are being portrayed, as it seems, in a universalistic way, in terms of time and space, as well as in the political and religious realms.

Geographically speaking, the reign of Yahweh covers all the world; politically, the sum total of nations is affected. Emphatic designation of his reign's territorial extension over "all the earth" (*kol ha-'areṣ*; cf. Pss 47:3, 8; 97:5, 9) corresponds to his overlordship over "all the Gods" (*kol 'elohim*; cf. Pss 95:3; 96:4) and obeisance of "all the nations" (*kol ha-'ammim*); cf. Pss 47:2; 96:3; 99:2), and "the peoples" (*ha-goyim*; cf. Pss 96:3, 10; 98:2). Is this mere exaggerating, poetical rhetoric which disregards reality and in fact only envisions the small world of local interests around one's own church steeple? Hardly so. Evidence of a universal outlook may come from that special term *tebel*, frequently used in the Psalms, meaning the "inhabited world," "full disk floating upon the primeval waters."[5] As such, *tebel* is

---

3. Ps 47:3, 8; similar titles and attributes in Pss 93:3; 96:4, 6.

4. Pss 47:9; 93:1; 96:10; 97:1; 99:1. Comparable is the enthronement shout for human kings (2 Kgs 9:13).

5. Pss 93:1; 96:10, 13; 97:4; 98:7, 9; and outside the kingship collection, Pss 24:1;

a synonym of 'aphse-'areṣ, "rims of the earth."[6] The universal perspective comes to the fore vividly in those cosmological (and eschatological?) judgment scenarios, extant also in two Yahweh kingship texts: Pss 96:10–13; 98:7–9). The first one is an opportune example:

> Say among the nations [goyim], "Yahweh is king!
> The world [tebel] is firmly established; it shall not be moved. He will judge the peoples ['ammim] with equity."
> Let the heavens be glad, and let the earth ['areṣ] rejoice;
> let the sea [yam] roar, and all that fills it;
> let the field [śade] exult, and everything in it.
> Then shall all the trees of the forest sing for joy
> before Yahweh; for he is coming,
> for he is coming to judge the earth ['areṣ].
> He will judge the world [tebel] with righteousness,
> and the peoples ['ammim] with his truth.
> (Ps 96:10–13 NRSV, except for "Yahweh")

The vocabulary of worldwide rule includes geographical and political terms. "Peoples" in this context refers to "foreign nations," they are here named goyim and 'ammim. Another most conspicuous one is le'ammim, "people," which occurs only in poetic/liturgical contexts, including in Ps 47:4.[7] All the people on the earth, is the seemingly preposterous claim, are subjects of Yahweh, Israel's God. This affirmation coincides with so many in ancient Near Eastern and Persian hymnic and political statements, made on behalf of imperial state gods and their human emperors, as we shall see. Geographical designations of our passage above include tebel, 'areṣ, yam, śade, and they all can carry mythical and universalistic connotations. One more expression belonging into this line is 'iyyim, "islands" or "coastlands," occurring quite frequently in Second Isaiah and once in the kingship psalms.[8] The cluster

---

33:8; 50:12; 89:12; Fabry and van Meeteren, TWAT 8:547–54. Both authors emphasize the late, i.e. exilic/post-exilic, use of the term and its uncertain etymological background. Derivation from the Akkadian tfbalu, "dry land," is possible.

6. Ps 98:3; cf. Pss 2:8; 59:14; 72:8; Isa 45:22; 52:10; Jer 16:19; Zech 9:10.

7. Thirteen times in the Psalter: Pss 2:1; 7:8; 9:9; 44:3, 15; 47:4; 57:10; 65:8; 67:5; 105:44; 108:4; 148:11; 149:7, and prominent in Second Isaiah (cf. Isa 41:1; 43:4, 9–10; 49:1; 51:4; 55:5). Preuß affirms that the word primarily means other nations in opposition to Israel and that it is typically part of scenarios describing Yahweh's world governance ("le'im," in TWAT 4:412–13).

8. Isa 41:1, 5; 42:4, 10, 12, 15; 49:1; 51:5; Ps 97:1. The notion is of inhabited places

of concepts which should be augmented by notions of enemies, opponents,[9] creation works and their liturgical backgrounds, garments and royal implements, etc., is indicative of a cohesive mental picture of one world under the "jurisdiction" of Yahweh, the creator of the universe. Noticeable are the inclusion of all peoples in a kind of final judgment and the partaking of foreign leaders in a kind of covenant ceremony:

> Clap your hands, all you peoples ['ammim];
>> shout to God with loud songs of joy.
> For Yahweh, the Most High, is awesome,
>> a great king over all the earth [kol-ha-'areṣ].
>> (Ps 47:2-3, ET 1-2)
> God is king over the nations [goyim];
>> God sits on his holy throne.
> The princes of the peoples [nedibe 'ammim] gather
>> as the people ['am] of the God of Abraham.
> For the shields of the earth [maginne-'areṣ] belong to God;
>> he is highly exalted. (Ps 47:9-10; ET 8-9)[10]

There is little doubt that Yahweh is being portrayed in the kingship psalms with colors taken from mythopoetic, priestly-liturgical, and royal-administrative backgrounds. In each one of these realms we may detect tendencies of construing the world as a unified entity. The open question is: In which way did the Hebrew psalmists work out this concept within the broader stream of ancient Near Eastern and Persian traditions? Again, we have to alert ourselves to the possible distorting influence of modern

---

at the far rim of the earth-disk floating on the primeval ocean. The globalizing aspects can be seen neatly, e.g., in Isa 42:10-12, a "summons to worship" for all the world: "Sing to Yahweh a new song, / his praise from the end of the earth! / Let the sea roar and all that fills it, / the coastlands ('iyyim) and their inhabitants. / . . . Let them give glory to Yahweh, / and declare his praise in the coastlands ('iyyim)."

9. In the kingship psalms, Yahweh's opponents are partly depicted, in a mythical way, as primeval forces of chaos who have to acclaim his sovereignty: "The floods have lifted up, O Yahweh, / the floods have lifted up their voice; / the floods lift up their roaring" (Ps 93:3).

10. The terms used for world leadership ("princes," "shields," v. 10) are highly poetical and honorific, but hardly used as titles in common language. "Shield," of course, belongs to the military sphere, and occurs as divine epithets, e.g., in Pss 18:3, 31; 33:20; 59:12; 144:1-2. "Prince," strangely enough, literally means "volunteer" or "benefactor"; the word is rooted most of all in cultic language. Perhaps the idea behind the designation is this: national leaders have to be wealthy, in order to be able to give freely and abundantly to God and their subjects; cf. Conrad, *TWAT* 5:237-45.

concepts of homogeneity in world interpretation, linked to a millenary history of monotheistic and scientific thinking.[11]

Benefits for Israel

Concepts of the world, "worldviews," are always rooted in determined social and cultural contexts. They are not abstract and disinterested designs, fallen from heaven like meteors. Even universalistic explanations of the world are being contrived from particular vantage points, usually from some center of real or imagined authority. Given an integral outlook on time and space, we should not hastily conclude that the basis and origin of encompassing views is equally far-reaching and universal. Immanuel Kant's material and spiritual home was a tiny city named Königsberg in a small kingdom called Prussia. It was from this angle that the famous philosopher designed his overall picture of the universe. His mental frame truly did not correspond with the horizons of his living place, but, on the other hand, it somehow was confined by the local, eastern European worldview. Vice versa, the concepts of the "kingdom of Yahweh" in the Psalter were nurtured by an insignificant people. Yahweh had a counterpart in "his" people of Israel. We thus have reason to look for the interrelationship between God and people, i.e., for the center of interest within the kingship psalms. Astonishingly, there is no royal institution visible in these psalms which could serve as an administrator of divine orientations.

In my opinion, our collection clearly bears witness to its origin and use, lacking a monarchic system of implementation. There are conspicuous occurrences of the first person plural in some texts, which make the best sense when attributed to the exilic or post-exilic community of faithful Judahites. Recent research leads to that conclusion.[12] The assumption is that a plurality of persons joining in hymn singing barely reflects vertical monarchic but rather horizontal community structures. In fact, the communal "we" seems to be extremely rare in comparable ancient Near Eastern sacral texts. In the Psalter, however, this stylistic form abounds. Examples taken from the kingship group are: Pss 47:4-5, 7; 95; 98:3; 99:5, 8, 9. Among these

---

11. Astrophysicists, for instance, seem to be compelled by Western tradition to search for the pinpoint, exclusive beginning of celestial "history," the "Urknall," to be localized exactly in time and space, a totally absurd undertaking for Hindu or Buddhist thinkers.

12. Two studies so far have pointed out this relationship: Scharbert, "Das 'Wir' der Psalmen auf dem Hintergrund altorientalischen Betens"; Seybold, "Das 'Wir' in den Asaph-Psalmen." I myself have extensively utilized the evidence in *Psalms, Parts 1* and *Psalms, Part 2*.

passages are invocations of "Yahweh, our God," affirmations that he "chose and saved Israel" and "put peoples [*leʾammim*] under our feet" (Ps 47:4),[13] and most of all a kind of liturgical summons to Deuteronomistic preaching:

> O come, let us worship and bow down,
>   let us kneel before Yahweh, our Maker!
> For he is our God,
>   and we are the people of his pasture, and the sheep of his hand.
> O that today you would listen to his voice . . . (Ps 95:6–7; NRSV)

It seems obvious that first the community is speaking or, respectively, a liturgist in the name of his or her congregation. Then, abruptly, it is Yahweh's own voice, communicated by some speaker or mediator of the divine word (vv. 7c–11), addressing directly the assembled crowd in the second person plural, pleading for obedience over against God's manifest will and orientation. Style, form, and content are very much like so many admonitions and warnings in the book of Deuteronomy and other Deuteronomistic literature.[14] Reading this text, we are entering, so to speak, the lecture hall of Judahite communities.

Given the *Sitz im Leben* of early Judaic worship services either in Babylonia or at home, the theological contents of the Yahweh kingship psalms fall in line. Israel, or the "pride of Jacob" (Ps 47:5), the "people of Abraham's God" (Ps 47:10), the "people of his pasture, sheep of his hand" (Ps 95:7), the "faithful," "righteous," and "upright in heart" (Ps 97:10–12), is the partner of that universal deity who is in real command of the extant, contemporary empire. "He has fashioned us, not we ourselves; we are his people, the sheep of his pasture," as Ps 100:3 aptly summarizes. Yahweh wields all powers over the nations; they are—just like Israel herself—offered a chance to acknowledge his rule (cf. Pss 47:5–9; 96:7–9). If they do not comply, adorers of worthless idols will perish or be compelled to praise the supreme god (cf. Pss 93; 96:5–6, 13; 97:6–7; 98:9). It is God's own people which is at the center of world affairs. On behalf of Israel, Yahweh's universal rule is being executed and administered. Israel's privileged position as a chosen people also transpires in Ps 93:5: The "decrees" or "testimonies" [*ʿeduth*] apparently refer to the Torah for all the world, while Ps 95 recounts the reception of

---

13. Within the kingship psalms, this is the only occurrence, but cf. Pss 2:1; 9:9; 44:3, 15; 57:10; 65:8; 67:5; 105:44; 108:4; 117:1; 148:11; Isa 34:1; 41:1; 43:4, 9; 49:1; 55:4; Preuß, "*leʾom*," in *TWAT* 4:411–13. The term "overbords the limits of Israel, in order to demonstrate Yahweh's power *over* peoples and nations" (413).

14. Commentators agree on this affinity to Deuteronomistic sources. A prime example is the preaching of Deut 29:9–14; 30:11, 15–20.

Torah in the wilderness (cf. Exod 17:1–7; 19–34). Significantly, in the kingship psalms there are hardly any polemics against the "other" gods, as we are accustomed to encounter in many prophetic texts (cf. Isa 13–23; Jer 46–51).

World Dominion in the Ancient Near East

Conditions of Universal Concepts

We have now to consider the background of ancient Near Eastern concepts of world government in order to understand better what the Psalms are talking about. An adequate point of departure is the cultural and religious history of Mesopotamia, Egypt, and Persia, which we can undertake only ephemerally and cursorily at this point. "Worldviews" in general to a large part depend on ways and degrees of social organization. We are hardly able to develop visions of family, clan, village, urban center, state, or nation without ever having experienced these specific forms of life. Therefore, the concept of government over a more or less unified world hardly can antedate real experiences with imperial states. Where and when are we allowed to talk about multi-ethnic entities which deserve the characterization of "empire?" Since when have imperial rulers claimed to occupy and rule over the "whole" of the earth? Consequently, our query is for developing political structures, their mental profiles and religious rationales.

It is a well-known fact that the ancient Near East has been the cradle of humanity in a very special sense. It was in the fertile crescent that, at about ten thousand years BCE, migrating groups of hunters and gatherers invented agricultural methods, turned sedentary, and formed larger settlements. By the fourth millennium BCE, the tightly organized political model of "city-states" under clannish or monarchic leadership had emerged, the history of which we are able to trace in written documents through the third millennium BCE. Inter-city and territorial political entities soon sprang up. And during the periods called "Early Dynastic" and "(Old) Akkadian" (roughly 2800 to 2100 BCE), the first larger conglomerations of power begin to appear. It is this trajectory of a social unfolding from agnatically construed, small-scale groups via tribal associations, neighborhood communities, various forms of state government towards multiple stages of imperial organization that does constitute the background of our search for effective ideas of world dominion under the rule, as it where, of gods and their earthly regents. Ancient Near Eastern texts, mostly of the royal and hymnic genres, make it abundantly clear that the developments of political bodies and their mental models from "natural" smallness to gigantic conglomerates really took place step by step in the three millenniums of the pre-Christian era, culminating with the Persian, Hellenistic, and Roman empires. Many details still remain clouded from our view, and quite often experts disagree in evaluating extant facts, but the varying notions of society and statehood in the ancient Near East stand out in the relevant literatures. Hebrew Scriptures and also the kingship psalms are part of this tradition, and hopefully can be placed into this wider context. I venture to point out a few relevant steps in the process, drawing chiefly on royal inscriptions of two millennia. Mythical and liturgical texts should be consulted as well, but limited space and time are prohibiting a fuller probe into these materials at this time.

Third Millennium Beginnings

For the Sumerians, "kingship" was the most logical form of government. It "descended from heaven," casting anchor, so to speak, in successive Sumerian cities like Eridu, Bad-tibira, Larak, Sippar, Shuruppak ("before the flood"), and Kish, Uruk, Ur ("after the flood").[15] The early and basic extensions of royal power were the limits of the respective city-state. Most frequently, the titles *fugal*, literally "great man," and *ensi*, "ruler, governor"[16] or perhaps "priestly prince," denoting political and religious competence, are combined with the native city, e.g., Urnanshe (ca. 2550 BCE),[17] *lugal/ensi* of Lagash or Lugalzagesi (ca. 2350 BCE), and *lugal/ensi* of Umma.

The ideological and theological background of Sumerian and Akkadian royal titles in the third millennium, of course, is very important for us. As long as the city-states existed side by side, each one adhered to its own deities. Growing prestige and power of some cities also elevated particular gods and goddesses to more prominent positions. The claims of higher authority of determined rulers and their divine city patrons or matrons intertwined, promoting each other mutually. Such an extension of divine power and authority certainly was concomitant with Sumerian outreaches to and conquests of the hostile mountainous regions to the north and east. All this means to say is that in pre-Sargonic times, Sumerian centers of power (city-states) were on their way to expand their spheres of influence towards the peripheries. They already legitimated their claims for dominion

15. The so-called "Sumerian King List" was probably compiled at the end of the third millennium utilizing older materials; cf. Jacobsen, *The Sumerian King List*; Edzard, "Königslisten und Chroniken. A. Sumerisch."

16. Hallo, *Early Mesopotamian Royal Titles*, 45; there had been in use a more archaic title, *en*, "overlord," down to the Akkad period.

17. Approximate dates according to Postgate, *Early Mesopotamia*, and the *Cambridge Ancient History*.

by theological affirmations, alleging superior authority of their own gods. The dominant city with its central temple becomes the hub of the world, as far as military and economic dominance are concerned.[18]

The empire founded by king Sargon of Akkad (ca. 2350 BCE), basically run by Semitic speaking ethnic groups who nevertheless seem to have been fully integrated into Sumerian traditions, takes further steps into the same direction. In large inscriptions, Sargon, "King of Agade," gives a comprehensive survey of all his battles won, cities and territories taken over. Kings are considered the vice-regents of sovereign highest deities, be they Anu, Enlil, Ishtar, Suen, or others. Conferring their divine power not only in the domestic sphere but also over other nations and kings to the elected one in some capital of Sumer and Akkad seems to be a topic as early as King Lugalzagesi of Umma, defeated thereafter by contemporary Sargon of Akkad.

We should be cautious, however. Later readers, especially we ourselves, working subconsciously with experiences of subsequent historical periods, tend to project a coherent and universal world order into ancient texts. Acknowledging an ideal construction of ancient worldviews from the imperial rulers' own vantage points (center to periphery), we do not really know whether these designs have been all-inclusive or not. Enemies are beaten down, their domains incorporated into the victorious state. The king triumphantly tells about his deeds, but does he really negate every possible other political competitor beyond the rims of his sphere of influence? Trade relations with distant peoples and cultures teach a different lesson. The tendency to claim all-inclusive authority apparently has been virulent in some way. But was it a rational and pragmatic motion? Or the other way around: our own concepts of "one God, one world" certainly have been shaped by a long Christian and scientific tradition of a completely homogeneous, mono-causal world. Obviously, it is difficult for us to abstract from this modern worldview. Looking at the ancient texts as pragmatically as possible, it seems that much of the energy of dominating all the earth, already present in these ancient rulers, was clad in mythopoetic concepts of winning and maintaining control within a large part of that world, comprising Mesopotamia and some of its neighboring territories to the east, north, and west, e.g., Elam, Mari, Ebla, etc. The rest of the world, which certainly was known to exist beyond the neighboring states, did not matter too much yet, being included in a vague way ("four corners," "all foreign nations," etc.).

---

18. Cf. Maul, "Die altorientalische Hauptstadt—Abbild und Nabel der Welt"; and George, "'Bond of the Lands': Babylon, the Cosmic Capital."

Second Millennium and into the First

After the decline of the Akkad Empire towards the end of the third millennium, some more locally restricted rulers figure prominently on the historical stage, like Gudea, King of Lagash and environs, famous for his temple building activities, and the third dynasty of Ur, dominating much of Mesopotamia and some eastern and northern territories roughly between 2100 and 2000 BCE. Apparently we cannot speak of real, universal political ambitions during this period, yet some of the older concepts linger on.[19] The extreme power going out from the temple and the presence of the mighty, heavenly god is quite often described as a "frightening glare" which "fills" the world.[20] Even if Gudea does not accumulate so many royal titles reaching beyond his home territories, the innermost drive to look outward from the center place into the world beyond is quite visible in the texts. And humanly speaking, it is familiar to all of us, especially in our individualized modernity.[21] Ur III rulers more or less fall into line with those of Gudea and their predecessors formulaic language as far as royal titles or the description of divine potentialities are concerned. They all, with the exception of Ur-nammu, use the title "king of the four corners."[22] Only the exact meaning, to my mind, is not clear at that point.

The second millennium—the periods of mere city-states having more or less passed by—is filled with hegemonial struggles between territorial states of comparable size and power; Babylonia, Assyria, Hatti, Egypt, Elam, Mari, Amurru, Mitanni, and others. The outlook on the world remains about the same: affirmations of superior or seemingly all-encompassing power, reality of wars with strong neighbors.[23] The monarch's functions, however, are

---

19. Cf. Sallaberger, "Ur III—Zeit." Political reality possibly contradicts religious belief, in that the rulers from Sulgi onward use the more ambitious title of "King of the four corners" (p. 180). But to me it remains dubious whether or not at this early time the formula had a universal connotation (cf. Hallo, *Early Mesopotamian Titles*, 49–56). The same doubt is even stronger in regard to the divine determination of royal names of the period. Divination of the king does not indicate a universal worldview of his subjects or courtiers (differently Steiner, "Altorientalische Reichvorstellungen im 3. Jahrtausend," 134), which appears to be a modern monotheistic projection.

20. Cf. Hartenstein, *Die Unzugänglichkeit Gottes im Heiligtum*, 69–76; and Podella, *Das Lichtkleid JHWHs*.

21. Richter, a psychiatrist, labels the modern human drive for total autonomy as an autistic effort to fill the vacuum left by the banishment of God from reality (*Der Gotteskomplex*).

22. Cf. Thureau-Dangin, *Die sumerischen und akkadischen Königsinschriften*, 191–96; and Sallaberger, "Ur III—Zeit," 123, 180.

23. Thus Hammurapi, in his prologue to the famous law stipulations, claims successive installment of the god Marduk, his capital city Babylon, and her regent Hammurapi.

circumscribed solely in regard to his own people and land. Administration of justice, in the first place, and protection against intruders, are all to the benefit of the "black-haired" Mesopotamians (Codex Hammurapi 1,1–41), not for anything like a world population. Nevertheless, Hammurapi's reign has been very intimately linked with the ascent of the god Marduk, and vice versa. Power was understood in terms of superhuman capability, endowed in the king, but still it was visualized more in actual national structures than in an overarching world society.[24]

The Assyrians brought a new, aggressive dimension into the world dominion concepts. Not only did they pointedly take up age-old traditions of empire, sometimes taking the rulers of Akkad as their spiritual and political forbears, they also developed their own mastery of war techniques, political organization, and religious ethos on behalf of imperial expansion.[25] The reasons for their peculiar ways of striving for and building up their hegemony may be sought in a mixture of ethnic traits, economic and political situations prevalent in the upper Tigris region, and faith in the supreme national deity, the (all)mighty Assur. Highest heavenly authority then is communicated to the royal administrator of Assur's rule on earth.[26]

24. It certainly would be of great interest to look at some contemporary non-Semitic-speaking nations, e.g., of Hittite or Egyptian provenance. Although there may be noticed Mesopotamian influences in Asia Minor and tendencies of deifying the living or deceased monarch, we are probably justified in stating that the worldviews in both neighboring cultures focused on the respective own lands, and that an outreach for universal dominance at least does not seem to have been a primary concern. For the Hittite kingdom, cf. Goetze, *Kleinasien*, 88–90, 135–46. The Pharaohs of Egypt, for their part, were gods or god-like, but even in the period of greatest expansion and opening up towards the foreign parts of the world (New Kingdom, about 1500–1100 BCE), Egyptians thought more in terms of isolation from barbarous "other ones" than of incorporating all territories until the end of the earth (cf. Assmann, *Ägypten: Eine Sinngeschichte*, 171–73, 232–42).

25. The widespread fame of Assyrians being cruel warriors and ruthless exploiters of their power position echoes in ancient Near Eastern documents, among them some prophetic writings (cf. Isa 10:5).

26. As, for instance, in one of the earliest inscriptions of the empire: "God Assur, great Lord, who properly administers all the gods, grantor of scepter and crown, sustainer of sovereignty . . ." (following are hymnic invocations of equally great, yet somehow subordinated, deities: Enlil, Sin, Samas, Adad, Ninurta, and finally Istar) "foremost among the gods, mistress of tumult, who adorns battles . . ." (then the king is introduced as) "unrivalled king of the universe, king of the four quarters, king of all princes, lord of lords, chief herdsman, king of kings" (Tiglath-Pileser I [1114–1076 BCE], in his hymnic introduction to an extensive triumphant inscription). Cf. Grayson, *Assyrian Rulers of the Third and Second Millenia (to 1115 B.C.)* (=Tiglath-Pileser 1, I, ll. 1–14, 29–30).

Noteworthy is the last part of the honorific list: Dominance is personalized to demonstrate dependence of foreign potentates on the Assyrian "Supreme-King." This feature coincides with the lengthy reports of battles and conquests; it is confirmed by

It was this supreme deity which commanded the Assyrian armies to march south- and westwards and occupy all territories. "By the command of Assur" is a constant legitimating phrase in extant royal inscriptions.[27] They are, consequently, painstaking in listing military achievements. They demonstrate a special sensibility for the central importance of the human king (titles, epithets, glorifications). And, most of all, they betray a keen awareness for "political (i.e. imperial) theory." The Assyrian governments tried to impose one and the same "language of obedience" in an ethnically pluralistic world, aiming at an ideologically homogeneous world empire. The Assyrians thus seem to have made significant progress towards modern homogenizing concepts of one worldwide empire. Small wonder, then, that they also developed further (especially since Sargon II [721–705 BCE]) not the term itself but the notion and brutal practice of "holy war," that is, of expanding the reign of their national god, laying the grounds, as it were, for later campaigns of this sort.[28]

Persian World Dominance

When the states of Asia Minor, Mesopotamia, Syria, Palestine, and finally also of the Nile valley broke down under the onslaught of Persian armies, a new empire was formed, the center of which was located to the east of the mountain ranges that limited Mesopotamia, on the Iranian highlands. It is worthwhile to note that the Achaemenian rulers took over a good many customs and rites, political experiences, and religious beliefs found in those ancient cultures they met on their way west. But it is equally obvious that they brought with them views and values of their home cultures, ranging as far as the old eastern Iran. Most of all, the oldest parts of the Avesta, the

---

Assyrian vassal treaties, the iconography of Assyrian palaces, and mythological and religious texts, all of which deserve closer attention. In the context of the whole royal report, the old titles "King of Kish" and "King of the four quarters," combined with the designation "unrivalled," now seem to aim at world dominance in a fuller sense than those inscriptions of the third millennium. Still, we have to distinguish between ancient and modern concepts of world rule, as the invocation of seven high gods suggests.

27. It is already Šamši-Adad I (1813–1781 BCE) who thus adduces divine instigation for world dominion. Other gods besides Assur naturally support these ambitions, as, e.g., Ishtar, "the controller of the entire heaven and underworld" (Grayson, RIMA, vol. 1, 58). Adad-narari I (1305–1274 BCE), e.g., boasts himself of many ambitious titles and epithets, and he describes himself and the interference of his deities like this: "capturer of all people, the king at whose feet the gods Anu, Assur, Samas, Adad, and Istar made all rulers and princes bow down" (Grayson, RIMA, vol. 1, 131).

28. Cf. Weippert, "'Heiliger Krieg' in Israel und Assyrien"; and Ruffing, *Jahwekrieg als Weltmetapher*.

sacred writings of Iranian religion, apparently go back to the very eastern parts of the Persian Empire. This also means that the religion and culture of the Achaemenians were different from those found in the Near Eastern regions. How did the ancient Persians deal with the complex nature of world rule? What was their design of universal power, if they held any concepts of this kind?

Concentrating on our subject matter, we may affirm that official religion, going back to Zoroaster and superseding older types of religious faith, clearly provided sufficient background for a worldwide government. Ahura Mazda, "wise Lord," "Lord of Wisdom," in this faith, was the only and universal creator of heaven and earth, all humankind, and all living beings. The message, communicated by the supreme deity to Zoroaster, his prophet, claimed to be valid for all people regardless of national or racial background. Faith in Ahura Mazda is meant to be proclaimed to all people on the face of the earth; there is no distinction of ethnic or national bodies. Humankind is divided only into those who will listen and adhere to Ahura Mazda's teachings and others who will disobey the call to "do, think, and speak" good. There are no national or ethnic strings attached to being a follower of the Truth. At the end of history or after one's own death, respectively, every human being will be judged according to his or her life's results. The crucial point is personal decision for the good principle, offered and demanded by the "Lord of Wisdom," implemented by Vohu Manah, the "good will" and Asa, the all-ruling "just world order." In contrast to Mesopotamian worldviews, it seems that Zoroastrian faith had neither geographical nor an ultimate dynastic center of gravity, in spite of the fact that Persian rulers felt commissioned by their national god. Their religious politics of relative tolerance to the faith of their subjects seem to presuppose that the universal "wise Lord," who never was called a "king" himself, was operating even in foreign cults under the names of alien deities.[29] Before this background, Persian emperors of the Achaemenian dynasty presented themselves as global rulers called and ordained by the creator of the universe, Ahuramazda.[30] In the wake of ancient predecessors, they proclaimed themselves "Great Kings," "King of Kings," "King of the countries," and they claimed that Ahuramazda gave to them "power/empire," with definite universal connotations.[31] Taken together with those affirmations which

---

29. Cf. Mary Boyce, *Under the Achaemenians*, 62–65.

30. The influence of Zoroastrian religion on political philosophy and practices among the Achaemenian rulers is much debated in scholarship. In spite of taking over much of Mesopotamian, Egyptian, etc., concepts, however, the great kings of the time did not hide their affiliation to Ahuramazda and Persian traditions.

31. The most famous instance is that of the monumental Behistun Inscription:

refer to the kings' reign over "countries," "races," and "all the earth," this terminology of dominion makes a strong case for an underlying concept of "one world"—"one rule." As already pointed out, crucial features in the last mentioned titles appear to be designed not so much from an ancient Mesopotamian perspective of city-states (center and horizon) as from a multi-national basis. The iconography of adoration and support, prevalent in Persian monumental art, points in the same direction.[32] In short, Persian religion and the political philosophy of the Achaemenid kings took another step towards a full-fledged idea of worldwide rule of one designated emperor over all the inhabitants of the earth. The theological basis for such thinking seems to have been a special faith in that exclusive god who created the universe and the principle of "good" or "best" human action. The other way around, belief in a universal god in the Persian tradition apparently grew out of experienced instability of social life. Zoroaster himself and his followers may have been on the move, as raisers of cattle, first in the eastern part of the country, then during centuries of "going west." The much older cultures of Mesopotamia originally must have exercised a special fascination for the "barbarians" of the East.

Yahweh Kingship within Ancient Near Eastern Traditions

Our task at this point, as I see it, is to evaluate the concepts of world dominion, found in the Yahweh kingship psalms, within the immense stream of imperial traditions of about two millennia extant in ancient Near Eastern and Persian traditions. This means that instead of raising the traditional quests for incomparable qualities of biblical faith, instead of postulating absolute uniqueness for ancient Israelite theological affirmations, I try to understand our particular subject within (not against) its environment. Summarizing provisionally some brief observations that may be drawn from the evidence touched upon (which, of course, needs much closer study), we may say:

Darius I states how he defeated his competitor, the rebellious Gaumata. In consequence of his victory, he says, "According to the will of Ahuramazda I became king. Ahuramazda gave the *xsaça* to me." Cf. Widengren, *Die Religionen Irans*, 139; and Ahn, *Religiöse Herrscherlegitimation im achamenidischen Iran*, 255–77.

32. Cf. Root, *The King and Kingship* in *Achaemenid Art*; and Heidemarie Koch and her vivid description of the reliefs of the apadona ("audience-hall") of Persepolis, delegations of twenty-nine peoples bring to the Great King the gifts of their regions and cultures, apparently peacefully, freely bearing their weapons (in Assyrian reliefs, foreign people usually appear as captives bowing down submissively), coming by their own volition (*Es kundet Dareios der König*, 97–120).

1. Ancient Near Eastern traditions of "world dominion" reflect various tentative points to interpret growing spheres of political (military, economic) influence. The Mesopotamian starting point is a given city-state expanding its reign. In the case of the Persians, occupation of large territories and effective organization of provinces together with a universal type of religious faith may have initiated the move towards world rulership. Both economic and religious motivations should not be underestimated: securing raw materials, controlling routes of commerce, subjecting other peoples to the rule of one's own deity, certainly were powerful forces and, at the same time, legitimizing ideas behind such drives for hegemony.

2. Only such states or national alliances could seriously claim world leadership that outranked possible competitors by a large margin.[33] Israel hardly had opportunities to cultivate such ambitions on account of her own royal history. Yahweh kingship psalms, however, preaching world dominion, do represent that special tradition which had developed in true empires since the Akkad and a few pre-Sargonic kings. Not even the Davidic-Solomonic "reign" was strong, large, and enduring enough to give rise to any true imperial notions. Israelite communities probably learned to think in terms of worldwide divine authority by contacts with real world powers and world politics. They probably took over those concepts living within the respective political systems.

3. The most logical phases in Israel's history to get involved with slogans and expectations of world dominance would have been the Neo-Assyrian, Neo-Babylonian, and the so-called post-exilic periods. Direct contact with troops and administrations of first class powers, with their economy, tributary systems, and religious demands, must have occurred from the eighth century BCE onward. The tacit influences of such contacts may be seen in the varied expressions of world dominion attributed to Yahweh. Open confrontation with great powers may have been less conducive to using imperial epithets in theology than times of amenable relationships like in the environments of Second Isaiah (cf. the embrace of Cyrus in Isa 44:28; 45:1–7).

---

33. M. T. Larsen counts six Mesopotamian states that justly may be called "empires": the kingdoms of Akkad, Ur III, and the reigns of Old Babylonian, Middle Assyrian, Neo-Assyrian, and Neo-Babylonian rulers ("The Tradition of Empire in Mesopotamia"). His criteria are: 1) permanent occupation of vast territories by 2) military garrisons, and 3) division of state into provinces (92). A "center–periphery model" of state administration prevails in one or another form (92–97).

4. Like some other neighbors of the Mesopotamian empires, among them also the Persians, Israelite theologians adopted a good many features of their mainstream governmental concepts for theological purposes. They had been developed from the city-state to a vision of ruling the "four corners" or the "totality" of the land. Gradually, such a concept came to include all known countries, among which there was no longer "any equal" in power and authority. From the Akkad empire to the Neo-Assyrian state, thinking about world kingdom moved in more or less the same mold, with contextual variations. Yahweh kingship psalms participate in this stream of tradition.

5. The Persian variant of world dominion utilized Mesopotamian concepts and rites, but it also included a new religious base and new cultural dimensions. Not a city-god like Enlil, Ishtar, Marduk, etc., with all their ties to one determined capital, but Ahuramazda, creator of the universe, lord of the good powers, judge of all humankind, victor in the final battle, was the divine overlord of the king. Yahweh remained the god from afar (1 Kgs 19), even if he took lodging at his favorite place, Zion. Yahweh betrays little allegiance to royal dynasties (cf. 2 Sam 7; Pss 2, 89, 132), none in the kingship psalms, but some affinity to Zion-Jerusalem. Most of all, Yahweh is tied to the individual faithful (cf. Ps 119), reveals himself through prophets, communicates to them his ordinances, judges all nations, demands justice for all, etc.

6. Persian ideas about world rule seem to have been structured more from the people, and the individual person, rather than from top to bottom, i.e. from king and court down to the mass of constituents. Both in Avesta and Hebrew Scripture it is the lay congregation, which is the partner of the deity, markedly also in the Yahweh kingship psalms (cf. Ps 95). Indeed, the universe seems to be construed on the basis of national and international societies. The decision for faith in the supreme goodness is paramount. Peoples, consisting of human beings, are supporting the king of the world.

7. Theologically speaking, Persian and Hebrew traditions allow for a certain democratic basic consensus. Personal decision for the right deity is initially important. Adherence to a certain creed, final judgment, importance of living right, the written word (lectures from Bible and Avesta, liturgical use of Scripture) are constituent features of both the biblical and Zoroastrian traditions. A prophet (Moses, Zoroaster, or others), as indicated, is channeling or mediating revelational words to everybody's home. Both creeds thus have an ecumenical outlook that goes hand in hand with the universal rule of the deities.

8. The discovery of a unified world, with all human beings and nations dependent on one ultimate source of life-giving authority, does not contradict earlier "democratic" notions of a plurality of autonomous entities. But there has to be a directing and protecting power which guarantees freedom of individuals and groups. The old world discovered this basic necessity of world organization. At the time this discovery, in fact, was abused for egocentric and chauvinistic ends. One city, one government subdued others and proclaimed itself the greatest. Israel's early contribution to the problem has been a spiritually dominating god, without reference to human vice-regents (exceptions are messianic concepts, like in Pss 2; 110; Isa 9:1–6; Ezek 34:23–24; Mic 5:1–5; Zech 9:9–10, etc.). Significantly, the Yahweh kingship hymns on first look are free from human mediation of Yahweh's rule. The kingdom of God in our psalm group comes with Yahweh himself and only with him (cf. New Testament allusions in Matt 4:17; Mark 1:15; Luke 10:9, etc.). Seemingly, the problem of dominance exercised by humans over humans has been avoided.

9. Yet divine rule over all the world, in itself a liberating concept that may guarantee equal standing for all creatures, has to be implemented by human agents, be they individuals, dynasties, or collective bodies of government. Monarchic and imperial structures are obsolete today, because "Western" cultures are based on human rights for each individual person. The burning problems of our present time call for effective leadership and controlling power through the United Nations. Self-appointed authority in world affairs in the long run cannot solve the enigmas of humankind.

5

Psalms and Sumerian Hymns

Presuppositions and Preliminaries

WHOEVER WANTS TO STUDY the aftermath of events or traditions is well advised also to study their first sprouts. That is to say: In our case of diving into the very rich and meaningful reception history of the Psalms it must be highly rewarding to consider the distant beginnings of psalm-like poetry in the ancient Near East or to take a glance upstream from where traditions kept flowing in biblical times, and to capture the spirituality and literary art, as much as possible, of those most ancient singers of chants and hymns. Traditions do change on their long trajectory through history, but they also, to some extent, carry with them the sedimentary materials of the territories and cultures through which they come flowing.

Sacred songs of the Eastern Mediterranean, including those of the Hebrew Scriptures, all share in a common heritage of poetry and enactment of poetry through at least three thousand years before Christ.[1] Notwithstanding regional differences the spiritual compositions from Egypt to the Hittite lands, from the Philistine coast to the Sumerian marshes have a firm joint foundation in general beliefs and mentalities quite characteristic for the inhabitants of the fertile crescent: The world receives orientation mainly from the heavenly abodes of the great gods above. The Netherworld is a dreary place for defunct beings with its own rulings. History has a beginning in bygone eons and starts afresh after a universal deluge. Humans are to be subservient collaborators of the deities and in fact they rather prove to be autonomous executors of divine will.

---

1. Efforts to determine the common cultural and religious foundations of biblical (Western) and ancient Near Eastern traditions have increased in recent decades, cf. Sasson, ed., *Civilizations of the Ancient Near East*; Hallo, *Origins*; Hallo, ed., *The Context of Scripture*, 3 vols., with Hallo's general introduction in vol. 1, XXIII–XXVIII.

The original forms and genres of spiritual poetry in the ancient Near East most probably were used in many kinds of cultic or liturgical setups, be they tied to sanctuaries and outright temple structures or to otherwise defined sacred spaces like niches in private homes or consecrated spots anywhere else. Much in contrast to modern literary production, texts written down in antiquity did not serve individual reading pleasures but public recitations. Ever since Hermann Gunkel and Sigmund Mowinckel[2] alerted the scholarly community to this fact exegetes have been wrestling with its concrete implications. To tear away any text even today from its life-setting(s), its involvement(s) in real, contemporary communication between agents, is an act of violence. Texts do receive their meaning not only from the recipients, be they listeners or readers, but from the exchanges, the interplay, and the performative paraphernalia of their being used in communication.

The hymns of the ancient world constitute one particular group of genres,[3] often juxtaposed to the complaints, laments, and supplication categories in ancient literature. Their *Sitz im Leben* in general are celebrations of joyful events like bountiful harvests, victories, escapes from serious dangers etc. The majority of hymnic texts that came down to us betray to have been perused in larger groups, to the accompaniment of musical instruments and/or choirs, with expert singers and players leading the performance. Such a characterization of the genre implies its primary importance for larger organized societies, while the petitionary prayers quite often belong into the realm of small primary groups.[4] The finality of praising the divine world in hymns seems not only to be to express thanks and rejoice over blessings received, but also to strengthen the benevolent divine powers. I want to focus on this part of Sumerian literature that is the oldest of mankind and the antecedent of Babylonian, Assyrian, and, among others, Hebrew tradition.

Sumerian Hymns

Definition and availability

Literally hundreds of editions and translations[5] of Sumerian literary texts have been issued during the past 150 years as the cuneiform tablets were

---

2. Cf. Gunkel and Begrich, *Einleitung* [ET *Introduction*]; Mowinckel, *The Psalms in Israel's Worship*; Eisen and Gerstenberger, eds., *Hermann Gunkel Revisited*.

3. Cf. Burkert and Stolz, *Hymnen der alten Welt im Kulturvergleich*.

4. Cf. Gerstenberger, *Der bittende Mensch*; Zgoll, *Die Kunst des Betens*.

5. Cf. the English collections: Jacobsen, *The Harps that Once . . .*; Foster, *Before the Muses*.

excavated and investigated in the large museums. To facilitate research and references I propose to work with the Oxford "Electronic Corpus of Sumerian Literature" (ETCSL) available in the internet.[6] This grand, but lamentably unfinished, collection of more than 400 texts was elaborated by a team of specialists until 2006 under the direction mainly of the late Dr. Jeremy Black. Looking for pertinent Sumerian hymnal compositions the question arises: Which ones qualify as hymns in this oldest literature of the world? Invariably, we are caught with our western, Christian understanding of "hymnic praise": A poetic composition addressed to the one and only God, in sheer admiration and without any hind thoughts. Sumerian praise does not fit this pattern. Just taking the Sumerian shout *zà-mí* ("praised be N.N," corresponding more or less to Hebrew *halleluyah*) as a formal criterion[7] and searching through ETCSL we are stunned by the widespread use of the formula, which frequently appears at the very end of the praising affirmations. What a wealth of meaning and moods comes to the fore! How varied are the objects of praise and its veritable contents. To be sure, there are poems which look familiar in tone, style, agents, contents, theological affirmations. But quite often the unnamed singer of praises elevates not only exemplar deities, but temple buildings, royal potentates, natural forces, agrarian tools. Many times the singer or speaker is mentioned by name, sometimes he or she will intone a hymn in unashamed self-laudation, be it a deity or one of the deified kings of the Ur III period and afterwards. The style and contents of praise-songs vary greatly, certainly also in consequence of the large time-span the texts are covering. The oldest examples date from about 2600 BCE, the latest Sumerian hymnic poem may have been written and used around 500 BCE. That means: During more than two millennia the Sumerian language, albeit no longer spoken in daily life since ca. 1900 BCE, was actively used in cult ceremonies throughout ancient Mesopotamia much like Latin remained the sacred language of western Christianity. In terms of laudatory contents and flow we find much diversity. Epic tales, reports of voyages, admonitions and counsels are part of hymnic texts. Liturgical rubrics are present in about half of the poems.[8] And Sumerian eulogies seem constantly to reflect a fluctuation of powers, a growing and waning of authority throughout the known world.

---

6. The website is: http://etcsl.orinst.ox.ac.uk.

7. About 150 occurrences in ETCSL in approx. 84 different texts, see below.

8. For a overview of Mesopotamian hymnic compositions, cf. Wilcke, in *RlA* 4 (1976–1980) 539–44; Wilcke, "Formale Gesichtspunkte in der sumerischen Literatur."

Objects of Praise

To give an impression of the diversity of praised objects/persons I shall give a few examples, identified by the letters A through D. The Keš Temple Hymn is one of the very oldest texts already extant in a fragment from the Abu Salabikh finds of the pre-Sargonic era (ca. 2500 BCE). It lauds the archaic temple and mother Nintud as well as her son Ašgi, both venerated at Keš: The temple itself is visualized in a perfect personal way.

> (A) House Keš, platform of the Land, important fierce bull! Growing as high as the hills, embracing the heavens, growing as high as E-kur, lifting its head among the mountains! Rooted in the Abzu, verdant like the mountains! Will anyone else bring forth something as great as Keš? Will any other mother ever give birth to someone as great as its hero Ašgi? Who has ever seen anyone as great as lady Nintur? . . . House roaring like an ox, bellowing loudly like a breed-bull! House in whose interior is the power of the land, and behind which is the life of Sumer![9]

Also the hoe is praised, even in direct address, as the founder of human culture in general. No other tool has had such an impact on civilization.

> (B) The hoe makes everything prosper, the hoe makes everything flourish. The hoe is good barley, the hoe is a hunting net. The hoe is brick moulds, the hoe has made people exist. It is the hoe that is the strength of young manhood . . . It builds the right kind of house, it cultivates the right kind of fields. It is you, hoe, that extend the good agricultural land![10]

Pre-eminent universal gods are praised frequently, because on them rests the responsibility for the world, and they are the divine forces which can be contacted by humans. Note the derivation of power from An, the primordial "father":

> (C) Lord of all divine powers, who establishes understanding, whose intentions are unfathomable, who knows everything! Enki, of broad wisdom, august ruler of the Anuna, wise one who casts spells, who provides words, who attends to decisions, who clarifies verdicts, who dispenses advice from dawn to dusk! Enki, lord of all true words, I will praise you! Your father, An the king, the lord who caused human seed to come forth

---

9. ETCSL 4.80.2, ll. 14–20, 28–30; Black et al., *The Literature of Ancient Sumer*, 326.
10. ETCSL 5.5.4, ll. 94–97; 99–100; Black et al., *The Literature of Ancient Sumer*, 314.

and who placed all mankind on the earth, has laid upon you the guarding of the divine powers of heaven and earth, and has elevated you to be their prince.[11]

A later hymn praises the outstanding goddess of Mesopotamia, Inanna. The singer's voice is more clearly articulated than in example C:

> (D) I shall greet her who descends from above, her who descends from above, I shall greet the Mistress who descends from above, I shall greet the great lady of heaven, Inana! I shall greet the holy torch who fills the heavens, the light, Inanna, her who shines like daylight, the great lady of heaven, Inanna! I shall greet the Mistress, the most awesome lady among the Anuna gods; the respected one who fills heaven and earth with her huge brilliance; the eldest daughter of Suen, Inana! For the young lady I shall sing a song about her grandeur, about her greatness, about her exalted dignity; about her becoming visible at evening; about her filling the heaven like a holy torch; about her stance in the heavens, as noticeable by all lands, from the south to the highlands, as that of Nanna or of Utu; about the greatness of the Mistress of heaven![12]

Four examples of Sumerian hymns which exhibit peculiarities of Mesopotamian spirituality as well as analogous conceptualizations of the divine to those of the Hebrew Bible. All of them consider the praised objects as centres of benign power so utterly needed for the sustenance of life.

Forms, Themes, Motifs

We may expect a specific range of characteristics in Sumerian hymns, to be sure, because of linguistic, cultural and historical peculiarities. On the other hand, there certainly are overlaps and analogies with Hebrew psalms. To indicate only a few:

The praised-ones are either addressed directly (2nd person singular) or mentioned in the 3rd person (as if recommending the exalted object to an audience) with statements of glorious achievements or of personal potentialities. "You are great, mighty, radiant, frightening" etc. are examples for the first type of address; the attributions, of course, likewise occur in 3rd person discourse. More narrative, epic statements recount the valour,

---

11. ETCSL 2.5.6.2, ll. 1–7; Black et al., *The Literature of Ancient Sumer*, 270–71.

12. ETCSL 2.5.3.1, ll. 1–16; Black et al., *The Literature of Ancient Sumer*, 263; cf. also the hymns of Išme-Dagan in Ludwig, *Untersuchungen zu den Hymnen des Išme-Dagan von Isin*.

wisdom, generosity of exemplar deeds, like creation, defeat of chaos powers, fertilization of the fields and herds, administration of artisanship, knowledge, and justice (cf. the above examples A–D). Statements of glory, authority, and power articulate positive experiences of the adorers but, at the same time, conjure up the persistence of that beneficial state of affairs. The "hoe is barley, net, mould, life of the people" etc. (example B) emphasizes ongoing and desired realization of its blissful effects. Enki guarantees the spiritual backbone of the world order (example C), Inanna provides light and heavenly blessings (example D).

Exuberance, music, cultic agitation of performers and communal participants are often referred to; they find their echo in the structure of language, that is, the poetic expression. The mysteries of Sumerian poetry are far from thoroughly known or maybe understandable. But poetic motion towards glorification can be felt even through translations, e.g., imperatives, wish form and elicit power. Metaphors suggest and implement authority (cf. bull roaring in example A). Epithets for the celebrated enactors of blessed motions abound. Hymns betray, by their forms, structures, imagery an upward surge away from destruction and distress which may loom behind jubilation.[13] The formal aspects of hymnic poetry are best analysed by Wilcke and Black.[14]

The powers envisioned certainly include all kinds of "political" and "natural" variations, but they also presuppose decision-making and ruling for the good on the part of divine beings or divine assemblies. The wilful sentences of the deities do have a certain preponderance, they call into being or else recognize a given pre-existence of what Sumerian theologians call *me, nam-tar, ĝishur, ešbar, inim* ("power," "fate," "plan," "decision," "word") etc. Thus volatile and neutral forces seem to be working side by side, the personalised deities being, however, the only powers to be communicated with (cf. example C). Both forms of divine authority need strengthening: "I will recite your holy song! . . . I will enumerate your divine powers for you!"[15] To "recite" and "declare" is a performative action that realizes that which is articulated.

A special detail of hymnic formulas is also an example of congruence and diversification in Mesopotamian tradition. The expression *zà-mí*, "lauded be" usually with following name or pronoun of the praised subject roughly has the function of Hebrew halleluyah. Are we facing an archaic hymnic-element common to many cultures and religions? The expression is

---

13. Cf. Gunkel and Begrich, *Einleitung*, 32–94 [ET *Introduction*, 22–65].
14. Wilcke, "Formale Gesichtspunkte"; and Black, *Reading Sumerian Poetry*.
15. ETCSL 4.07.2, ll. 63 and 65; cf. Zgoll, *Der Rechtsfall*.

quite frequent in the hymnic texts. I count 153 cases in ETCSL contained in 84 different texts. "Praise be to D.N." at the end of a composition therefore declares the poem to be a powerful song; it may have been used in praising liturgies. There certainly is an archaic ring about this formula, and whenever it occurs in the body of a given text this impression is underlined. Zà-mí belongs to the oldest Sumerian hymnic vocabulary. It denotes a powerful song of praise suited for special worship opportunities, maybe on the official level of state-cult or wider community life.

Praise in the Sumerian tradition is much more than emotional liturgical action or reverberating gratitude of god-fearing people. By necessity it includes involvement (or even sponsorship) of humans ready to acknowledge divine volatility but who also know of their own co-responsibility. The believers' participation in governance and sustenance of the world most clearly appears in praise liturgies. They in fact strengthen the divine work and therefore must be kept going (particularly in temple services) without cessation. King Šulgi is particularly concerned to guarantee ongoing hymn singing, also in order to keep alive his own semi-divine memory.[16]

The question of comparability or common roots in Ancient Near Eastern hymnology has been discussed at various opportunities and still would have to be investigated further concerning a good number of items and from different perspectives. Suffice it here to select just one issue, as *pars pro toto*: What about Israel's peculiar habit to praise Yahweh's extraordinary historical interventions in the struggle for survival in Egypt and Canaan, and his seeming exclusiveness in relation to Israel? (cf. Exod 15; Deut 32; Judg 5; Pss 78; 81; 105; 135; 136; also Pss 46; 48; 76; 132, etc.). The answer may be: Some of Israel's hymns celebrate those well-known saving feats of her God that guaranteed the formation of the confessional Yahweh-community they were composed and used in. Sumerian hymns, likewise, glorify the extra efforts of local and highest gods to save and protect and promote their own clients, be they governments of cities, states or empires. Personal and familial hymns seem to be fairly unknown in the Sumerian tradition, but likewise in the Hebrew Scriptures.[17] Exactly in this partisanship for the group of adherents Yahweh, purportedly being the universal ruler over all humankind, behaves like a particular Mesopotamian deity.

---

16. Cf. ETCSL 2.4.2.05, ll. 240–257; cf. Klein, *Three Šulgi Hymns*.
17. Cf. Crüsemann, *Studien zur Formgeschichte von Hymnus und Danklied in Israel*.

Theologies

Theological implications of generative praise include the concept of competing deities rather than a purely monotheistic and all-powerful, purely inclusive and exclusive Highest God. We may leave aside, at this point, the inherent suspicion that pure monotheism is an illusion anyhow and never really can be practiced. What we find in the Old Testament and ancient Mesopotamian hymnic literature, likewise and on all counts, are different forms of monolatry. In this vein, Sumerian hymns apparently direct their praises—in determined situations—to the highest ranking divine entities. There seem to be, on state- and empire-level, no eulogies to lesser, that means: local and familial deities. Vice versa, prayer petitions from the lower levels of society are usually directed to higher ranking gods. Among the Sumerian great deities, forming the ruling pantheon of a city or state, the dominant ones are being addressed exclusively or in concert with their colleagues. Interestingly, the zà-mí formula often calls the praised one "father" (e.g., Enki; Enlil; Nanna etc.), female addressees are titled "holy" (Ninisina; Inanna; Damgalnuna). Sometimes, several deities of the pantheon are mentioned, but the hymnic flow as a rule goes to the leading figure in the group, to the point, that the prominent god is lauded by his colleagues in the pantheon. There is, consequently, a monolatric dynamics in hymnic praise (cf. ETCSL 1.1.3, ll. 81–83; ETCSL 4.05.1, ll. 100–108). The first text just cited describes how the Anuna-gods pray to Enki, after he has pronounced a big self-laudation about his achievements (ETCSL 1.1.3, ll. 61–80).

The other side of the coin in Sumerian theology we already exposed above: The possible dominance of one deity in a given situation does not indicate absolute power. On the contrary. Divine forces, be they conceived of personally or impersonally participate in the moulding of history, and the share praising communities have in the interplay of potencies is considerable.

A few Old Testament psalms fit into the same scheme. They consider Yahweh as the leading or presiding highest deity, cf. Pss 58 and 82 (but also Gen 1:26; Deut 32; Job 1–2; 1 Kgs 22). This means: The idea of a divine council with the highest God presiding over an assembly is present in the Old Testament. Also, powers like "justice," "peace," "grace" do play a fairly independent role especially in the Psalms (cf. Pss 85:11–12 [ET 10–11]; 45:5 [ET 4]; 89:15 [ET 14] etc.), and in Ps 29 the "sons of God" have to "deliver glory and strength" to the supreme deity.[18] Only later on, the lofty absolutely

---

18. NRSV translates Ps 29: "Ascribe to Yahweh, O heavenly beings, ascribe to Yahweh glory and strength" (v. 1). The verb, in the imperative (*hab* from *yhb*) really does not mean a theoretical act of recognition but the active, labor-some effort to elevate the

sovereign "God of Heaven," akin to the Persian Ahura Mazda, is unrivalled acting, however, always in accordance with impersonal powers, but really does no longer need edification by human praises. Nehemiah 9 and Ezra 9 are prayers of penitence; they begin with a hymnic part, but soon move to endless confessions of sin and deep contrition. Praise becomes blocked or submerged in the overwhelming feeling of sinfulness.

Of course, the concepts of God in Sumerian hymns and Hebrew psalms are still different. But where are the points of dissension? The fact that the Sumerian pantheon does consist of a number of deities, male and female, who are nominally known, and of a good number of impersonal properties, which all freely interact according to human patterns, and usually come out in favour of their worshippers, this is only a marginal point of variegation. Some layers of the Hebrew Scriptures adhere to very similar patterns. The break with Mesopotamian concepts of God obviously occurred only under Persian rule, when Yahweh turned to be the unimaginable, all encompassing God provoking deep fear and apprehension, and choking free, hearty praise (cf. Pss 90 and 139).

Conclusions

The brief foray into ancient Sumerian hymnic literature to my mind makes clear, that the biblical hymns belong into the wide stream of Ancient Near Eastern praise tradition. Hebrew psalms must not be studied in splendid isolation from the rest of cuneiform (and other) liturgical remnants of Mesopotamian cultures and religions. Patrick Miller and others have ably demonstrated how the songs and prayers of the Old Testament can be fruitfully related to the patterns of ancient Near Eastern singing and praying.[19] Of course, as has been pointed out, the differing modes of tradition, the specific life situations, and, above all, the varying social and religious organisations in Mesopotamia and homeless, stateless Israel have to be considered.

The heart of the matter, it seems to me, is our theological pre-disposition to perceive and evaluate hymnic texts (to limit my statements to this genre) outside the Bible. If we part from the exclusiveness and incomparability of all "heathen" expressions of praise, we postulate an abyss between Old Testament and foreign texts. This stance is impossible at least in the case of hymnic materials, as Gerhard von Rad stated long ago: The psalm-genres belong in the category of "human responses" to God 's action, and therefore

---

status of the lauded one. "Bring here, deliver" power and strength! The adorers have to submit to the adored and hand over authority to him or her!

19. Cf. P. D. Miller, "The Theological Significance of Poetry."

cannot claim qualitative otherness in regard to outside religious and their answers to their divine challenges. In my opinion there is neither any logical nor theological justification to place biblical human responses outside human history, although some Old Testament scholars still follow this line of reasoning.

The ancient hymnic tradition anteceding Israel's coming into existence clearly shows a pronounced interaction between the highest Gods and their adherents and protégées. Traces of this dynamic relationship can be found also in the Hebrew Psalter. In the most recent poetic compositions of the Hebrew Bible, however (if we can trust our dating predilections), we may find much less overt and forceful praise and much more devout submission under the all-present, simply overwhelming power of the universal Lord. He really does not need any human elevation any more. Thus, e.g., the so-called "didactic" psalms which I consider products of the late OT faith-community of the Persian Period, dispense more or less with empowering praise of God, expressing instead feelings of stunned awe and devout submission.

To put the OT hymns into the perspective of a much older hymnic tradition will also help us to evaluate the later reception history of the Psalms. Motives and conceptions of pre-biblical times will shine up from under Yahwistic paint. The towering figure of Israel's God receives a more ancient Near Eastern profile. And there remains to be studied a whole range of problems concerning the transmission history of sacred songs (scribal schools!), the *Sitz im Leben* of hymns,[20] and their theological impact on doctrine and conceptualizations of the divine. All these issues affect Psalm research to this very day, including the deliberations of our present conference: "Jewish and Christian Approaches to the Psalms."

---

20. Mowinckel, *The Psalms in Israel's Worship*; Burkert and Stolz, *Hymnen der alten Welt im Kulturvergleich*.

6

Navajo Chants, Babylonian Incantations, Old Testament Psalms

A Comparative Study of Healing Rituals

Introduction

PRAYER MAY BE STUDIED from different angles: as a purely personal expression of individual faith or a collective effort to approach the divine; as predominantly verbal articulation of sentiments or as part of a ceremonial whole; as poetic effusion or magical incantation. No doubt, different kinds of prayer do provoke various approaches. When it comes to curative supplications, however, widely used over historical times and across cultures, the questions of individual vs. communal, emotive vs. liturgical, aesthetic vs. performative functions become more succinct and also more important. There certainly always have been, in the history of prayer, ad hoc supplications of endangered persons borne out of despair and severe frustrations, but prayers formulated carefully to meet the needs of patients and transmitted in the public realm (as, e.g., the individual complaints of the biblical Psalter) have been preserved and used for more than one sufferer. In this case the query should be whether or not the words of such prayers originally had been part and parcel of concomitant rites. With good reasons, anthropologist Gladys A. Reichard affirms in her classic study that "the subject of prayer" may be "treated separately from the general discussion, but it must at no time be thought that it is independent of the ceremonial or religious whole."[1]

---

1. Reichard, *Prayer*, 3.

Ritualization of vital human (but also animal) interactions has long been recognized as a very important feature in many areas of life. The "Myth-and-Ritual" school in the 1940s to 1960s (e.g., S. H. Hooke, Aubrey R. Johnson, Aage Bentzen, Geo Widengren, Sigmund Mowinckel) focused on cultic ritual around sacred kingship in ancient Middle Eastern cultures. More recently, ritual research became a distinct branch of behavioral, anthropological, sociological, and cultural disciplines, very important also for arts and religion.[2] Nowadays it is common belief that rituals permeate life and faith in all cultures. This does include healing procedures. In fact, there may be traceable developments or connections from ancient practices to our modern medical treatments, in spite of considerable changes wrought by modern science and technology. Of course, the comparability of rites has to remain a matter of debate. There should not be hasty identifications of cross-cultural traits, but analogous performances are well to be noted and evaluated on the basis of sociological equivalences.

My proposition, then, is this: since ritual healing is a peculiar and widespread medical practice, it should be possible to look for analogies in ceremonial procedure and specifically to do a comparative study of the patient's prayer in the middle of such performances. I have chosen, from scores of existent examples, the well-documented Navajo chants as a starting point. I move towards antiquity, selecting the Babylonian incantations, best documented of their kind, for a second steppingstone. Last, but not least, I present my research on Old Testament complaints of the individual in the light of the former healing rituals. Prayers embedded in ceremonial procedure require a keen attention to a host of circumstances, personnel, and paraphernalia of the pertinent rites that can be done only in a shortened, condensed way. However, theological as well as esthetic dimensions of ritualized prayer must not be ignored.

Navajo Ceremonials

Healing Chants

Vast anthropological research on ritual shamanic healing in general has been going on for some decades.[3] Numerous cultures and religions around the globe have been using ceremonial prayer to combat evil powers and restore well-being to patients suffering from diverse ills. Navajo healing practices are outstanding in their well-researched quantity of recorded

---

2. Cf., e.g., Bell, *Ritual*, 1–22; Grimes, *The Craft of Ritual Studies*.
3. Cf. Bell, *Ritual*, 115–20; Futterknecht, *Heilung in den Religionen*.

specimens.[4] Navajo life as a whole has been saturated with shorter or longer rites for many areas of activity (agriculture, husbandry, hunting, rites of passage, home-building, and so forth). Night-long chants (or "sings") are major efforts to procure well-being, ban the evil, recover health; they require a fully educated, expert "singer." Wyman and Kluckhohn, on the basis of Navajo testimony, grouped dozens of ceremonials into six categories: Blessing Way (the most prominent chant, preserved in at least four local variants),[5] Holy Way, Life Way, Evil Way (they split up in numerous components to be performed in their own right), War Ceremonials, and Game Way (both all but extinct already in the thirties).[6] Each chant predominantly—because of proven effectiveness—but not exclusively, served determined purposes. Thus, for example, some chants of group II (Holy Way) were administered in the following cases: "Hail Way" "for persons injured by water, for frozen feet or parts, for muscle soreness, tiredness, lameness";[7] "Water Way" "for producing rain, for paralysis, for resuscitation from drowning, deafness";[8] "Shooting Way, Male Branch" "to cure prenatal effects of an eclipse, any disease caused by lightning, e.g., colds, fevers, rheumatism, paralysis, abdominal pain";[9] "Mountain Top Way, Male Branch" against "'porcupine sickness', constipation, anuria, gallbladder trouble, internal pains, 'bear sickness', mental disease."[10] As is to be expected, there always has been, in strictly oral Navajo tradition, a great flexibility and interchangeability of words, songs, and rites at the discretion of the singer and also their clients.

Navajo medicine men, still procured by a good percentage of the native population, are being trained through personal apprenticeship in some of the approximately 30 one-to-nine nights rituals, performed in a Hogan (traditional log cabin; admitted are only family-members or close friends). The patient sits on a sandpainting depicting holy *yeibeshe* beings or holy plants, while medicine men are performing acts of purification and exorcism, as well as narrating texts of Navajo sacred myths. Prayer-sticks (see below) and prayers, spoken by chanter and patient, hold vital roles in the

---

4. Cf. Wyman and Kluckhohn, *Navajo Classification*; Kluckhohn and Wyman, *Introduction to Navajo Chant Practice*.
5. Cf. Wyman, *Blessingway*.
6. Cf. Wyman and Kluckhohn, *Navajo Classification*.
7. Cf. Wyman and Kluckhohn, *Navajo Classification*, 22.
8. Cf. Wyman and Kluckhohn, *Navajo Classification*, 22.
9. Wyman and Kluckhohn, *Navajo Classification*, 24.
10. Cf. Wyman and Kluckhohn, *Navajo Classification*, 25.

ceremony. A public, nightly dance, a real social affair lasting into the early hours of the new day, completes the rites.[11]

Navajo chants have been, as mentioned before, under intense study for more than one hundred years. Ever since Washington Matthews (1843–1905), a U.S. medical doctor with a southwest army detachment, started to dedicate time and energy to learn the native language and explore Navajo traditions,[12] interest of the white man has been great in all their lore. Matthews himself published the first comprehensive report about a Navajo ritual in 1902.[13] Since then, numerous editions of a considerable number of Navajo chants have appeared, in English translation and also partially in the native tongue.[14] These publications constitute a valuable treasure of sources. Yet, one has to be aware of what kind of sources they represent: White anthropologists persuaded Navajo medicine men to break their absolute discretion in regard to the holy tales and rites. They dared to narrate the full content of a given ceremony, night by night; some were mechanically recorded.[15] What we have, however, are hardly the complete rituals but verbal narratives, told to white (and very empathetic) scholars. They, in turn, translated the Navajo narration into English, trying to make accessible indigenous worldviews and faith-patterns to American minds. Interpretations of rites, religious concepts and feelings, sacred time, space and equipment, works of art, dresses, gestures, and so on are helpful instruments in this task of comprehension. And some rare films of complete ceremonials are valuable avenues to understanding. Therefore, we should not only rely on verbal communications. All the knowledgeable details about performers, situations, and paraphernalia, in particular, for the matter of prayer, sandpaintings, and prayer-sticks, need to be taken into account. Still, for "westerners" the Navajo world is an alien one, and the greatest experts who submerged themselves into their spiritual universe readily confess to have remained strangers in it. This is true for about every instance of transcultural understanding.

---

11. Cf. Kluckhohn and Wyman, *Introduction to Navajo Chant Practice*; Reichard, *Navajo Religion*, 279–353; Faris, *The Nightway*, see index "dancers"; "dances."

12. Cf. Matthews, *The Night Chant*, XLVII.

13. Matthews, *The Night Chant*, re-edited by Farella.

14. Cf. Haile, *Waterway*; Wyman, *Blessingway*; Wyman, *Mountainway*; Luckert, *Navajo Mountain*.

15. Cf. Faris, *The Nightway*, 6–24.

Prayer in the Center

Even with these shortcomings in mind, a very noteworthy phenomenon with Navajo healing chants is indeed the position and function of prayer in the pertinent rituals (e.g., the most famous ones: Nightway; Beauty Way; Shooting Way, male and female branch, etc.). As a rule, the verbal parts of any healing ceremony consist of mythical narrations or episodes, in prose or poetic form, and outright prayers/supplications, all chosen by the medicine man and the patient for the particular occasion. In general, the mythical texts give information about how the rituals were created or composed by divine beings and what their effects were like for suffering people. The prayers are inserted into the ceremony by the shaman. They carry some, perhaps much, of the burden to accomplish betterment, restoration of health, and good standing among the people. Berard Haile[16] described praying in the ceremonial this way: "as a rule the singer says the prayer in a singing tone and pauses briefly after a clause to allow the patient to repeat it." This means the sufferer's supplication occurs under the supervision of the shaman; he is responsible for its precise recitation, because the text, in ultimate analysis, is a gift to the healer, most likely received in a vision, of the holy ones. But the patient has to pronounce the words himself (cf. Babylonian: "let him recite") in order to make them truly his own concern and articulation. Ceremonial songs, on the other hand, need not to be repeated by the patient, even if they carry similar power as prayers.[17]

To give a concrete example of prayer in a Navajo ritual: Father Berard Haile of the St. Michael's Franciscans gathered information about the Waterway chant in 1929 from a medicine man named Black Mustache Circle. The narration was published in 1932 and reprinted much later.[18] "Waterway" was used originally against "venereal and skin diseases."[19] One prayer, spoken by the healer to the patient in a conjuring mode, runs this way:

> Water monster of the Water-bottom White spot, Young Man Chief, I have made your sacrifice, I have prepared your smoke. / This very day your power, which you may exert over him, you will remove from him! You have removed your power from him. / You shall carry it far away from him! You have carried it far away from him! Far away you will return with it! Far away you have returned with it!/ May he nicely recover this very day! May

---

16. Quoted by Faris, *The Nightway*, 63.

17. Cf. Reichard, *Prayer*.

18. See Haile, *Waterway*, with an appendix by Karl W. Luckert, *Navajo Mountain*, 135–52.

19. Haile, *Waterway*, 135.

the pains in him nicely cool off this very day! / May sickness nicely move away from him! May he nicely walk about! / May he walk about with his body thoroughly cooled! May he go about with his body thoroughly lightened! / May he go about full of energy! May he go about with no sickness on him! May he go about immune to sickness! / With his front in nice shape, may he go about! With his back in nice shape, may he go about! / With all below him in good (nice) shape, may he go about! With all above him in nice shape, may he go about! With all his surroundings in nice shape, may he go about! With his speech always pleasant, may he go about! / As one who is Long-life Happiness One may go about! Pleasant it has become again (four times). (The prayer then is repeated to 21 other Holy People).[20]

The author remarks on the same page: "The informant has given the text of the prayer as recited for the patient. Actually, the prayer is repeated word for word by the patient and throughout the prayer the I-form must be used."[21] We recognize some elements known from OT complaints: Address to the divine people, strong wish forms for good health, affirmations of confidence that relief has been granted. Astonishing is the all-inclusive view of health and well-being: body, mind, and surroundings are meant to improve and gain a wholesome status.

Gladys A. Reichard, who not only took part in the non-public sections of healing rituals but also several times assumed the role of the "sung-over-patient,"[22] describes the forms, functions, and inner meanings of Navajo prayer. It is her ambition to synthetize the elements into a symbolic network of religious performances interacting with the divine beings:[23] "Prayer, like sand-painting, is a fundamental feature of the ritual. It must of course be looked at as a part of the whole to which it belongs, but it may also be considered by itself, because it richly demonstrates all that a Navajo does in his ritual, his fears, his aspirations, and his attainment."[24] Formally, the prayers expose elements similar to those known from Babylonian and Hebrew supplications. Reichard's prime example is the lengthy prayer of Male Shooting Way comprising 399 lines, organized in litany-structure and five main parts.[25] The first four open with invocations of Holy Man, Holy Woman, Holy Boy, Holy Girl (ll. 2, 78, 163, 247) preceded by reference

20. Haile, *Waterway*, 64.
21. Haile, *Waterway*, 64 n70.
22. Cf. Reichard, *Prayer*, 2.
23. Cf. Reichard, *Navajo Religion*.
24. Reichard, *Prayer*, 3.
25. Reichard, *Prayer*, 58–93; Navajo and English versions.

to a local "At Rumbling Mountain," an important "geographic symbolism" difficult to decipher.[26] The fifth segment (ll. 326–399) is sort of the anticipation of being cured, comparable with some Hebrew psalms (cf. Ps 22). Invocation of the Holy Ones is followed by a self-presentation and pleas for protection:

> Line 1: At Rumbling Mountain, 2: Holy Man who with the eagle tail-feathered arrow glides out, 3: This day I have come to be trustful 4: This day I look to you (for help) 5: With your strong feet rise up to protect me, 6: With your sturdy legs rise up to protect me, 7: With your strong body rise up to protect me, 8: With your healthy mind rise up to protect me, 9: With your powerful sound rise up to protect, 10: Carrying the dark bow and the eagle tail-feathered arrow with which you transformed evil . . .[27]

The battle against evil powers molesting the patient can only be won by being close to the benevolent healing forces and by identification with the Holy Ones (ll. 22: "your child I have become"; l. 34: "Just as you are the one who is holy because of these things"; l. 35: So may I be holy because of them" (61). Evil has to be banned from individual parts of the sufferer's body ("from the tips of my toes," "the tips of my body," "the tips of my fingers," "the tips of my speech," ll. 15–18).[28] The wrestling with bad forces, in conjunction with the Holy Ones, we may rate as plaintive supplication (ll. 11–36, 59–61). After this, the prayer more and more speaks about a successful termination of the ritual. Evil sorcery has gone (ll. 37–44).[29] "Behind you I survive" (ll. 45 on 61). The affirmations of ll. 37–69 certainly still have a conjuring undertone, but they aim at restoration of former health or "beauty" (wholeness, happiness, order, health etc.). The final lines (70–76)[30] of the first prayer-section are fully confident of victory (parts 2 through 4 follow a similar setup, part 5, ll. 326–399 is a powerful song of praise on recovered "beauty"):

> Line 70: My mind is safe. 71: My mind is safe. 72: Restoration-to-youth According-to-beauty I have become again. 73: Restoration-to-youth According-to-beauty, 74: Natural Boy I have become again, 75: It has become beautiful again, 76: It has become beautiful again.

26. Reichard, *Prayer*, 26.
27. Reichard, *Prayer*, 59.
28. Reichard, *Prayer*, 59.
29. Reichard, *Prayer*, 61.
30. Reichard, *Prayer*, 63, 65.

So the sequence of elements in this prayer: invocation, self-presentation as supplicant, initial plea, plaintive supplication or entreaty, affirmation of confidence (praising anticipation of success) are quite comparable to the structure of individual complaints in the OT Psalter. Reichard has the following main divisions: Invocation—petition—benediction,[31] with intricate subdivisions in forms of repetition, summary, increment of line-couplets and strophes, ditto: unnumbered appendix of twenty-five structural analyses.

Being an empathetic eyewitness and active participant in Navajo ceremonies, Gladys Reichard observed and interpreted a host of particularities in ritual performance and worldview, always admitting Western preconceptions potentially to bar a full understanding of Navajo thought and feeling. Thus, for example, she tries to explain their vision of good and evil: Navajo duality is not a separatist but an inclusive antagonism. "Good is evil, and evil is good," depending on "presence or absence of control." Likewise, "That which harms a person is the only thing which can undo the harm."[32] In consequence, the evil powers first have to be called and identified with before they can be driven out and dismissed. In this context, the rite of "tying knots represents the 'tying in of evil.'"[33] Prayer, according to Reichard, has an important place in ritual; it is an extraordinary part, indeed. Words are an essential form, but they are often identified with thought and deed and also with sandpaintings, prayer sticks, strewing of pollen (9s; cf. a layman's simple prayer: pollen plus a muttered "may it be beautiful").[34] Prayers must be recited correctly, word by word; otherwise, the supplication could cause damage instead of wellbeing. With their endless repetitions (or variegated litanies) memorization is a very difficult task. One of the prayers observed by Reichard lasted for one hour and forty minutes (12, 14s). Two basic intentions of prayer may be distinguished: Type I being a call for protection, good luck, sustenance, fortune, etc.; and Type II imploring the holy ones for deliverance from evil, always connected with exorcistic pleas and actions (13s, 15s, 22s, 31–33). "Prayers to get a person out of danger, that is, exorcistic prayers, and those to deities most difficult of persuasion seem to have the greatest elaboration" (41). The number of symbols used in ceremonials for Reichard is astounding. Numbers do play a role, for example, measuring out the frequency of repetitions (46); colors have a deep meaning for identifying beings, human and divine, and forces like weather phenomena, mountains, waters, sounds of words (prayer as poetry) and winds, geographical places

---

31. Reichard, *Prayer*, 41–49.
32. Reichard, *Prayer*, 5.
33. Reichard, *Prayer*, 6.
34. Reichard, *Prayer*, 13.

(of the Navajo territory!), directions of the wind-rose, animal potencies and so forth are all integrated into the world vision which guides prayer performance (cf. Reichard 26s; 29s, 36s, 46, etc.). It is small wonder that each ceremonial in itself, as well as the interconnections of sings, and their local variations seem inexhaustible.

Implements of Prayer

The conjuring tone of the prayer may call the attention of modern readers. The magic notion is increased when the ritual performance is taken into account. Navajo medicine men concentrate not only on the wording of prayer and songs, but have to fabricate special "prayer-sticks" (Navajo: *kethawn*)[35] for each occasion to accompany the rites. These symbols of power consist of little pieces of reed or wood, adorned and empowered by various effective additions, feathers, pollen, colors, and little stones. Researchers have listed a large number of forms and meanings of these sticks.[36] The prayer quoted earlier in context is introduced like this: The healer takes

> one stick at a time, he sprinkles the full length of it, saying: 'From now on may you nicely do restoring. May you do restoring this very day.' At once he applies it to the person for whom the ceremony is held, from his soles up to the top of his head. Some he puts into his mouth, some he sprinkles out, and this is done that he may continue to walk on it. Then he (the singer) puts the prayer-stick into his hand. The one first in rank one places at the bottom. After which, placing them one on top of the other, that last (prayer-stick) comes uppermost. Then there, facing the (patient), he sits down and speaks.[37]

Prayer-sticks, it seems, are enhancing the spoken words; this can be observed in various situations of the ritual. Gladys Reichard, for her part, emphasized the "invocatory" and "talking" functions of the implement. The first one in her sight "carries a compulsive invitation to the deities to attend the ceremony. If the sticks are made properly and deposited according to deific decree, and if the prayer is repeated without a mistake, the gods

---

35. Matthews, *The Night Chant*; this spelling follows Matthews.

36. Cf. Franciscan Fathers, *An Ethnologic Dictionary of the Navajo Language*, 396–98; Matthews, *The Night Chant*, see index, p. 323, sub *Kethawns*; Reichard, *Navajo Religion*, 301–13.

37. Haile, *Waterway*, 63; immediately followed by the prayer cited above.

cannot refuse to come."[38] Magic object and spoken words do complement each-other. Does this conjunction devaluate the spoken prayer?

A similar attention in regard to performed prayer should be paid to the sand paintings of the medicine man. They are prepared with utter care and concentration, representing holy people who are asked to assist in healing, viz. in the neutralization of evil powers. Materials used (colored dusts and powders, including pollen), techniques of fabrication, time and persons adequate for execution, figures and scenes depicted, behavior of the medicine man are all minutely regulated, although healer and patient do have some liberty to choose from many models. Since the painting, worked out on the floor of the ceremonial hut, serves as a sitting ground for the patient (the sing is being performed "over him or her") has to be destroyed after finishing the ritual and carried away into desert or running water to eliminate the evil absorbed by it, there exist only photographs and (water colored) copies of such works.[39] Distrust of copying the sacred paintings was particularly strong among Navajo medicine men. In 1963, a film was produced of a whole ritual and three persons of the inner circle of those in charge died within the following year, rumors stated that the holy people had taken revenge for the disclosures. Still, much information of ritual sandpainting has been gathered. Navajo supplicatory prayers are also intimately connected to the art of creating non-sustainable but energy-laden pictures of the Holy Ones, an art taken up by many a Navajo brush and chisel artist like Carl Gorman (1907–1999),[40] whom I interviewed in 1963. Musical expressions (intonation; rhythm; syllabic differentiation; instruments, etc.)[41] would be worthwhile to be investigated.

Myth, Song, and Prayer

Another remarkable feature of Navajo chants is the overwhelming mass of mythical narration filling ritual space. The medicine man recounts episodes and stories of the Holy People, who, in ultimate analysis, were the inventors of ritual and the first composers of pertinent sacred songs and prayers. They, in turn, instructed human healers to use the text materials and taught them to tell abundant tales of the divine world. Katherine Spencer in her

---

38. Reichard, *Navajo Religion*, XXXV.

39. Cf. Matthews, *The Night Chant*, 34–36; Franciscan Fathers, *An Ethnologic Dictionary of the Navaho Language*, 398–99; Reichard, *Navajo Religion*, 694–717: reports on sandpainting and prayer performances; Faris, *The Nightway*, 109–56

40. Cf. Greenberg and Greenberg, *Power of a Navajo*.

41. Cf. Reichard, *Navajo Religion*, 279–84.

doctoral study of Chantway myths gives, among other things, the compact mythical plots of seventeen complete rituals,[42] among them the Waterway ceremony,[43] from which the prayer above was taken. (Spencer distinguishes three different versions; we stay with the Haile edition.) One main line of the narration tells about a hero under the care of two old grandmothers, who is being ridiculed by the people because of a disfiguring skin disease. He takes revenge by seducing married women, has to flee from Dark Thunder, "visits super-naturals in the sky and elsewhere and learns the ceremony."[44] The long-winded tales punctuated by differing motives fill hours of ritual performance. Sacred songs and prayers and possibly ritual acts stand out from this flow of words.

Songs in the Navajo culture accompany all sorts of human activities. Those pertinent to ceremonial chants possess a special holy quality;[45] they derive from mythical episodes where they frequently are compositions of the gods, handed over to adorants. "In myth an ever-recurring theme is loneliness. Crying originated in loneliness and from crying came a song."[46] "The primary function of song is to preserve order, to co-ordinate the ceremonial symbols; a secondary purpose must be enjoyment . . ."[47] Songs have much in common with prayer, but they are less significant and less "dangerous" in that they are not direct communicative instruments between humans and divine beings. In any case, songs also create a "zone of protection that gives comfort."[48] Songs possess various properties and they are considered forms of wealth if owned by families or the community as a whole.[49] As far as healing rituals are concerned, they support the aims of the whole performance: "Songs of exorcistic rites express strong emotion—vengeance, triumph in victory, retribution."[50]

Medicine Men, Chanters

Elaborate healing rituals like the Navajo chants cannot be mastered by everyone. Like in many other cultures, the office of "healer" requires long

---

42. Spencer, *Mythology and Values*, 100–218.
43. Spencer, *Mythology and Values*, 107–16.
44. Spencer, *Mythology and Values*, 108.
45. Reichard, *Navajo Religion*, 279–300.
46. Reichard, *Navajo Religion*, 284.
47. Reichard, *Navajo Religion*, 288.
48. Reichard, *Navajo Religion*, 288.
49. Reichard, *Navajo Religion*, 289.
50. Reichard, *Navajo Religion*, 292.

years of preparation and final recognition by the community he or she wants to serve. "The term *hatqáli*, chanter, implies that the bearer of this title is conversant with one or more of the chants, its prescriptions, songs and requisites . . . Persons of an especially retentive memory and natural alertness are selected as pupils by an elderly shaman."[51] "The chanter studies with his teacher for many years, learning by rote every tiny detail. Meantime, he collects a bundle of sacred objects: special prayer sticks, herbs, and the Navaho 'jewels' of turquoise, white shell, abalone, and jet. He finally is graduated in an impressive ceremony and begins practice for himself."[52] Experienced diagnosticians, consulted by patients and working with different divinatory means, propose adequate curing rituals. On request of the patient's clan, the chanter then agrees to payment offered for his service and determines an opportune date for the treatment. The only conclusion: Sophisticated rituals like Navajo curing chants can be performed only by well-prepared experts. This truism is valid for all medical care through ages and cultures, and it is well attested also in Babylonian sources from the second and first millennia.

To summarize: Curing rites and the expert personnel who have been observed in real life, the performers of which have been interviewed by researchers, open up wide horizons transcending those offered by the study of ancient manuscripts. Thus the Navajo example tells us vividly how healing has been and is being done, in the cultural and natural environment of the "people" (Navajo: *diné*) who, according to their "emergence myth," once upon a time came up to their sacred lands, marked by four holy mountains in Arizona, New Mexico, and Utah. Patients in need of expert treatment undergo a diagnostic procedure, are being recommended an appropriate "chant" against the evil of their illness or else for their general well-being, and the curer takes action observing all the intricate rules of his profession. The ritual unfolds, after purifications, in three to nine nights of preparing prayer sticks and sandpaintings, chanting, rattling, bathing, tying knots, drumming, story-telling, singing, offering, and praying. The carefully formulated prayer, gift of the gods and property of the expert, is the central part of the whole. Interestingly the Navajo concept of "beauty" (*xójóni*), meaning a comprehensive state of well-being and happiness, is the declared goal of most prayers.[53] Prayers have a decisive place in the performances comparable to the patient's supplication in Babylonian incantation rituals.

---

51. Fransciscan Fathers, *An Ethnologic Dictionary of the Navaho Language*, 381; cf. Underhill *Red Man's Religion*, 224–40.

52. Underhill, *Red Man's Religion*, 228.

53. Cf. Reichard, *Prayer*, 31; Wyman and Fontana, *Beautyway*.

Magical components should not block comparisons with biblical prayers and rites, because, after all, Gladys Reichard may be right: Prayer is always "the Compulsive Word."[54]

Babylonian Incantations

Inner-biblical evidence of shamanic healing is interesting and alerting, but all by itself cannot establish the origin and further use of shamanic supplicatory procedures in Israel. External evidence does perhaps help a little. First of all, the existence of numerous cuneiform petitionary texts (of collections called, e.g., *šuilla, eršaḫunga, eršemma, dingir-šadibba, ki-utu, maqlu, namburbi, šurpu,* etc.)[55] proves beyond doubt that on the Sumero-Babylonian side professional rites for the treatment of many different disorders were common. Quite often, a supplicatory (and incantational) prayer, with very analogous elements over against Old Testament complaints of the individual (invocation; praise; affirmation of confidence; lament; petition, vow etc.), was a central piece in the ceremony. The leader of the performance always was a trained specialist, called *mašmaššu, āšipu, kalu*.[56] We have to be aware, however, of the fact that ancient Mesopotamian societies were different from tribal social organisms. Sumerians and Akkadians formed the first urban, class-structured, highly diversified, trade-ridden, empire-oriented, and anonymous commonwealths.

Fighting Ominous Evils

Stefan M. Maul, for example, describes carefully and in great detail the ritual of the Babylonian series *Namburbi*.[57] This incantation series is dedicated to the "dispersion of ills, which are threatening by bad omens" (*namburbi*, "its dispersion"). An extensive Sumerian and Akkadian literature of evil portents and deep-seated anxieties looms in the background of such healing rituals. After a thorough diagnosis of the patient's afflictions and the expert's suggestion of a relevant cure,[58] the incantation expert (*āšipu*) as well as the sufferer had to undergo a period of purification and "sanctification"

---

54. Reichard, *Prayer*.

55. Cf. Maul, *Zukunftsbewältigung*; Cunningham, *Deliver Me from Evil*; Heeßel, *Babylonisch-assyrische Diagnostik*; Lenzi, ed., *Reading Akkadian Hymns and Prayers*; Frechette, *Mesopotamian Ritual Prayers*.

56. Cf. Lenzi, ed., *Reading Akkadian Hymns and Prayers*, etc.

57. Maul, *Zukunftsbewältigung*, 37–113.

58. Cf. Heeßel, *Babylonisch-assyrische Diagnostik*.

by taking ablutions and obeying dietary rules forbidding determined dishes.[59] During the night before the ritual was staged, the *āšipu* prepared the "holy water" (*agubbû*) for ablutions using intricate ingredients.[60] A prayer for its effectiveness was in order.[61] A specialty of the *namburbi*-ritual was the formation of an image (a figurine) being able to substitute for that object which had shown the evil portent to the patient.[62] The healing ceremony itself started with a sacrifice to three highest gods (Ea, Šamaš, Asalluḫi) who were to be entreated to undo the bad omen,[63] a very complicated procedure involving a small altar (*paṭiru*), a choice of incenses on a special stand (*nignakku*), and sacrificial materials, prayers, and magic formulas. Interestingly, this sacrifice at the home of the patient, consisting of vegetables and drinks, "always occurred at early dawn."[64] The offering-site was fenced off and imagined evil persons were admonished: "Wicked tongues shall turn away" (a direct address of potential enemies, also found in Pss 4:3–5; 6:9; 52:3–7; 58:2–3; 62:4, 11).[65] After the sacrifice had been accepted, according to Maul's interpretation, and the high deities had assembled (perhaps represented by statues), the decisive part of the ritual began, a "juridical fight" before Šamaš, sun-god and judge.[66] In Maul's understanding, the conjurer (*āšipu*) and the patient fight against the object that carried the evil portent, pleading for a reversal or dispersion of its destructive power. The patient had to approach the sacred sacrificial site, stepping on to a carpet of garden-herbs (*šammū kirî*) with their purifying capacities.[67] They, so to speak, sucked in the evil powers threatening the patient. But an essential part of the "law-case" was the verbal petition for liberation from bad portents spoken by patient and conjurer.[68] This liturgical, fixed prayer "in many rituals first was spoken by the conjurer for the patient. The latter, then, had to recite it after the conjurer."[69] Those fixed "sacred" words (which were thought to be

59. Maul, *Zukunftsbewältigung*, 39–41.
60. Maul, *Zukunftsbewältigung*, 41–46.
61. Maul, *Zukunftsbewältigung*, 45.
62. Maul, *Zukunftsbewältigung*, 46–47.
63. Maul, *Zukunftsbewältigung*, 48–57.
64. Maul, *Zukunftsbewältigung*, 48; cf. Ps 5:4: "O Yahweh, in the morning hear my voice, in the morning I sacrifice to you [*ʾeʿerak leka* = I arrange for you] and watch out for you"; small altars have been found in many ancient Israelite homes
65. Maul, *Zukunftsbewältigung*, 55; a direct address of potential enemies, also found in Pss 4:3–5; 6:9; 52:3–7; 58:2–3; 62:4, 11.
66. Maul, *Zukunftsbewältigung*, 60–71.
67. Maul, *Zukunftsbewältigung*, 61–66.
68. Maul, *Zukunftsbewältigung*, 67–69.
69. Maul, *Zukunftsbewältigung*, 67.

the gift of the gods) "were then repeated three, sometimes seven times. But in addition, the affected person had the opportunity [according to the ritual instructions] to articulate his or her personal affliction, pleas and wishes before the divine judge... Such a 'free prayer' certainly did have a liberating effect just like the oral confession in the catholic church."[70] An elaborate discussion of the "transfer of evil to the substitute figure,"[71] the "removal of the substitute," which now is the carrier of the evil,[72] and final purifications of patient and his environment[73] as well as re-integration of the saved one into his social group and further prophylactic measures constitute the rest of Maul's treatise.[74]

The supplication, spoken by conjurer and patient, had a central place in all the concomitant rites and words. One example of a *namburbi-*ceremony must suffice:

> 1) Incantation: Šamaš, king of heaven and earth, 2) lord over right and justice, 3) lord over the Anunna-gods, lord over the spirit of the dead, 4) whose "Yes" no other god 5) can change and whose decree 6) cannot be altered. 7) Šamaš, to revive the deadly ill, 8) to free the bound one, 9) is in your power! Šamaš, 10) I, your servant 11) N.N. son of N.N. whose 12) gods are Marduk (and) 13) Zarpanitum, 14) am standing before you now, yes, you. 15) I hold on to your seam. 16) Because of that evil which came out of the snake appearing in my house. 17 It did catch a prey. 18) I did see it. 19) Therefore I am afraid, terrified 20) and constantly put into panic. Let me pass 21) this evil, then 22) I shall always praise your great deeds, 23) and extol you! 24) People who shall see me 25-26) shall eternally praise you! Text of the incantation.[75]

The structural elements of the prayer are clearly visible: Praise of Šamaš (ll. 1-9), self-presentation (10-14), affirmation of confidence (15), complaint (16-20a), petition (20b-21), vow to praise (22-23), witness to others (24-26a), scribal note (26b). With some particularities standing out (denomination as "incantation"; praising invocation; insertion of personal name; scribal note; lack of imprecations), the elements and their arrangement correspond to the ones found in Hebrew complaint psalms. Other

---

70. Maul, *Zukunftsbewältigung*, 69.
71. Maul, *Zukunftsbewältigung*, 72-84.
72. Maul, *Zukunftsbewältigung*, 85-93; cf. Lev 16:5-22.
73. Maul, *Zukunftsbewältigung*, 94-100.
74. Maul, *Zukunftsbewältigung*, 101-13.
75. Maul, *Zukunftsbewältigung*, 297 (my trans. from the German ed.).

Babylonian petitionary rituals, like *šuilla, eršaḫunga, eršemma,* and so on, show very similar prayers of the patient/conjurer in the center of the healing ceremony.[76]

Priests and Singers

Babylonian society, as mentioned before, was based on urban literate and administrative tradition. Written documents almost exclusively came to us through scribal schools of royal and temple administrations reflecting principally, as it were, the social structures, habits and beliefs of urban classes. There has existed, since Sumerian times, a very elaborate system of liturgical ceremonies, dedicated, most of all, to the preservation of dynastic power. Priests, singers, and composers of hymns were employees of the urban or territorial ruler; the sacred place was the state-temple, grandiosely exemplified by a hymn of Šulgi, second king of the third dynasty of Ur (2094–2047 BCE). Astounding is the richness of (mostly unidentified) liturgical genres that permits conclusions as to the wealth of ritual performances!

> Line 14: I, Šulgi, the king whose name is suitable for songs, 15: intend to be praised in my prayers and hymns . . . 20: At the command of my sister Ĝestin-ana, 20: my scholars and composers of . . . have composed 22: *adab, tigi* and *malgatum* hymns . . . 17: about how wise I am in attending upon the gods . . . 23/29: they have composed *šir-gida* songs, royal praise poetry, *šumunša, kunĝar* and *balbale* compositions . . . 38/31: They composed for me *gigid* and *zamzam* songs about my manual skill . . . (ETCSL 2.4.2.05)

Royal ceremonial art was temple- and palace-bound and has to be distinguished from the patient-oriented activities of the afore-mentioned "incantation-experts," the professional curer and diagnostician. *Mašmaššu, āšipu,* and *kalu* were long-trained professionals, in possession of the proper healing rites, powerful implements and conjuring texts, and ready to serve—for adequate remuneration—those people in need for medical and magical help. Both aspects, physical and mental health in antiquity always went together. Various types of incantations already have been alluded to.[77] Each conjurer may have been specialized in one or a few kinds of ritual, because—just

---

76. cf. Cunningham, *Deliver Me from Evil*; Lenzi, ed., *Reading Akkadian Hymns and Prayers*; Frechette, *Mesopotamian Ritual Prayers.*

77. Cf. Abusch, *The Magical Ceremony Maqlû*; Cunningham, *Deliver Me from Evil*; Frechette, *Mesopotamian Ritual Prayers.*; Heeßel, *Babylonisch-assyrische Diagnostik*; Lenzi, ed., *Reading Akkadian Hymns and Prayers*; Maul, *Zukunftsbewältigung.*

like in the case of Navajo chanters—there were numerous details to know and perform carefully. Little is known about the relationship of healers with the temple staffs. Presumably the fields of curing people and keeping up public order are wide apart, although there may have been points of contact, possibly in the area of receiving visions or auditions from the deities. Since private homes of "conjurers" have been discovered by archaeologists the possibility of freelance healers has been debated anew. In any case, the professional curer of pre-historic times apparently had survived in Mesopotamia even within urban bureaucratic societies.

Prayers of the Patient

All known Mesopotamian rituals concerned about individual well-being, be they of the protection (prophylactic) or the healing type, cherish a personal prayer, sometimes with personal name of the supplicant to be inserted at the beginning. The rites as a whole carry determined purposes, of course. They have been fashioned and tested by the enchanter specifically to ward off certain dangers caused by evil powers or to heal well-defined ills of a person. To give one more example of personal prayer, besides the *Namburbi* one cited above, a specimen of the *Šuilla*-series directed towards the healing goddess Gula may be quoted:

> 1: O Gula, most exalted lady, merciful mother, who dwells in the pure heavens, 2: I call out to you, my lady, stand near-by and listen to me! 3: I seek you out, I turn to you, as the hem of my god('s) and my goddess('s) garment, I lay hold of your (garment's) hem, 4: Because judging the case, handing down the decision, 5: Because restoring and maintaining well-being are within your power, 6: Because you know to save, to spare and to rescue. 7: O Gula, sublime lady, merciful mother, 8: Among the myriads stars of heaven, 9: O lady, to you I turn, my ears are attentive to you. 10: Receive my flour offering, accept my prayer. 11: Let me send you to my angry (personal) god (and) my angry (personal) goddess, 12: To the god of my city who is furious and enraged with me. 13: On account of oracles and dreams that are hounding me, 14: I am afraid and constantly anxious. 15: O Gula, most exalted lady, through the word of your august command, which is supreme in Ekur, 16: And your sure approval, which cannot be altered, 17: May my furious god turn back to me; may my angry goddess turn again to me with favor. 18: May the god of my city who is furious and enraged with me, 19: Who is in rage, relent; who is incensed, be soothed. 20: O Gula, most

exalted lady, who intercedes on behalf of the powerless, 21: With Marduk king of the gods, merciful lord, 22: Intercede! Speak a favorable word! 23: May your wide canopy (of protection), your noble forgiveness be with me. 24: Provide a requital of favor and life for me, 25: That I may proclaim your greatness (and) resound your praises!

26: It is a wording of a lifted hand [*šuilla*] to Gula.

27: Its ritual: You prepare an assemblage of offerings in front of Gula . . . you libate first-rate beer. You recite this incantation three times and the supplicant's (lit. "his") prayer will be heard.[78]

Like many other prayers in the Mesopotamian tradition, this *šuilla* has a scribal colophon (l. 26) and a short ritual prescription (ll. 27–28) indicating rites to be performed and words to be spoken. The addressee of these last two lines may be the conjurer. "You recite" then suggests his letting the patient repeat the prayer line by line. The body of the prayer shows the familiar structure of invocation and initial plea (ll. 1–3), affirmation of confidence (ll. 4–6), adoration and praise (ll. 7–10), petition (ll. 11–12), complaint (ll. 13–14), invocation (l. 15–16), petition (ll. 17–24), vow to praise Gula (l. 25). In comparison to Navajo prayers, the *šuilla* to Gula may put more emphasis on lauding the deity, asking for mediation between gods of different rankings, and emphasize a little harder the ailments of the sufferer, but the basic scheme of a patient's prayer is visible. In conjunction with overwhelming evidence for expert performance of healing rituals in ancient and present-day cultures, we may consider this ceremonial system a fairly constant anthropological feature.

Ancient Israelite Healing

The biblical Psalter offers a good number of "individual complaints" which on first sight already seem to fall into the pattern of "patient's prayer" studied in the foregoing sections of this paper. Whether or not these outside or "alien" analogies can have any bearing on the interpretation of the relevant psalms depends, firstly, on inner-biblical evidence, and, secondly, on the admission of foreign "proof," or better, intercultural comparability.

78. Lenzi, ed., *Reading Akkadian Hymns and Prayers*, 254.

Personnel and Rites

Hebrew Scriptures house a good number of names for persons dedicated to the mediating office between humans and the divine. Most impressive is the list of Deut 18:10–11, containing eight or nine (as it were: banned) professions: *ma'abir beno ubitto ba'eš* (one "who makes a son or a daughter pass through fire"—probably later addition); *qosem qesamim* (diviner / by arrow-shots? Lot-casting?), *me'onen* (soothsayer, magician / by observing clouds?), *menaḥeš* (diviner / by observing oil on water?), *mekaššep* (sorcerer / by which means?), *ḥober ḥaber* (spell-caster / from *ḥbr* = bind together, ban), *šo'el 'ob* (necromancer), *yidde'oni* (spirit of divination, / *yd'*, to know), *doreš hammetim* (consulter of the dead /coincides with *šo'el 'ob*?). The names suggest a plurality of mediating functions, the exact connotations of which remain in the dark. We are, apparently, in the middle of spiritual (in the original meaning) strategies. Did the transmitters of the text still understand all the names and implications? Mantic and magic functions are in the foreground; they probably belong in a wide sense to the curing profession. There are no extensive narrations about curers (but see Elijah and Elisha below). The most detailed story about a "cursor" of enemies is that of Balaam Num 22–24. A direct professional identification, however, is lacking. The vocabulary of Deut 18 only dimly echoes in this tale (Num 23:23: *naḥaš* and *qesem*). Shamanistic traits appear most of all in Num 24:3–4, 15–16: Balaam hears and sees God and future events and thus is able and commissioned to give oracles (*mašal*; *ne'um*) to his client. Any specific or general label for curer, doctor, therapist, however, is not at hand. "Doctor"—often used for Hebrew *rope'*—is inadequate. The verb *rp'* means "restore" and not "be erudite." From Gen 20:17–18; Exod 15:26; 2 Chr 16:12; Pss 41:5; 103:3, etc. one cannot deduce that only Yahweh himself was considered the healer. Professional healers in all cultures perform their work in collaboration with the deity. Akkadian *asûm*, perhaps "bandager," "curator of wounds" and *āšipum*, "conjurer" (Sumerian loanword: *mašmaššu*) are different medical experts, often working together.

Narrative and *prophetic* literatures offer, however, some illuminating evidence. The Elijah/Elisha cycles contain on the one hand the Deuteronomistic vision of early prophets fighting vigorously for Yahweh, the exclusive God of Israel. On the other hand, they preserve some older strata of two "men of God," apt to deal with spiritual powers, also and particularly in favor of afflicted people. Elijah's engagement for the "widow of Zarephath" is typical and legendary (1 Kgs 17:8–24). The "man of God" (*'iš [ha]'elohim*; in later tradition transformed into *nabi'*) provides miraculous sources of flour and oil for the starving widow and her son. The second part of the story tells the wondrous resurrection of the dead boy. Here we have, with some Yahwistic overpaint, the authentic figure of itinerant helpers and healers, true mediators between humans and the divine. The grateful widow recognizes Elijah's identity: "Now I know that you are a man of God" (1 Kgs 17:24). The subject of helping and healing ills in a shamanic way is pursued through the Elisha legends (cf. 2 Kgs 2:19–22; 4:38–41, 42–44; 5:1–19; and in particular 4:18–37—re-animating the dead boy—the motif of which has been copied and elaborated from 1 Kgs 17:8–24, or vice versa). In Isaiah we find an episode showing the prophet healing, alongside his word-mediating prophesy, by a "lump of figs" to be applied to Hezekiah's boil (Isa 38:21). Job 33:23–26 features a *mal'ak*, a "messenger and mediator (*meliṣ*)" who visits the sick bringing relief through intercession and prayer. All these passages offer hints of healing practices in ancient Israel, but only dimly so. There is no full-fledged report on healing a patient: The healing of Naaman, the Syrian general (2 Kgs 5), and the priestly incantation over a wife suspected of adultery (Num 5:11–28) offer but fragments of ceremony. Interestingly enough, the frustrated Naaman spells out what he had expected from a healer: "I thought that for me he surely would come out, and stand and call on the name of the LORD (*yahweh*: textually uncertain) his God, and would wave his hand over the spot, and would cure the leprosy" (2 Kgs 5:11).

Even less leader-focused narrations about healing cannot do without mentioning the experts in the field. Thus 1 Kgs 14:1–18 involves the blind *prophet* Ahijah who is expected to give a diagnosis from the distance and perhaps suggest a curing treatment for Jeroboam's sick child. The payment for good counsel is considerable (v. 3). But contrary to expectations the prophet, visualized in a Deuteronomistic messenger profile, pronounces a harsh verdict over Jeroboam, the child, and Israel (vv. 6–16). In a slightly different vain, 2 Kgs 1:2 tells of injured king Ahaziah seeking divine support from Baal-Zebub, the Philistine God of Ekron. Certainly, intermediation of some priest or holy man is presupposed, but not explicitly mentioned. The theological framework again is Deuteronomistic (cf. 2 Chr 21:15, 18–19, containing a rare description of illness: cancer?). Leviticus 14:3–7 has a priest interacting with the patient, obviously for purity reasons and diagnostics. Isaiah is involved with Hezekiah's illness also as a prophetic messenger (2 Kgs 20:1, 4–5 // Isa 38:1, 4–5). Various texts mention sickness just in passing (cf. Gen 48:1; 1 Kgs 15:3; Dan 8:7, etc.); others emphasize empathy with the patient including visits and presents to the sufferer (cf. 2 Kgs 20:12; 2 Chr 22:5–6). In short, narrative and prophetic literatures indicate the gravity of disease and loss of strength for somebody, but do not focus on those situations and the desired cure and rehabilitation. What, then, can we glean from these texts in regard to general attitudes over against the impact of illness, its causes and desirable cures, and the professional healer?

Complaint Psalms and Their Origin

We turn to individual ailments and their contextual frame in the Psalter.[79] Treatments or cures of sickness viz. psychic or social disorders are never described in full in the Hebrew Scriptures. Narrators and transmitters were not interested in details; they did not intend to compose handbooks for medicine men or women. More by chance we learn that wounds were bandaged after perhaps receiving some cleansing and herbal coverage (cf. 2 Kgs 8:29; Isa 1:6; Jer 51:8; Ps 147:3; Sir 27:23). Compressions were applied (Isa 38:31), meals and drinks prescribed (Exod 32:20; 2 Kgs 2:19-22; 4:41). Occasionally, a given passage will mention ritual procedure, mostly prayer ("crying out to the Lord": cf. Pss 5:2-4; 22:2-3; 39:13; 54:3-4; 57:2-3; 61:2-3; 107:4-6, 10-13, 17-19, 23-28; 130:1-2, etc.). The involvement of spiritual forces and deities in all dangerous, life-threatening situations was quite natural in ancient times. They, in ultimate analysis, did cause illness and misfortunes, and this fact made incantations and prayers necessary. We gleaned from the more extensive medical literature of ancient Babylonia as well as from Navajo tribal ceremonies that healing by ritual power was widespread and, in most cases, the only relief for sufferers.[80]

The most important inner-biblical evidence of shamanic rituals, then, could, in fact, be the "laments" or "complaints of the individual" or "prayers of personal supplication." Form critics count thirty to forty specimens of this genre in the Psalter.[81] Although no ritual prescriptions have been preserved alongside OT psalms, we still may look for some indirect evidence of liturgical embedding, that is indicative of a specialist's participation. Three selected complaints/supplications of the individual may serve as examples for the testimony of the Psalter.

Psalm 38

Often designated a "prayer in grave illness," Ps 38 paints quite a complex picture of the patient's suffering.[82] Physical decay is threatening (vv. 4-5), "wounds grow foul and fester" (v. 6), social ties have broken down

---

79. Cf. Gerstenberger, *Der bittende Mensch*; Maul, *Zukunftsbewältigung*.

80. Cf. Faris *The Nightway*; Maul, *Zukunftsbewältigung*; Lenzi, ed., *Reading Akkadian Hymns and Prayers*; Futterknecht, *Heilung in den Religionen*.

81. Cf. Gerstenberger, *Psalms, Part 1*; Gerstenberger, *Psalms, Part 2*.

82. Cf. Gerstenberger, *Psalms, Part 1*, 160-65.

(vv. 12–13), and the analysis of these ills (which may go back to an anterior evaluation of a diagnostician) clearly states, that the patient had committed sins against his deity (vv. 4–6). In fact, the introit of the psalm (vv. 2–3) is of unusual urgency, omitting a formal invocation! It does start abruptly with an admission of guilt:

> O Yahweh, do not rebuke me in your anger,
>> or discipline me in your wrath.
> For your arrows have sunk into me,
>> and your hand has come down on me.
>> ... because of your indignation. (vv. 2–3, 4b)

This prayer is to be followed by a formal statement to be guilty:

> I confess my iniquity;
>> I am sorry for my sin. (v. 19)

The structure of the poem, its theological depth, analytical oversight, profound knowledge of human anxieties, and literary language all point to a professional author, not to a layman's hasty composition. Did temple-singers like Asaph or Korah (cf. 1 Chr 15; 16; 25, etc.) deal with healing of the sick? We do not know. Interestingly enough, the language of entreaty and imprecation is carefully chosen (vv. 2–4, 10, 16–17, 22–23; note the direct addresses: *yahweh*, *'adonai*, *'elohay* and the condemnatory wish in v. 17). Also, the variety of symptoms (vv. 4–6, 12–13) suggests that this prayer was used for multiple cases of severe disorder, all laden with the verdict of "sin." Only repeated practical use would explain such a feature. Likewise, the repeated use of one prayer would testify to the origin and handling of the text by a professional healer. In the same vein, the theological insight into the intricacies of sin and punishment and the nature of God's indignation, retaliation, and forgiveness lead to an expert's reflection and composition. Again, recognition of misconduct ("sin") in regard to the deity did require, and would have been in this case, a professional diagnosis and verdict previous to the healing ritual (cf. Lev 13:7–8).

Psalm 55

Psalm 55 is a supplication in the midst of social mobbing.[83] There is no inkling of guilt or remorse, neither of physical illness in this prayer. Instead, the well-known "enemies" in the Psalms are blamed for the supplicant's

---

83. Cf. Keel, *Feinde und Gottesleugner in den Psalmen*; Fortune, *Sorcerers of Dobu*.

mishap/bad luck/deep consternation (e.g., ʾawän; ʾemot mawät).[84] The evildoers are likened to wild animals (v. 11; cf. Pss 22:13–14, 17; 59:7, 15–16) or outright demons (cf. Ps 91: "terror of the night," "arrows that fly by day," "pestilence that stalks in the darkness," "destruction that wastes at noonday" vv. 5–6), which kill people. And, more serious still, the allegation is that close friends joined their ranks (Ps 55:13–15), a motif of utmost forlornness. If diagnosis of the ailments of a sufferer got to this point, attributing the whole situation to hostile people (remember medieval accusations of witchery in Europe!)[85] certainly an expert in exorcisms was necessary to counteract this evil. To my mind a prayer of people haunted by unnamed and diabolized enemies clearly needed expert assistance. The affairs presupposed, which are close to open ostracism (that is, they are public events), require a publically acknowledged treatment. Also, curses against the originators of evil (Pss 55:10, 16, 24; 109:6–20) have to be handled with utmost care, comparable to dealing with dangerous modern medicines, so that they may be harmless to the supplicant himself. Indeed, the presumed *Sitz im Leben* (life-situation)[86] of OT complaint psalms as well as form and content of the relevant prayers are significantly marked by ceremonial healing practices conducted by expert healers.

Psalm 88

Psalm 88 seems to be a very special case of a desperate call from the abyss.[87] Leaving aside the question of whether or not the complaint is fragmented (note the abrupt ending of v. 19: "my companions are in darkness") it seems to wrestle, in a Jobean way, with God himself, who is directly accused of having caused the supplicant's trouble: "You have put me in the depths of the Pit . . ." (v. 8); "you have caused my companions to shun me . . ." (v. 9). The very heart of the matter is uncertainty about the reason of the estrangement: "Why do you hide your face from me?" (v. 15; cf. "My God, my God, why have you forsaken me?" Ps 22:2). Not the supplicant's errors, nor the evil minds of enemies or demons, caused the calamity at hand, but God himself. The motivation to pray, then, is to appease an angry deity (like in a series of Mesopotamian supplications), a rather risky task which presupposes much experience and prudence in dealing with the divine. The situation of this type of suppliants is dreadful because they combat the Deity him- or

---

84. Cf. Keel, *Feinde und Gottesleugner in den Psalmen*: he identifies more than ninety different designations of destructive agents.

85. Cf. Seybold, *Krankheit und Heilung*; Schmitt, *Magie im Alten Testament*.

86. Cf. Gunkel and Begrich, *Einleitung*, 175–83 [ET *Introduction*, 123–30].

87. Cf. Barth, *Die Errettung vom Tode*.

herself. In our Christian understanding such a struggle is near impossible in itself. Antique experiences were different, as stories like that of Jacob in Gen 32:23-32; the prophet Jeremiah in Jer 12:1-4; 15:10-18; 18:19-23; 20:7-18; some psalmists like those in Ps 44; and the exemplar sufferer in the book of Job abundantly demonstrate. Yahweh could be contested or even accused. Nevertheless, the direct confrontation with Him was audacious and highly risky. Therefore, it required the skills and experiences of a healer or shaman-type professional.

The prayers of our OT Psalter, as mentioned, do not clearly indicate professional authors of psalms and rituals or leaders of ceremonies. Could *lamnaṣṣeaḥ* (cf. Pss 4:1; 5:1; 6:1; 8:1; 9:1, etc., fifty-five times in the Psalter; NRSV translates: "to the leader") hide a reference towards a shamanistic healer? Or does it mean "choirmaster" indicating a conjuration by music?[88] The profiles of sufferers in the psalms certainly do not preclude a congenial interpretation in the light of Mesopotamian petitionary prayers embedded in concomitant ritual.[89] A brief look at the superscriptions of the Old Testament psalms does not help any further in determining original uses of Old Testament complaint psalms of the individual, save perhaps Ps 102:1: "A prayer of one afflicted, when faint and pleading before the LORD" (*Yahweh*), which seems to allude to a temple-situation (cf. 1 Sam 1:9-18, Hanna praying at Shiloh). Allusions to situations of utmost danger and in some "biographical" references to the David story (cf. Pss 3:1; 18:1-2; 34:1; 51:1-2; 52:1-2; 54:1, etc.) presuppose a personal, more informal entreaty before the divine far from any sanctuary. Present Hebrew "headlines" of psalms in their majority seem to integrate, by their main contents, wording, imagery, and the pertaining text into some temple-setting. The same intention can be found in 1 Kgs 8:31-53, a lengthy (exilic in origin) treatise about prayer and temple in Jerusalem. Privately and congregationally, Israel is supposed to direct its requests to Yahweh's abode in Jerusalem, on the spot or from afar. In some layers of tradition, the temple therefore has become a "house of prayer" (cf. Isa 56:7, quoted in Mark 11:17, etc.).

Complaints in the Canonical Psalter

The arguments for a liturgical and expert of the "individual complaints" may sound somewhat convincing to many readers. Do they suffice, however, to explain these prayers or songs in their present context, a written and canonized book of Psalms? Have these psalms of suffering people in

---

88. Cf. *TWAT*, 5:569: instruments, melodies, etc.
89. See below; cf. Gerstenberger, *Der bittende Mensch*.

their written form, integrated into a "prayerbook," become autonomous, or better, the property of a faith community which no longer admitted conjurers and healers with their modes of approaching deities? Did these prayers turn into meditative literature instead of performed incantations? Can we imagine an early Jewish community that incorporated, on the basis of a strict monotheism, every sign of heterodoxy into their patterns of service to Yahweh alone, be it in congregational worship or new forms of casual celebrations or religious education? These and other questions are widely debated nowadays in Old Testament scholarship.

Answers to these queries should be thoroughly considered and critical. The Psalter surely has suffered some reworking and accretion in the name of Yahweh, the exclusive God of emerging Judaism. Notable are the Torah Psalms: 1, 19, 119; the Yahweh-kingship and Zion songs; or some history and Hallelujah poetry. But the bulk of prayers and songs in the Psalter has remained more or less untouched. In particular, the large group of complaints of the individual is still recognizable as supplications of the distressed and marginalized. The name of Yahweh is used hesitantly, e.g., in Pss 42–83; enemies and evildoers often muster demonic traits. In short, the minimum that can be stated is this: Probably, complaint psalms in the Hebrew Psalter were used as petitionary prayers also in later times, when emerging Judaism used the book of Psalms in their weekly synagogue services. Perhaps congregational leaders and early rabbis had taken the place of ancient exorcists and conjurers.

Outlook

The study of Navajo songs and Babylonian incantations has brought to light some cultural, religious, and spiritual dimensions in which healing the sick and endangered has taken place. Seriously sick or distressed persons in all probability cannot take care of themselves. Over against mostly unseen potencies of destruction, they need expert assistance from someone who knows how to deal with those evil powers in order to regain their health and good spirits. Prayer (agnostics possibly do substitute meditation and debate within oneself for it), which serves to clarify the human position and purpose in this world, becomes a central event for corporal and spiritual rehabilitation. The prayers studied in this paper, coming from distant ages and cultures, all speak vehemently about the anxieties of humans in regard to deadly dangers and painful living conditions. Ceremonial experts lead the patient's prayer; there may be room for individual outpourings of grief and hope.

The goal of a guided prayer in line with the whole ceremony is to be saved from the abyss, to reach a happy state of mind and physical well-being. Navajos frequently call it life's *xójóni* ("beauty," "harmony," "good order"), Babylonians *salīmu* ("peace") or *šimtu damiqtu* ("good fate"), Hebrews *šālōm* ("wholeness, wellness, peace"). It can best be realized in a common effort by all people concerned in case of illness or disorder, by medical and spiritual experts within the community of friends, relatives, supporters; that is, in the solidarity of good will and self-understanding. The common goal of ritual prayer, then, seems to be identical or at least comparable in all the three cultural realms studied above. Take the Navajo attitudes towards the desired state of wholeness as an example, because testimonies are so overwhelmingly numerous, having been recorded and interpreted by hosts of deeply interested and empathic observers. (Clear enough is also the fact that these observers unequivocally are wearing the glasses of Western cultural experiences and values, but most of them have been conscious of this unavoidable situation.[90]

The Navajo world was (and is, although in modes of change) an infinitely complex organism of living beings and powers collaborating, ignoring, and feuding with each other. From time immemorial this has been the state of affairs as the emergence-myths of the "People" (*dine*) from the netherworlds tell. The much-desired condition, naturally, would be that of a calm, well-provided, happy life of individuals, clans, and people, but evil powers constantly would disrupt the good order devised and communicated by the Holy People. Good and evil, for their parts, were not separated into fixed beings (with the exception of primordial Monsters, killed by warrior gods) but persisted gradually and variably in all kinds of beings:[91] "few things are wholly bad; nearly everything can be brought under control, and when it is, the evil effect is eliminated. Thus evil may be transformed into good; things predominantly evil, such as snake, lightning, thunder, coyote may even be invoked. If they have been the cause of misfortune and illness, they alone can correct it."[92] The chant-ceremonials given or inspired by the Super-Naturals, are probate means to counteract evil, restore harmony and beauty, and drive away damaging spirits. Humans, under the leadership of ceremonial experts, are co-agents with helping powers. They have a part in causing the calamities by disturbing malevolently or unwittingly good order and they actively engage in repairing the situation in prayer and ceremonial practices.

90. Cf. Faris, *The Nightway*, 11–16.
91. Cf. Reichard, *Navajo Religion*, 4–7.
92. Reichard, *Navajo Religion*, 6.

> The causal factors which bring about a violation of established order and beauty are very much a human affair. In the attempts to re-order, there are supplicating features addressed to Holy People, of course, but their attendance at the healing ceremonies is, if such ceremonies are done properly, very compelling—indeed, they cannot resist attending. And if all is done properly, this attendance and this healing and this blessing and these offerings and these expressions of rigid propriety, beauty, and order bring about and restore a condition of *hózhó*, literally, holiness that is the harmony sought—a beauty, a balance in an order set out in Navajo history and recapitulated in ceremony.[93]

Keeping in mind the overall vision of "beauty, harmony, order" to be attained in ritual and prayer, we have to evaluate all the ceremonial activities of medicine men and participants as expressions of carefully dedicated art. Every rite, beginning with all preparatory actions, has to be executed in awe and utmost diligence over against the wholeness of being. Outstanding examples of this attitude include the production of the sandpaintings and prayer-sticks: The sacred actions involve, as all the rest of the chant performed, powerful materials, holy words, ceremonial outfits and implements, deep knowledge, clean conscience, proper time and space, traditional (inspired) songs and narrations, rhythm and music, and participation of a friendly group. The patient's prayer is the topping middle-section of the whole performance, and all together the chant is truly a work of art, an intricate spiritual edifice surpassing our individualistic and mainly esthetic understanding of the term.

It would be worthwhile to investigate Babylonian and ancient Israelite healing ceremonies on account of such inclusive vision of wholeness to be aspired in salvation and rehabilitation of suffering patients. For the Babylonian incantations we may point at the meticulous care required of the ritual expert when executing his tasks.[94] Israelite psalms quite often refer to "fullness, joy, beauty, happiness, integrity" of life to be regained by supplication and salvation through the grace of the lord Yahweh (cf. Pss 4:7–9; 5:12–13; 11:7; 13:6; 16:2–11; 17:15; 22:25; 26:11–12; 27:13; 30:12–13; 31:20–25; 32:10; 35:27; 36:6–11; 40:17–18; 41:13; 52:10; 56:13–14; 59:17–18; 62:6–9, etc. Some passages come close to describing even God in terms of "glamour" and "beauty" (cf. Exod 24:9–11; Pss 50:2; 104:1–2; Isa 60:1–3; Ezek 1:26–28; Hos 6:3).

---

93. Faris, *The Nightway*, 15.
94. Cf. Maul, *Zukunftsbewältigung*, 37–156.

7

Singing a New Song

On Old Testament and Latin American Psalmody

The History of a New Song

MUSIC—BE IT VOCAL OR instrumental—has always played an important role in all kinds of religious rituals throughout all known cultures. Sound and melody, rhythm and movement are integral to many forms of worship. The reasons for this ornamentation and mystification of the divine services lie hidden far back in pre-history. Among them certainly count notions of power and magic, of participation in superhuman spheres and articulations of innermost longings. The silent speech of heavens and times (Ps 19:2–5; note: verse numbering is according to Hebrew tradition; NRSV etc., differs), the shouts of divine beings providing strength for the Lord of hosts (Ps 29:1, 9; Isa 6:3), the acclamation of nations, rivers and mountains (Pss 96; 98), all may be thought of as musical events. Being itself, we are led to suppose by religious experience, is of a musical fiber. Therefore, it is all very natural to approach God in songs and rhythms.[1] The Jewish-Christian tradition has developed along with other elements of liturgy like blessings, scripture-readings, and sacramental acts, a special kind of sung prayer or hymn. It does have counterparts in many other cultic traditions, to be sure, but the width and depth and diversification of this stream of communal prayer is astonishing. Already in the last century some industrious scholars collected

---

1. Cf. Bowra, *Primitive Song*; Wyman, *The Mountainway of the Navajo*; and Heiler, *Das Gebet*.

more than a hundred thousand Christian hymns and spiritual songs.[2] The number today must be multiplied by a considerable factor, especially if Jewish songs of all ages and the liturgical poetry of the new continents are to be included, as they certainly should be. Already in New Testament times the vivacity of that old psalmic tradition made itself felt in ever new songs. There are numerous citations of new Christian hymns in the New Testament writings themselves (cf. Luke 1:46-55, 68-79; 2:29-32; Phil 2:5-11; 1 Tim 3:16; Rev 1-12; 6:10; 7:10, 12; 11:17-18; 12:10-12; 15:3-4; 19:1-8). Also, New Testament authors intensively and pointedly speak about the singing of hymns, attributing to it great importance in regard to personal edification and congregational fortification (cf. 1 Cor 14:15; Eph 5:19; Col 3:16; Jas 5:13; Rev 5:9; 14:3; 15:3). The diversity and newness of early Christian vocal music is witnessed to by the classification of "psalms, hymns, and spiritual songs," which certainly indicates different functions and forms of this poetry in congregational liturgies.

The Christians had inherited the custom of psalm-singing from Jewish liturgical usage. But how had it arisen in that parental creed? From the earliest times (cf. Exod 15:21; Judg 5) and in particular since the exilic period (cf. Ps 137; Lam 1-5) Israel had been approaching Yahweh in a great variety of religious ceremonies, not only by sacrifices and offerings, but also in hymns and lamentations. The amplitude of forms and expressions is due also to local and regional differences and temporal changes. Individuals as well as neighborhoods and communities would voice their concerns over against Yahweh. Sometimes, under determined (for us hardly verifiable) conditions this way of vocal, liturgical articulation took precedence over all the other forms of worship (cf. Ps 51:17-18). Sometimes it was abused and therefore severely contested (cf. Amos 5:23; 6:5). At any rate, psalm-singing very early had become a hall-mark of Israelite faith. It had, to be sure, more ancient roots in pre-Israelite religious life. It came out of the rites of passage and healing ceremonies of family and tribal religion, out of hymns and chants used in Canaanite festivals, out of nomadic songs used for pilgrimages and wanderings. All these influences grew together and were joined with the liturgical customs of Yahweh worship.[3] The national, Yahwistic creed had gradually been installed in the sanctuaries throughout the promised land. Only very much later it became centralized at the Jerusalem temple, and with this new development there appeared new hymns (cf. Pss 46; 48; 76; 132).

---

2. Cf. E. E. Koch, *Geschichte des Kirchenlieds und Kirchengesangs*; Wackernagel, *Das deutsche Kirchenlied*; Rambach, *Anthologie christlicher Gesänge*; and Dreves and Blume, *Analecta hymnica medii aevi*.

3. Cf. Cross and Freedman, *Studies in Ancient Yahwistic Poetry*.

From the distant beginnings we have to trace the march of the new singing in praise and lament to our present day. Here and there in the course of the history of Jewish-Christian worship we recognize peaks of psalmic poetry and hymn-singing. If critical investigation is correct, the time of the Chronicler (fourth/third centuries BCE) already was such a high time. The authors tell us emphatically about levitical singing in Jerusalem. While they project the beginning of this liturgical habit back to the period of David (1 Chr 16; 25), in reality it is their own situation which they are portraying. It is their own congregational, synagogal worship which they want to legitimate.

More popular and closer to the small church-group and the house-community of old was the singing of the primitive Christians (cf. Mark 14:26; 1 Cor 14:15; Eph 5:19; Jas 5:13; Rev 5:9; 14:3). Although there was some discussion in the early church about the permissibility of music in worship—adamant purists tried to limit liturgy to word and sacrament—hymn-singing broke through. Not restricted to Old Testament psalms, this hymnody adopted the rich eastern and western traditions and reached impressive heights, e.g., in the work of Ephraim, the Syrian church poet, or Ambrose, bishop of Milan, in the third and fourth centuries CE respectively. Some of their hymns are still used today (e.g., "O Jesus, Lord of Heavenly Grace," by Ambrose of Milan) with unbroken spiritual force.

Medieval Jewish spiritual poetry was strong and constantly invaded liturgies, challenging the official, scripture-oriented psalm-singing.[4] Purviewing more rapidly the history until our own days, we see many more periods of singing and spreading the gospel by musical means: the Reformation century with its jubilant discovery of the new/old message of grace and reconciliation; Methodist renewal of the church; awakenings and revivals in Europe, the United States, Africa, and Asia. Last, not least, there is the astonishing rebirth of psalm-singing in the churches of Latin America and other so-called (with hideous arrogance!) "Third World" countries. A new song has arisen in these parts of the world, under incredible pain and in deepest misery, against oppression and despair, in Christian hope and certainty of the Kingdom of Heaven.

To recognize better the core of Jewish-Christian hymnody, to see what this "New Song" is, we want to study some aspects of Old Testament singing and compare to them the new song in Latin America where this author has lived and taught for some years.

---

4. Cf. Elbogen, *Der jüdische Gottesdienst*; and Maier, "Zur Verwendung der Psalmen in der synagogalen Liturgie."

Aspects of the New Song

What has Old Testament hymn-singing been about? How did the "New Song" arise and what does it imply? We should be aware of the fact that Old Testament psalmody used rather fixed poetic, stylistic, liturgical, and theological patterns. These patterns were dependent on tradition and ceremonial purposes and on those social and religious groups who were sponsoring the rites. Modern psalm-research has proved beyond reasonable doubt that Old Testament psalmody in no case was a private, poetic affair of isolated individuals. There is nothing like our seemingly "private" poetry in ancient times. Nor is there very much of it in modern times. If an atomized industrial and urban society today adores at times idiosyncratic, individualistic art, this does not mean that art is less public than in antiquity. Among the Hebrews, in any case, we do not know of one single individual writer or poet. Not even Jeremiah or Baruch belong in this category. All Old Testament literature is community-oriented, destined to be used in groups and congregations.

The psalms were used in some ceremonial setting or other which of course underwent considerable change through the centuries: social shifts and rifts occurred as the transitions were made from nomadism to agrarian ways of life, from clan and tribal society to monarchy, and on to the loss of statehood and an existence in dispersion and dependence. Clearly a bedouin tribesman has different needs and expectations, different beliefs and superstitions from those of a peasant in his seasonal routine. A citizen and royal functionary worships in another way than a craftsman in the province under foreign dominion. Is this, then, the point for the "New Song" to arise, as response to new social situations (cf. the Zion-hymns mentioned above)? Should we consider the "New Song" in Israel as a kind of protest-hymn like the ones which came up in our churches, sung by young people, civil-rights-, anti-war-, and peace-movements, and which settled down in a large quantity of pamphlets apart from official hymn-books?

This is by no means true for the Old Testament "New Song." Changes of social structures by and large took a long time to occur and be recognized, if ever. Even abrupt turmoil like the downfall of Jerusalem in 587 BCE and its consequences were lamented in very traditional forms (cf. Lamentations). The structural upheaval hardly plays a role in these laments, perhaps even passes unnoticed. The expression "sing a new song" in the Old Testament (Pss 33:3; 40:4; 96:1; 98:1; 144:9; 149:1; Isa 42:10) must have a meaning which differs from our own expectation. We should be aware that "new" in our languages and cultures may mean a substitution for things past, but to the effect that a steady progress may be enjoyed and consummated by the things implementing the "new" situation. The jargon of advertising is an example. The word "new" promises more of the old with better means and lesser pain, work and investments.

Not so in the Old Testament psalms. It is not the newness of the prayer which is aimed at, nor the continuous usufruct of the old. We marvel: the "New Song" consists of old words. But the situation, the reality, has radically changed in comparison to what existed before. There may have occurred a salvation experience of a distressed individual or an endangered community. Psalms 40:4 and 144:9 seem to presuppose this wonderful upheaval of oppressive reality. The psalmist sings praises because he is saved. He has passed through despair and death (cf. Ps 107 and its descriptions of deadly realities, or Pss 22; 38; 69, etc.). In typical thanksgiving situations the adorant looks back into the abyss. These situations mark a miraculous renewal of life, a reversal of the death-reality, a victory over evil. On a larger and seasonal scale this same overthrow of bad powers is being celebrated in festal hymns like Pss 96:1 and 98:1. Small wonder that the same word may also be used in order to articulate eschatological hopes for a new world to come (cf. Isa 42:10; 65:17–25). Not continuation and growth, but salvation and new beginning, return and renewal are the reference points for the psalmists from the beginning. The words of the songs may be old. But reality, which carries the great intervention of God, is brand new. Therefore, the judgment of R. North puts things upside down: "The totality of existing reality, as already in existence, continues to be, only in a revitalized form . . . it is a kind of creation which, however, accentuates more the dynamic motion of ongoing existence than its substitution by something new."[5] It seems to me that the modern predicament of being drugged by newness without pain has been read into the Old Testament texts.

The criteria for the Old Testament "New Song," consequently, are these:

1. It was intoned against death and evil in order to support and make possible full human life.

2. It was voiced in communities small and great, but never in the privacy of a chamber or office.

3. It anticipates boldly, against all evidence, the coming of God's liberation, the new and just world.

---

5. North, *TWAT*, 2:775.

Latin American Revival

In Latin America there has been going on for some decades now a revival of religious singing. A truly new song has come up. Thousands of spiritual poems have been composed especially in the base-communities. Sometimes the authors are unknown, the songs are folk-songs, the language may be idiomatic or slangish. But spiritual compositions may be found through all layers of society and all linguistic levels. Even renowned poets and singers, commanding a vast audience, like Pablo Neruda and Victor Jara in Chile; Mercedes Sosa in Argentina; Carlos Drummond de Andrade, Chico Buarque de Holanda, and Maria Bethânia in Brazil, and many others known to include the spiritual dimension in their work. These intellectuals certainly are no opportunists; they simply respect the religious foundations of all life.

The background for this new singing, and paradoxically the fertile soil for it, is an economic and political decay of astounding proportions. Agrarian and mineral exploitation of the continent has, of course, been going on practically since discovery, conquest and colonization. But with the exception of short price-booms for certain export-goods, like rubber, copper, cotton, wheat, soy, meat, etc., the more recent efforts of industrialization have resulted in a rapid accumulation of wealth in the hands of a very thin layer of upper-class people and a deadly impoverishment of large segments of the population. Infant mortality in 1985 was about 62.9 per thousand live births according to the Brazilian Institute of Geography and Statistics. In 1980 more than 25% of the population over fifteen were illiterate. Starvation and disease plague the millions without land in the countryside and the *favelados* (slum dwellers) around the large cities. "In 1980, the richest 10% of Brazil's population generated almost half (49.6%) of the country's GDP, while the poorest 50% accounted for only 13.8%."[6] Unemployment, substandard housing, lack of educational facilities, faulty health care join the list of calamities and make a full, vicious circle of inhuman living conditions. It is virtually impossible to escape from it. The majority of the people, that is 70–80 percent, lives—no, it rather dies—on 20–30 percent of the national income. A worker has to toil for 10–20 hours in order to gain the money that buys him one kilogram of meat. He has to work for a full month to buy one pair of decent shoes. The children who survive very often are weakened physically and intellectually to such an extent that they never can develop fully their human capacities. Profiteering by a few at the cost of the majority goes hand in hand with a ruthless destruction of nature by uncontrolled use of chemicals and unscrupulous extraction of all natural resources.

---

6. Hoffmann, "Desigualdade e Pobreza no Brasil no Período de 1979–1990."

Another background is equally or more important, however. Since 1968, in the wake of the Second Vatican Council, the bishops of the Roman Catholic Church have been analyzing the economic and social situation of their continent and trying to formulate responses to it. On the basis of their analyses, the bishops have flatly denounced the existing reality and the system which led into this situation as unchristian and dehumanizing. This stand of the official church was the signal for a free proliferation of base-communities and the green light for the new Latin American song. The Vatican, by the way, seems to fear increased alienation in Latin America. Therefore Rome tries to contain liberation theology and intimidate "leftist" priests. Nevertheless, the popular movement within the church is still strong, especially in Brazil. And there are thousands of new church hymns growing in that hopeless environment of poor congregations. Their beauty and force very often is breathtaking. Following the criteria of Old Testament psalm-singing given above we should note the following.

The Forces of Evil

The forces of evil are constantly being identified and denounced in these new hymns of Latin American Christians. There is no other way to proceed. Dogmatic affirmations about that "evil within a person" or the "all pervading sin" (cf. Ps 14; Rom 3:9–20) fail to do justice to the calling of Christ in that concrete situation. Mere dogmatic truths never will do, because the gospel is a living truth. Injustice has to be named. Taking the enemy descriptions of Old Testament laments as a point of departure Ernesto Cardenal writes:

> My God, my God, why did you abandon me?
> I am a caricature of a man, despised by everyone.
> They make fun of me in their papers,
> their armored cars close in on me.
> They point their machine-guns at me,
> and I am surrounded by wire, by electric fences.
> Every day I have to attend to their roll-call,
> they burned a number into my skin.
> They took photos of me between the barbed wire,
> all my bones may be counted as in a radiography.
> They took my personal documents,
> they pushed me naked into the gas-chamber,
> and divided my clothes among themselves . . .[7]

---

7. Cardenal, *Salmos* [ET *Psalms*].

This is indeed a stark and comprehensive description of that devilish reality that can be witnessed in Latin America and other parts of the world. Most importantly, in this poem it is the military, dictatorial abuse of power which is being denounced, in accordance with the mythical and archetypal enemy descriptions of Ps 22. This deadly and oppressive reality must be unmasked, combatted and overcome in the name of Christ!

The identification of the causes of misery has nothing to do with sowing hatred or envying the upper classes for their possessions and privileges. The songs and liturgies are amazingly sober in Latin America. They even portray the economic pressures which induce the landowner to dismiss his farm-workers and turn to more profitable cattle breeding or to switch to large-scale, mechanized plantation methods. The peasants understand this development to a certain extent, but they experience subhuman treatment and they lose their little subsistence in spite of the protection which the law wants to provide (a farmer has a title to the land which he has cultivated for more than ten years, a right not respected by great landowners). Typical are the spiritual songs of the farmhands of Goiás, one of the central states of Brazil.[8] They tell the stories of threat, humiliation, force, and expulsion, which are the daily bread of the lower-class people there. The hymns sometimes show a deep knowledge of economic machinations which come from the cities. Mining companies, banks, traders promote their interests by invading Indian reservations and national parks, buying large areas legally or illegally and expelling defenseless natives or squatters. Again it is the experience of sheer and brutal force, the total contempt for the most fundamental human rights which is most shocking. The underprivileged know that this kind of predatory economy is sacrificing millions of human lives, destroying all the environment and in the end will be suicidal even for the rich. Therefore, the poor in their hymns sing against death and destruction, feeling responsible for the whole of creation.

> I am baptized,
> therefore I have the duty
> to put myself to service
> following our Lord.
> He set the example
> of justice and truth,
> of union and friendship,
> of freedom and love.[9]

---

8. *Cantos dos lavradores de Goiás.*
9. *Cantos dos lavradores de Goiás*, 10.

These are words of farmhands in the wider Amazonian region.

The other side of the coin is the unimaginable suffering of the people. Quite in line with Old Testament descriptions of misery, reflections upon the situation of the exploited recur in many hymns beside the identification of the evil-mongers.

> Hear us, our God,
> you are the strength of the weak and lowly.
> Hear our clamor which is burning our intestines.
> We are the miserable of the earth,
> that's the way they call us.
> It is hard to live only by your two hands,
> when a gang of exploiters is after you.
> We live in shacks of dirt and boards.
> When it rains our children weep.
> Cold weather bites into our bones.
> We have three chairs to sleep on,
> our household is a tiny compartment.
> Our children grow up naked without and within.
> They are the ones who steal food on the market place.
> Everyone condemns us and looks at us with disgust,
> and we have to swallow our black hatred in order not to explode.
> We eat rice and beans if we can.
> We all eat from one plate until the dish is finished.
> We work two hours away from home,
> we have to rise at four in the morning.
> They keep us like starved dogs;
> our big-bellied bosses do not consider us humans.
> We already start to think like them,
> we come to the point to lose all hope . . .[10]

In spite of the harsh tones which may offend us, these songs are real Christian hymns and by no means chants of an ideological class-struggle, as the new Vatican instruction against liberation theology might suggest. No, here is that militant love of Christ at work which we find through the Bible: in psalms, prophets and the gospels themselves (cf. Amos 1–6;

---

10. *Os salmos da vida,* mimeographed sheets without names and dates (Caxias do Sul, 1980), 4.

Isa 5; Jer 22; Matt 23; 25; Luke 18:18–27, etc.). Paulo Freire explains very well how conscientization and liberation of the poor for the sake of Christ also implies the conscientization and liberation of the rich.[11] And Dom Hélder Câmara, impressive in his simplicity, humanity, and understanding, in one of his nocturne meditations puts it this way:

> You, O God, are the father of which kind of poor?
> Without any doubt
> of the helpless,
> the oppressed,
> of those without rights and voice.
> But please, do not forget
> the other kinds of poverty:
> those deprived of love,
> deprived of their dreams,
> deprived of faith and hope,
> deprived of peace.
> In your boundless mercy
> also take care
> of the poorest of poor,
> the poor rich ones.
> They embrace the shadows of power,
> they live all along
> under the illusion
> to live intensively:
> But they do not live at all.[12]

Theologically speaking, the New Song in Latin America is in line with Old Testament and New Testament psalmody. It is its declared goal to overcome the inhuman, devilish forces of the dark, to begin a new life, to realize the good creation of God. The new hymns sing against death, they proclaim the victory of life. This kind of identification of evil and announcement of the new age can be done legitimately, however, only from the depth of suffering, of utter deprivation (cf. Pss 69:2–3; 88:5–7; 130:1).[13] The same words

---

11. Freire, *Pedagogia do oprimido* [ET *Pedagogy of the Oppressed*].
12. Câmara, *Mach aus mir einen Regenbogen*, 85. [ED: trans. by Gerstenberger.]
13. Gerstenberger, "Enemies and Evildoers in the Psalms" [Chap. 8 below].

of psalms and hymns used in a position of power would become cynical instruments of exploitation.

Community-building

The new songs of Latin America are never individualistic or private in our sense of the words. They are fully integrated into the life of the community, no matter whether or not the author is known, well-known, or anonymous. Bishop Pedro Casaldáliga, who has been living and working with the natives and poor in Mato Grosso, Brazil, for many years, once told me of the origin of a little hymn which is widely sung all over Brazil. The author's name usually is missing on the mimeographed sheets which serve as hymnals. The small farmers of some village in Mato Grosso were clearing a piece of forest in a joint effort to provide living space for some families. And the bishop was helping them physically and spiritually. Dom Pedro after a while was asked to prepare the coffee for the group. While he was doing this there occurred to him this song which has become a real church hymn:

> We are a people of human beings,
> God's people are we.
> What we want is land on earth,
> land in heaven we've got already.
> We want to work in the fields,
> love we want to plant.
> Peasant, the land is ours,
> united, as we are, in the Lord.[14]

The "we" in the hymn is conspicuous. The movement of rural and urban base-communities discovered, as one aspect of the liberating gospel, that there may be and must be fraternal love between the exploited, instead of distrust, envy and strife. Solidarity among the poor was experienced as the first gift of God. Many Old Testament psalms show the same strong social cohesion as absolutely vital to a person. The psalmists complain, for instance, about the breaking of social ties in misery or sickness (cf. Pss 35; 40; 55; 88). They yearn for rehabilitation and re-integration.[15] Complaint really had the function of reconciling the sufferer with God and thereby re-establishing the broken social ties. Another example is the delimitation of the orthodox community after the exile, the warding off of "godless," "crooked," and "foreigners" (cf. Pss 10; 12; 37; 49; 73; 94; Neh 13). The same

14. *Nos lavradores unidos, Senhor*, 42.
15. Cf. Gerstenberger and Schrage, *Suffering*.

holds true for Latin American hymns. They do cultivate—although not glorify!—the righteousness and love within the base-group, recognizing very well also human frailty, faults and sins in one's own group. And they discover, theologically speaking, the divine value of poverty and lowliness. Power and glory are not the most significant attributes of God, but humility, sympathy, patience. In accordance with the overwhelming witness of the whole Bible, the Lord is at the side of the despised, persecuted, and helpless, suffering with them. "You are the God of the poor" is the title of a hymn from Nicaragua. Its second stanza runs:

> You go hand in hand with my people,
>
> you fight for them, in country and city.
>
> You line up in the worker's camp,
>
> to get your salary paid.
>
> You are eating there on the lawn with Eusebio,
>
> with Pancho and Juan José.
>
> You scratch your pan
>
> when there is too little honey in your food.

And the first and fourth stanzas summarize:

> You are the God of the poor,
>
> you are simple and human.
>
> You are sweating on the road,
>
> you are the God with the sun-burnt face.
>
> Therefore I talk to you
>
> just like my people used to talk:
>
> You are the laboring God,
>
> you are Christ, the worker.[16]

The new consciousness of one's own dignity, due to God's descent into this world which signalizes a loving and not a condescending participation in human affairs, comes out in many songs. It is part also of the eucharistic prayer of the Catholic Church at San Cristóbal de las Casas in México. Together with praise of God and memory of all the suffering in the world, the congregation mentions the lowly ones, thus portraying their own community:

> We do not forget your beloved ones,
>
> the farm-hands with their thousand sorrows,

---

16. Reiser and Schoenborn, *Sehnsucht nach dem Fest der freien Menschen*, 36.

> the peasants without land and harvest,
>
> the worker without a job,
>
> the carpenter without wood,
>
> the woman robbed of her dignity,
>
> the woman defiled and abandoned,
>
> all those who are persecuted
>
> for the sake of righteousness and fraternity.[17]

Not surprisingly, the sense of being wronged by existing power structures also results in assertions of one's own rights and demands. The "Songs of the farm-workers of Goiás" not only contain moving stories about the sufferings ("The cost of living," complaining about inadequate wages; "Mirror of reality," telling examples of expulsion from one's own land)[18] but also offer confidence in final justice and restitution. The assertion is that the claims of the people are right before God and men, and that they therefore constitute a force which must win victory without violence. In that sense, for example, Gustavo Gutiérrez also speaks of the "Force of the poor." The hymnic admonition says:

> Open your eyes, my friend:
>
> We will walk together!
>
> Only through the force of our union
>
> we will be liberated.[19]

Of course, we immediately suspect that these affirmations are mere "trust in flesh" and theological heresy. We should remember, however, that all the hymns here cited are deeply embedded in Christian communities who are well aware of their relation to God, and who are offering their cooperation at the lowest level of impotence. In the same vein many an Old Testament hymn ventures to speak about human participation in the liberating acts of God (cf. e.g., Judg 5; Ps 18). The same is true for the civil rights song "We shall overcome." The other danger we fear is political rebellion camouflaged as spiritual protest. In particular, northern Christians smell the Marxist menace in every movement which might threaten the industrialized states' privileges and wealth. (The Westerners usually do not realize that the Easterners are plagued by the same fear, and that the world is in reality not divided in East and West but in Northern and Southern hemispheres). Well,

17. Reiser and Schoenborn, *Sehnsucht nach dem Fest der freien Menschen*, 49.
18. *Cantos dos lavradores de Goiás*, 11, 13.
19. *Cantos dos lavradores de Goiás*, 17.

there is hardly any truly Marxist ideology in Latin America. The sensibility against socialist domination is as great as against capitalist exploitation. And the challenge to the rich comes from the gospel of Christ, not from a Marxist philosophy.

Exuberant Hope

The most pervasive and illuminating feature of new Latin American hymn-singing is the exuberant hope for the new world to come, which already has been touched upon here and there. The New Song in fact heralds the new reality of justice and love. In singing together, people—minority groups, impotent masses, exploited and suffering individuals—anticipate the new life which still is absent in their respective realities and environments. This also has been the experience in peace- and civil-rights-movements. The element of hope against all outward evidence is the most impressive fact in Latin American singing. Here is the prayer of a Christian condemned to death under the Somoza regime in Nicaragua, on the eve of execution:

> Tomorrow, my son, everything will be different.
> Oppression will vanish through the back door
> which will be closed forever
> by the hands of new persons.
> Small farmers will laugh on their sites,
> they will be tiny, but they will be their own.
> The worker's daughters no longer need to prostitute themselves,
> nor the daughters of the farmer.
> They will work in dignity
> and earn their food and clothes.
> Weeping will cease in the house of the poor.
> You will laugh with joy,
> and your laughter will be carried away
> by roads and streams and lanes.[20]

Or compare that vision contained in the "Psalm of a liberated man," another example of the popular collection of "Psalms for life":

> I want to be a messenger of hope,
> the light shining in my eyes,

---

20. Reiser and Schoenborn, *Sehnsucht nach dem Fest der freien Menschen*, 176.

passionate unrest in my weak hands,

disquieting strength of God in my words.

I want to be a sower of freedom,

among the people, my brothers,

in order to build his kingdom on this earth, so good and so much ours.

I want to proclaim peace,

with feet not profaned by gold.

I will not walk on paths of injustice,

I will not tolerate the oppression of the other poor . . .

I will not sell my heart for lies,

I will not keep silent when truth is called for . . .[21]

The hope to be found in Latin American hymns is the hope of the Christian church which Christ himself has sparked through his coming, living, suffering, dying and through his resurrection. Jesus himself lived in an anticipating hope of the kingdom to come (cf. Matt 9:15; Luke 23:43; John 6:35; 8:36; 11:25). And the Latin American Christians see the Reign of God sprout like a tiny seed in their own midst.

The New Song Has Power

These very few examples of Latin American singing should demonstrate that the biblical tradition of the New Song against death and in favor of life is being continued triumphantly on that poverty-shaken continent. The new hymns, in fact, *are* the force of God. They are instruments and material of the new time. To show this I may list a few incidents, involving New Songs and the reaction against them from the side of the powers of death.

After the slaying of Father João Bosco Penido Burnier on October 11, 1976, at Ribeirão Bonito, Mato Grosso, by a police sergeant, the congregation celebrated mass and sang its hymns in sadness and defiance.[22] The colonists expelled from their land at Alagamar, Paraíba, or at Ronda Alta, Rio Grande do Sul, and other places resisted the pressures to make them disappear into the slums. Their only weapons were protests, petitions, prayer, worship and singing. And they won at least partial victories. Father Reginaldo Veloso was sentenced to two years in prison in 1981. He had composed a new hymn with the first line running: "Vito, vito, vitória . . . ,"

21. *Os salmos da vida.*
22. Casaldáliga, *Creio na Justiça e na Esperança*, 135ff.

commemorating the expulsion by the government of the Italian priest Vitor Miracapillo, who had been living in too effective solidarity with the poor of his congregation. In spite of all these reactions—and they cannot be expected to be otherwise—Latin American Christians are sure that police power in the long run will lose out against the New Song of Christ. Antonio Haddad put it this way in a mass composed in 1976:

> Vem Senhor, vem Senhor,
> vem libertar o teu povo.
> Apesar da fome aguda e da sorte que não muda,
> sem casa para morar e sem onde se empregar
> este povo ainda, espera a tua vinda.

> Come, O Lord, come, O Lord
> come and free your people.
> In spite of sharp hunger and a fate which does not change,
> without house to live in and without job to take care of
> this people still waits for you to come.[23]

---

23. Translation by Erhard Gerstenberger.

8

Enemies and Evildoers in the Psalms

A Challenge to Christian Preaching

Human Conflicts and Faith

How to deal conscientiously with adversaries has become one of the most crucial issues of our times. There may be problems of greater gravity, such as the ruthless exploitation of the poor countries by Industrial states, waste of natural resources, pollution, and destruction of our natural habitat, scientific progress with ensuing manipulation of mind, life, and death. None of these enigmas, however, poses—within the limits of this decade—questions so explosive and deadly as do the friend-foe relations, especially in international affairs. Survival of mankind depends on satisfactory solutions of the many conflicts which are lingering on in our societies and between nations and continents.

Christians all over the world—and therefore in quite different historical, economic, and political contexts—are searching for orientation in the desperate decisions of life and death. Can the Bible, can the Psalms offer some help? Will they assist in defining the nature of human conflicts, in analyzing the phenomena of hostility, and in discovering viable paths to escape war and secure peace? The Psalter, it is true, does speak a great deal about enemies and evildoers.[1] But Christian tradition normally has shunned the teaching of the psalms in this regard. There are even editions of the Psalter that delete all references to enemies and revenge. Their publishers want to offer a "clean" book of prayer. And the Psalms are all but

---

1. Cf. Keel, *Feinde und Gottesleugner*.

missing in homiletical series of pericopes, perhaps for liturgical, perhaps also for ethical reasons. Obviously, Christian conscience has been shaped by passages like Matt 5:30–42 or Rom 13:1–7. Resistance to evil, or active and possibly even violent combat of injustice, seems to be excluded from Christian choices. The only legitimate Christian attitude seems to be patience and brotherly love (cf. also the Parable of the Weeds, Matt 13:24–30).

But it is really an open question whether or not Jesus and his followers wanted to give up the militancy of love. They certainly did transform ethical thinking of their time putting love and not self-preservation in the first place of the hierarchy of values. But they never denied the existence of enmity nor of class-distinctions (cf. Matt 23:13–32; Jas 5:1–6).[2] Furthermore, the New Testament must not be read outside or without the Old Testament. In fact, the Bible of primitive Christianity was nothing else but the Old Testament. And this original Holy Scripture is indeed very much concerned about political and economic situations, about justice, peace, and war. The enemy problem therefore is at the center of Old Testament ethical concepts. How is it that the evil came into the world? Why do persons, sometimes brothers, and people hate each other? Can Israel exterminate wickedness together with the evildoers?

Speaking in a general way, Old Testament authors recognize very well multiple forms of enmity and wickedness on many levels of society. One thing is common to all manifestations of wrongness: Enemies and evildoers are, in the first place, the authors of malignancy. They cause mischief and death, or, at least, act as responsible agents of evil. Everybody who fulfills punitive or destructive functions may be called enemy. Thus Esau (Gen 27ff) and Saul (1 Sam 18ff), with or without just cause, persecute their respective rivals, turning themselves into "enemies" for them. God himself may be considered a foe (Job 19:11; Isa 63:10). On the national plane, Israel's neighbors at one time or the other all qualify as ferocious enemies, starting with the Philistines of the tenth century BCE and not ending with the Babylonians of the sixth century BCE (cf. 1 Sam 13ff and 2 Kgs 24–25). The normal reaction of the people in times of emergency is that of life and death antagonism (cf. Amos 1:3—2:3; Exod 34:10–16; Deut 20; 1 Sam 15:32–33; 2 Sam 8:1–2; Isa 63:1–6). Each text, to be sure, has its own peculiarities, because it comes out of a peculiar historical, social and religious setting. Thus extermination-proposals of the late Deuteronomistic school are rather abstract and theoretical in comparison to historical reality (cf. Exod 34:10–16 and Deut 20 in contrast to Judg 1 and Josh 9; 1 Sam 15:32–33 as juxtaposed to 2 Sam 8:1–2). Nevertheless, they do demonstrate a certain,

---

2. Schottroff and Stegemann, *Jesus and the Hope of the Poor*.

even if ideological, state of theological thinking. It had been common practice in the ancient Near East, markedly so since the Assyrian Empire, to regard other autonomous nations as absolutely incompatible with one's own aspirations of hegemony. This notion of absolute dominance seems to have been condensed into Deuteronomistic theological reflection, although from a later, exilic, and thereby defensive point of view.

The Evidence of the Psalms

We turn to the Psalter seeking the dialogue with those psalms which mention enemies and evildoers and their suppression. We want to draw conclusions from these texts for our own time and our preaching today. Of course, actualization of ancient testimonies of faith is not an easy task. It presupposes clear recognition of that by-gone situation of old which brought forth the text at hand, it presupposes an honest and thorough analysis of our own situation, and, last not least, it demands a constant journey of mediation between the two poles separated by millennia. The Psalter's witness concerning the enemy-problem is contained mainly in three types or genres of prayers:

Complaints of the Individual

Personal complaints very often mention those unjust, deadly adversaries who seek to destroy the life of the supplicant (cf. Pss 3:7; 5:9–10; 22:6–8; 35:1–8, 11–16, 19–26, etc.—verse numbers according to NRSV, not to MT!). The most drastic example perhaps is offered by Ps 109. There, vv. 9–20 open up a real Pandora's box against those wretched criminals who caused the distress of the supplicant. Among the malicious and revengeful wishes are these:

> May his days be few . . .
> May the creditor seize all that he has . . .
> Let there be none who would help him . . .
> May his posterity be cut off . . . (vv. 8–13)

The final summary comes close to a formal malediction: he loved to curse; let curses come on him!

> He did not like blessing; may it be far from him!
> He clothed himself with cursing as his coat,
>   may it soak into his body like water,
>   like oil into his bones! (vv. 17b–18)

It is important to note: The prayer speaks up against wrongdoers; it is a cry from below (cf. Ps 130:1): it was being articulated within the fixed liturgical framework of a service for such individuals who suffered unjust persecution (cf. Pss 7; 17; 26). Other complaints of the individual go back to curing ceremonies (cf. especially Ps 38).[3] As far as the wrongdoers are concerned, they are seen as enemies of God (cf. Ps 5:4–6) and as being eaten up by their own mischief (cf. Ps 109:17–18). This last feature indicates a general belief in automatic retribution or self-produced punishment.[4]

National Laments

National laments in a very similar fashion attack the enemies. Thus Ps 74 describes the brutal destructions wrought by invaders and suffered principally in Jerusalem (vv. 4–8), then invokes the help of Yahweh (vv. 18–23). And Ps 83 explicitly calls for a radical punishment of those who devastated the land of Israel:

> My God, make them like whirling dust,
>> like chaff before the wind. (v. 13)
> Do thou pursue them with thy tempest
>> and terrify them with thy hurricane! (v. 15)

The revengeful wish which most painfully comes to mind in the context of national laments is that of Ps 137:8–9:

> O daughter of Babylon, you devastator!
>> Happy shall he be who requires you
>> with what you have done to us!
> Happy shall he be who takes your little ones
>> and dashes them against the rock!

Indeed, here we are confronted with an intransigent, merciless condemnation of the oppressors. It is noteworthy, though, that national laments much more than individual complaints accuse Yahweh himself directly as being chiefly responsible for the defeat and misery of his people. (cf. Pss 44:9–22; 89:38–45).

There are, consequently, some differences in the treatment of enemies if we start comparing the two genres, as well as individual psalms among

---

3. Seybold, *Das Gebet des Kranken im Alten Testament*.
4. K. Koch, "Is There a Doctrine of Retribution in the Old Testament?"

themselves. There is more historical reminiscence and more direct accusation of God in national lament, and there is more interpersonal fighting in individual complaints. But on the whole, the patterns of treatment are alike. Starting from their own painful experience of degradation and misery, Israel's entreaty goes to the Lord: He is to intervene and destroy the authors of their suffering.

Victory and Royal Psalms

The third type of psalms is essentially different from the two genres just mentioned, although it certainly has some relationship to national complaints. This third group in which the enemy sometimes looms large is constituted by victory and royal songs. They do not come out of a state of misery and weakness but of a position of strength. They belong to rituals of jubilation and highest self-affirmation. After victorious battle Israel gave thanks to the Lord, and in the olden days women composed and presented victory songs toll of taunts against the defeated foe (cf. Exod 15:21; 1 Sam 18:7; Judg 5; Ps 68). Furthermore, the king, during Israel's monarchic age, became the permanent representative of the victorious God. Ideally, the king was the supreme guardian of justice, and the relentless revenger of all injustice (cf. Pss 45:3-7; 72:9-11). This general conviction grew into programmatic affirmations especially on the occasion of the day of coronation. We probably find remains of coronation liturgies within our biblical Psalter, most of all Pss 2 and 110. Both poems contain references to the enemies. Yahweh's promise to the newly enthroned Davidic ruler includes powerful verdicts against neighboring peoples:

> Ask of me, and I will make the nations your heritage,
>> and the ends of the earth your possession.
>
> You shall break them with a rod of iron,
>> and dash them in pieces like a potter's vessel. (Ps 2:8-9)

And, equally strong:

> Sit at my right hand,
>> till I make your enemies your footstool.
>
> ...
>
> The Lord is at your right hand;
>> he will shatter kings on the day of his wrath.
>
> He will execute judgment among the nations
>> filling them with corpses;

> he will shatter chiefs
>
> over the wide earth. (Ps 110:1, 5–6)

Evidence from the Psalter could be amplified considerably in all three categories of enemy-treatment. Suffice it to have mentioned a few examples.[5] They tell us impressively how important it is to watch out for historical and social life-settings of each individual psalm.

Understanding the Ancient Situations

What can we learn from the Psalm's treatment of enemies and evildoers? Focusing on the two basic situations, that of being oppressed and that of being in control of one's adversaries, we may say the following:

In the first place, all biblical complaints, be they national or individual, have been articulated on a low, if not the lowest level of existence. Downtrodden people who are facing certain death are trying to win the support of God. Prayer, within a ritual of petition or curing, is the last resort to survive a threatening catastrophe. The description of misery in all relevant psalms gives a vivid impression of the urgency of the plea (cf. Pss 22:6–8, 12–18; 38:3–8; 44:9–16; 89:38–45). His inferior position does not give any chance to the supplicant to revenge himself with his proper hands. Only God, the guardian of justice, can turn the tide, can restore health and good fortune, bring back former bliss and security.

But this can be done, according to ancient beliefs, only by overcoming the forces of evil which caused the trouble. Living in a personalized world, Old Testament psalmists had to pray against those, mostly anonymous but willful, destroyers of their lives, be they human or superhuman.[6] Seen in this context and abstracting from our mechanistic worldview the psalmist's complaint, petition, and imprecation against enemies becomes a logical entity which is even plausible on the theological plain. Revenge, violence, submission of evil forces, eradication of the causes of suffering, all this does not directly emanate from the afflicted person. It would be entrusted to Yahweh, the supreme judge.

On the surface, we do no longer take part in a personalistic worldview as did our forebears. In general, we know to explain a given disease or misfortune by citing impersonal agents or natural laws as the primary causes. We see microbes at work or bio-chemical processes. We make psychic,

---

5. For comprehensive analyses of Psalms and Lamentations, see Gerstenberger, *Psalms 1*; Gerstenberger, *Psalms 2*; *Lamentations*.

6. Cf. Gerstenberger and Schrage, *Suffering*, 15–16.

political, economic, and social developments responsible for many kinds of evil. Do we still need, after all, the image of an "enemy" or "evil-doer" to cope with our desperate situations? Do we still need a personal God to help us out? The questions are not rhetorical. We cannot dismiss the results of modern science which helped us to analyze objectively the manifold situations of misery. Even more, it can be a criminal act of negligence if we tried to amend the distress of anybody by prayer alone. God has given to us the means of rational analysis, and we have to use them.

Strangely enough, however, the enemy-problem does not disappear from the scene. It gets dislocated and reformulated, to be sure, but it stays on and acquires new dimensions. It is an uncontestable fact that human responsibilities are invariably interwoven with the mechanisms of cause and effect. Therefore, it remains valid to ask for responsible persons and groups in any given situation of misery, more so, because human competence and capability have increased in an astounding measure during the last centuries. Applying all this to our own cases of distress and complaint we must admit: On the lowest level of existence, in the fore-rooms of death, in the torture-chambers of our times, it is imperative to identify those who are guilty of destruction and dehumanization.[7]

We enter a totally different realm when reading those royal and state-psalms which seem to promote, in an ideological way, domination over other peoples. Sure enough, a just victory over an oppressive enemy can spark exuberant joy which goes hand in hand with mockery of the defeated (cf. Judg 5). But very easily the borderline to haughty self-glorification is being crossed. Political control over other nations, growing wealth of one class, inherited privileges of an elite invariably produce that "Arrogance of Power" which is so obvious in all present-day international relations. We dare say that any kind of "power" or "dominion" (cf. Gen 3:16; Pss 8:7ff; 110:1) deprives the dominated of some of his inherent rights and possibilities of life, just like the wealth of someone necessarily causes the poverty of somebody else. Deprivation brings about disrespect of the lowly, which is the counterpart of the arrogance on the side of the mighty. All of a sudden, we see enmity growing among the rich and powerful against the oppressed and weak. It is a faked animosity which partly grows out of the oppressor's bad conscience which he projects over and materializes in the exploited.

There is no doubt that our coronation-psalms do participate in the ideology of power even if they should be post-monarchic compositions. In this case they represent a Jewish dream of superiority and dominion, and such a dream may flourish even in periods of depression and defeat.

7. Cf. Cardenal, *Psalms*.

A Christian evaluation of the two basic hostilities, that from below upwards and that from high above downwards, is now in order. In the first case, solidarity with the poor and powerless calls for resistance and militancy, if not out-right rebellion against existing power-structures. The enemies are the mighty, the exploiters and oppressors, dictators and cynics, patriarchs and technocrats. Christians have to rally with the oppressed, identify the enemy above, call him by his real names, pray to God to bring him down, organize resistance, conscientize the exploited.[8] It would be unchristian to cover up brutal domination with abstract ideas of love and brotherhood. Millions of people all over the world are in this position of utter deprivation. Ethnic minorities, women, children, deficient or "abnormal" people, and the masses of Third- or Fourth-World inhabitants belong to this category. Their militancy against oppressors and exploiters is justified.

The other situation is to create enemies by way of oppression and exploitation. Here things become very difficult, because traditional Christian preaching glorifies "power given from God," not admitting its dehumanizing effect. Many texts of the OT, however, are highly critical of arrogant power (cf. 1 Sam 2:1–10; Ps 110). Are we right, then, to classify the royal aspirations of Pss 2 and 110 as arrogant? Or is the authority of the Davidic king sanctified by his being a representative of Yahweh himself? Who could be the bearer of a similar mandate in our own days? In my opinion, we can no longer advocate the exercise of "just" and "absolute" power by any human dignitary. Power is an attribute of God alone. Nobody may usurp divine prerogatives (cf. Gen 3; 11:1–9). Also, our democratic ideals forbid power-concentration with individuals or groups. We must, therefore, decide against the possibility to create enemies from above downwards. These enemies always have legitimating purposes; they serve to enhance one's own power-position. Another question is the role and defense of human government which does not pretend to be omnipotent. Here we have to be careful to protect whatever promotes life and dignity, and to combat all those seductions to exceed constitutionally fixed limits of authority.

The Corporate Dimension

There is another point in this very complex picture of friend-foe relations which deserves closer attention. Looking at it we will discover certain structural analogies between the Old Testament texts and our own situation. Ancient man experienced and visualized society as consisting of corporate entities, and more likely than not, ethical thinking started from these entities

---

8. Cf. Freire, *Pedagogy of the Oppressed*.

instead of from isolated individuals. Families, clans, cities, nations, tribes, villages, neighborhoods could be considered expanded persons, corporate personalities, which had an existence of their own and created their peculiar spheres of life and destiny. Individuals took part in this greater entity without being able, with the possible exception of the king or titular head of the community, to direct its course.[9] Enmity, consequently, in virtually all cases is a social phenomenon, even if it afflicts individuals or starts from them. Blood-revenge is a family or clan affair (cf. 2 Sam 21:1-9), and personal insult can signify national disgrace (cf. 2 Sam 10:1ff). Small wonder, then, that in the Old Testament most hostilities have the appearance of group-conflicts. In other words: The enemy-problem at all times is very much tied up with structural antagonisms. But how can we cope with these collective aspects of enmity and wrongdoing?

It should be clear that merely individual ethics by no means are sufficient to deal with the aspirations and anxieties of corporate bodies.[10] The precepts "Love your neighbor" or "Do not resist evil" are counsels directed exclusively to persons with heart and soul. They may realize them within the familiar context of person-to-person contacts. Corporations do not function that way. They are anonymous and obey their own technocratic rules of competition, profit, and dominance. Managements of big companies, political leaderships especially of the industrialized nations, military headquarters, the "market of consumption and production," and many similar organisms do play the game of naked or camouflaged power. They corporately feel engaged in a life-and-death struggle for the survival of the fittest according to the laws which we summarize under the title Social Darwinism. Hostility seems to be a built-in principle of our Western group-relations. The enemy-problem, therefore, is not just a question of outward-directed group relations, but at the same time a structural enigma of our own society. And: Enemies in fact always had super-individual traits and methods.

Old Testament authors, particularly the psalmists, were well aware of the corporate structure of society and the conflicts that arise from it. Naturally, they could not know how serious is our present-day situation. The structural antagonisms of our day are likely to result in a cataclysm that may wipe out human civilization at any moment. That means to say: Group and national enmities can no longer play a regulative role; they no longer have any positive function. The psalmists certainly did not know our situation (only apocalyptic theologians of old in a way anticipated the agonies of our world, cf. Dan 7; Mark 13; the book of Revelation). Yet they somehow were

---

9. Cf. Robinson, "The Hebrew Concept of Corporate Personality," 49ff.
10. Cf. Niebuhr, *Moral Man and Immoral Society*.

looking for a solution to humanity's age-old torments. The answer is a vision of peace which comes out especially in the Zion-hymns. They were sung at some annual festival in Jerusalem. Their message is: Weapons are scrapped, and God will take over government on earth.

> Come, behold the works of Yahweh,
> > how he has wrought desolations in the earth.
> He makes wars cease to the end of the earth;
> > he breaks the bow, and shatters the spear,
> > he burns the chariots with fire!
> "Be still, and know that I am God.
> > I am exalted among the nations, exalted on the earth!"
> Yahweh of hosts is with us;
> > the God of Jacob is our refuge. (Ps 46:8–11)

Unfortunately, but understandably so, this beautiful picture of final and eternal peace is still tinted a little bit by Jerusalemite, Judaean, and Jewish particularism that expects the submission of the enemies and the hegemony of their own group as preconditions of ultimate bliss.[11]

How to Approach Our Own Conflicts

We have to summarize and meditate once more on what we found out about enmity and evil in the psalms. We want to do it while focusing our attention on our own situation. Scientific thinking, automated industrial production, refined medical techniques, vast increase in world population, near exhaustion of vital resources, development of world-wide economic and political systems, ideological faith in democratic, socialist, Christian, Muslim ideals—these and other factors mark our world today and make it different from Old Testament and Ancient Near Eastern worlds. However, there remain enough human and social analogies to warrant the possibility of comparative studies. Certainly, we cannot simply transfer experiences of Old Testament times into our own environment, to be repeated right here. But the faith of our spiritual precursors in one solitary God may be tested in our own dangerous presence. This can be done only in closest possible contact with reality.

---

11. Cf. Mowinckel, *He That Cometh*; Stolz, *Strukturen und Figuren im Kult von Jerusalem*; Steck, *Friedensvorstellungen im Alten Jerusalem*.

The Identification of Enemies

The identification of enemies, that is, of causes and causers of evil, may be easier and more difficult today than in antiquity, easier, because scientific methods permit fixation of many objective factors which give origin to misery. And these items can be manipulated to the relief of the afflicted. It may prove more difficult to describe with precision the personal or collective ingredients in the evils of our times. And more intricate still: According to modern insights the borderline between good and evil runs pretty much across all human beings and all known social systems. In its essence, this view of evil as being part and parcel of existence (be it in form of deficiencies or of bad qualities) is quite biblical. But it has been replaced, in much of Christian ethical thinking, by fallacious, dualistic ideas, as if good and evil could be separated neatly into two parties, that of the saved ones and that of the condemned. We have to wind back the biblical perspective of one world which at best awaits its future division and purification (cf. Matt 13:24–30; 25:31–46). While this human history is still in operation, there simply is no way of singling out cleanly and definitely the guilty ones. The shocking consequence of this statement is this: I/we do participate in all and every kind of wrong which may exist on this globe. In one or the other instance all of us are oppressors, liars, murderers, adulterers. This is what Jesus wanted to communicate to the scribes when he pointed at the accused woman: "Let him who is without sin among you be the first to throw a stone at her" (John 8:7). In the same vein, some journalists wrote at the occasion of the sentence against Adolf Eichmann, the technocratic, meticulous mass-murderer of Jews: "Eichmann is not only a determined person; he also is a little bit within ourselves."[12] In dealing with the enemy-problem we have to expect, therefore, one or the other accusation against our own persons. This inversion of roles—we cannot possibly stay only in the accuser's bench—is a sobering experience, but a necessary one if we want to do justice to biblical faith in our time.

Human Justice

The facts just described do not impede, by any means, legal denunciation and persecution of enemies and evil-doers. There is hardly any misery on this earth that would not be caused also by human agents. Except for some earthquakes and hurricanes, virtually all catastrophes are man-made. Identification of those who are more responsible for this or that misery or

---

12. See, e.g., Arendt, *Eichmann in Jerusalem*.

catastrophe than others is a necessity of human justice. But evidently, this justice has to be administered with due caution and humility. Haughty condemnation of any criminal or enemy-group is not at all justified. It would not take into account the existing guilt of those who judge and condemn. Death-penalty, being an absolute, irrevocable punishment, should be excluded from possible reactions to evil. Christians should support all modern tendencies to administer justice with the ultimate intention to rehabilitate the culprit and re-establish friendly relations to former enemy-groups. This very goal is not at all unknown to biblical psalmists, as Pss 51 and 46 may demonstrate. Utter destruction of the enemies—as, for example, in Ps 109—probably was understood as an emergency-measure aiming at eradication of the causes of suffering. If we today are well enough informed about the material, neutral causes of misery and injustice, why not direct all our zeal to exterminating such causes and recuperate human beings entangled with the evil? Such endeavor indeed would coincide with Christ's commandment to love even the enemy (Matt 5:43–48).

The Brazilian pedagogue and theologian Paulo Freire under these auspices has even developed a Christian concept of present-day class-struggle.[13] Other revolutionary thinkers have joined him in his effort to define militancy against world-wide oppression within the limits of Christ's love for all men. The undeniable fact to start from is this: Century-old, brutal exploitation of hundreds of millions of human beings can no longer be tolerated. God himself does not tolerate this kind of oppression (cf. Ps 12:5). It is, in ultimate analysis, suicidal for mankind. Economic and political deprivation of the greater part of the world population means not only dehumanization of the oppressed but also total distortion of the oppressor's humanity. Whoever lives on the subsistence of others loses his own humanity, the essence of which is solidarity with fellow men. The oppressor, then, has to be considered a bloodsucker or dehumanized man (cf. Ps 10). Class-struggle, according to Freire, has to begin with the conscientization of the disprivileged masses. They are crippled human beings, it is true, who suffered tragic losses of human opportunities. But they have kept a more intense feeling for human dignity than the rich oppressors who are being suffocated by their robbed wealth (cf. Matt 19:24). Consequently, the poor have to fight for their own liberation, and for the liberation of the rich as well, because the oppressors cling desperately to their wealth and privileges, not admitting that they are under their dehumanizing influence. Thus, the world-wide enemy are the privileged classes and nations; they have to be brought down to a human level of existence, and the starving and tortured

---

13. Cf. Freire, *Pedagogy of the Oppressed*.

masses have to be elevated to that same level. Such conceptualization of the enemy-problem is behind all the liberation theology of Latin America and other oppressed countries.

The Overthrow of Evil

Comparing, finally, the effectuation of enemy-submission and overthrow of evil in antiquity and today, we have to confess that we are lacking by and large the adequate cultic rituals employed so widely in the Ancient Near East. We are administering, as it were, a whole lot of therapies, mainly on the personal and small-group level. Such therapies include all medical and juridical consultations, all psychoanalyses, psycho-therapeutic efforts, and all methods of group-dynamics and meditation, and every one of them has its own ritual. In a way, those modern therapies are comparable with what we find in individual complaint psalms. But they are, for the most part, very individualistic in their essence, and they practically all occur outside the Christian community. In fact, Christian churches have kept astonishingly few services and offices destined to help the individual and his group in times of distress. Roman Catholic confession is such a remnant, just like Protestant "cure of soul" in confessional conversation. But where are the prayer-services for the divorced and lonely, for persecuted minorities, exploited workers, alcoholics, dope-addicts, jobless, poor, women, the aged? Thinking along the same line, Christian churches possess even less ceremonials to treat conflicts with those outside one's own group. Sure enough, there are worship services being held in times of emergency, like the Cuban Missile Crisis of 1962. But such occasions are rare; special worship services on their account are even rarer. This fact in itself proves the nonexistence of liturgical implements to cope with outward enemies. The same is true for the century-old North–South conflict of industrialized and colonized countries.[14] This topic enters into our sermons and services mostly with the rich man's charitable and humanitarian ring: Let's give a nice offering for those poor guys down in the other world. That our wealth produces the poverty in the Third World, and that charity is not the right response to the misery there are bypassed. Our services normally do not try to identify the oppressor, that is us ourselves, as do the psalms. We do not preach the solidarity with the exploited masses, as Jesus certainly would have done. Our communities did not wake up yet to combat the very structures of exploitation and worldwide injustice.

---

14. Cf. the presidential report: Barney, ed., *Global 2000*.

We do claim without hesitation, that our Sunday services represent the heart of a Christian congregation. This can be true only to the extent in which worship includes or embraces present-day reality. If the enemy-problem is missing in our services, because of some Christian bashfulness, an important part of reality is missing. We are living, after all, in a world filled with hostilities of all kinds and all social levels. Inclusion of the enemy-problem, on the other hand, is very meaningful for congregation and worship. And I mean it as a theological statement. By ritualization, we could say, a problem is torn out of its individualistic context and put into the realm of community, otherwise uncontrollable emotions are now being controlled. Ritualizing a problem within a worship service, furthermore, provides the opportunity to experience and enact all its implications before God. That means in our case: Enemies are now being treated not simply eye to eye in a deadly group-conflict, but in the presence of a supreme judge. This judge being for us the universal Lord, the Father of all mankind, the God of Jesus Christ, there is at least a chance for our treating ourselves and of outward enemies in a fair and loving way.

9

Delight in the Torah

The Book of Psalms

Śimḥat Torah: From Festive Joy to Adoration of Torah

THEOLOGICAL CONCEPTS AND RITUALS take their time to develop. And they never stop to grow and change their appearance. Thus the precise term *śimḥat torah* ("joy in/of Torah") comes up in Jewish tradition only after the Talmudic age (second to sixth centuries CE). The Old Testament Psalter does mention *śimḥah* as festive excitement quite frequently, thirteen times altogether.[1] But the technical term *śimḥat torah* is not yet present. It does occur in Jewish writings only more than half a millennium after the Psalter had been put together.

From that late time onward until today the Jewish festive calendar[2] carries one special day or event designated as "joy of/in/over Torah." This day of programed, exuberant joy about the most precious gift of God to his people may be considered an outgrowth of the ancient autumn festival, the development of which we may observe in the ancient texts. Exodus 23:17 does mention it as the last of three annual agricultural feasts: "You shall observe the festival of in-gathering at the end of the year" (Exod 23:16b NRSV). The younger priestly documents of Lev 23 rename the event into "feast of booths" (*ḥag hassukkoth*, Lev 23:34):

---

1. Cf. also synonyms like *gil* ("rejoice," 14 times in the Psalter), *rnn* ("make cheerful noise," 12 times), *'lz* and *'lṣ* ("jubilate," 10 times), *śuś* or *śiś* ("enjoy," 8 times); Wagner, *Emotionen*; Staubli and Schroer, *Menschenbilder*; Zernecke, "Freude."

2. Cf. Exod 23; 34; Deut 16; Lev 23, in that order; cf. Otto and Schramm, *Fest und Freude*; Fohrer, *Glaube und Leben im Judentum*; Vorpahl, "Sukkot."

You shall live in booths for seven days; all that are citizens in Israel shall live in booths for seven days; so that your generations may know that I made the people of Israel live in booths when I brought them out of the land of Egypt. I am Yahweh, your God. (Lev 23:42–43)

Just as the very old, probably pre-Israelite festival of *maṣṣot* ("unleavened bread"; cf. Exod 23:15; Lev 23:5–6) was superseded by memories of Israel's exodus from Egypt, the agrarian autumn festival receives new contents in its references to salvation and provision by God during the wilderness wanderings. We may call this a "historization" of formerly timeless seasonal visions of a peasant population. Growth and changes of festive emotions are obvious. Interestingly, prescriptions of the feast of booths in Lev 23:33–43 already include a special reference to "rejoicing (*śmḥ*) before Yahweh" (v. 40) so we may well assume: The autumn festivities in Ancient Israel were marked by special notions and performances of joy and gratitude for the natural and historic gifts of God to the people. The list of daily offerings during the festival of booths in Num 29:12–39, because of quantity and quality of sacrificed animals, underlines the particular importance of this celebration.

A particular day eulogizing the Torah as the object or reason of communal jubilation was appended to the feast of booths only near the sixth century CE. We do not know where it happened first, but the custom spread through Jewish communities worldwide. After the booths have been removed and people have gone back to live in their homes they come together in the synagogues for singing, dancing, reading of Torah's first and last chapters, done by especially appointed members of the congregation, so-called "bridegrooms of Torah."[3] Torah-scrolls take the center of the stage. The words of God through Moses spark ecstatic joy which is also transformed into charitable and encouraging gifts to nearby persons. Why this separate emphasis on Torah as the ultimate source of delight, if already the feast of *Sukkoth* breathes grateful excitement about Torah-reading? How can a written document of old assume the symbolic value of the presence of the living God? Obviously, Torah had become, over centuries of spiritual musings and insights, documented in Mishnah, Talmud, and countless corollary Jewish writings, the embodiment of divine benevolence.[4] This supreme symbol of faith needed an extraordinary, unique celebration of its own, named *Śimḥat Torah*, "delight of/in/over Torah." Late references to this festive occasion do not explain its theological and emotional dimensions taking them for

---

3. Cf. de Vries, *Jüdische Riten und Symbole*, 97–100.
4. Cf. Fohrer, *Glaube und Leben im Judentum*, 42–48.

granted. If we want to fathom that distinct, supreme joy we well may turn to its roots in the Old Testament. Such a procedure is like investigating the seed and roots of a beautiful blossom in order to determine its qualities. The Psalter, and some other texts, to be sure, do offer a full share of theological information in this regard. But before we take on the inquiry we have to touch another preliminary topic.

The Ambivalence of Torah

Are there any beings, is there anything in this world totally, unequivocally good and pure? Everything does have its pros and cons. Every coin, so a proverbial saying, presents two sides. Nothing in our lives, not even the most beautiful moments, are perfect bliss. The book of Ecclesiastes is full of precautions against any unilateralism of joy and happiness. The Old Testament as a whole presents here and there the threatening side of Torah, cf. e.g., 2 Kgs 22:8–20; Lev 26:14–33; Deut 27:14–26; 28:15–68. If Israel does not obey the rules of Torah, God will punish his people in the most cruel fashion, by lack of rain and vegetation, defeat in battles from their enemies, hunger and thirst, epidemics, revolts, violence of all kinds, to the most extreme consequences imaginable: cannibalism within starving families (Deut 28:54–57).

How does this horrifying aspect of Torah come about? It has spread through much of the "historical" books of the Old Testament, the Prophets and parts of the Writings. Thus the so-called "Deuteronomistic Historian" who reworked Joshua through 2 Kings built on the theory that Israel and its kings had been trespassing the prescriptions of Torah all along, accumulating guilt after guilt during the reigns of Saul, David, and Salomo, as well as their successors, until God himself could no longer dissolve their ugly load of apostasy. In spite of Josiah's serious efforts to renew the covenant and undo all the foreign cults (2 Kgs 23:1–20):

> Yahweh did not turn from the fierceness of his great wrath, by which his anger was kindled against Judah, because of all the provocations with which Manasseh had provoked him. Yahweh said: "I will remove Judah also out of my sight, as I have removed Israel, and I will reject this city that I have chosen, Jerusalem, and the house of which I said, My name shall be there." (2 Kgs 23:26–27)

There is at least one important passage in the historical books of the OT which contradicts the doctrine of a double-pronged Torah being a terrible threat to the transgressor and a blessing only to the faithful: Neh 8, the narration of the first reading of Torah at the occasion of the autumn festival. Ezra, the priest and "scribe skilled in the law (*torah*) of Moses" (Ezra 7:6)[5] reads from the "Book of the Torah of Moses" (*seper hattorah mošeh*) for six hours (Neh 8:2) with Levites translating the scholarly Hebrew into daily Aramaic and all Israelites, young and old, women and men, participating in the reunion. The reaction of the audience is sheer panic. Therefore

> Nehemiah, who was the governor, and Ezra the priest and scribe, and the Levites who taught the people said to all the people, "This day is holy to Yahweh, your God, do not mourn nor weep." For all the people wept when they heard the words of the law (*torah*). Then he said to them: "Go your way, eat the fat and drink sweet wine and send portions of them to those for whom nothing is prepared, for this day is holy to our Yahweh; and do not be grieved, for the joy of Yahweh (*ḥedwat yhwh*; *ḥedwah* only 1 Chr 16:27 and Neh 8:10; the word is close to Aramaic *ḥdʾ*) is your strength." So the Levites stilled all the people, saying: "Be quiet, for this day is holy; do not be grieved." And all the people went their way to eat and drink and to send portions and to make great rejoicing, because they had understood the words that were declared to them. (Neh 8:9–12)

What a different understanding of Torah! There is no separation of sinners and fulfillers of Torah. All are invited to receive the gracious gift of God regardless of their spiritual status. *Ḥedwat yhwh*, a synonym of *śimḥat yhwh*, refers to God's own pleasure in bequeathing a joyful day to his people, without any restrictions. Possibly, the expression even hints at the Torah-scroll which was so important in the autumn festivities. In any case, Torah, in this passage, does not cause fears but pure joy. How is such a dichotomy in interpretation possible? The fearsome Torah seems to be intimately connected with the notion of "covenant, treaty" (*berit*), which needs to be kept and guarded in order to effectively provide good relations between treaty partners although *berit* is not mentioned here. The relationship of Israel to Yahweh in this pattern of thinking often has been compared with political accords of Near Eastern political powers. In Neh 8 there is no reference to "covenant"! Theologically speaking, covenant in the OT may have these stern connotations, although there are other variant models of thinking assuming more gracious, onesided relationships with the God of Israel.

Anyway, we learn that there have been, over time and through different segments of Jewish congregational life, different notions, experiences,

---

5. Cf. Hieke, "Esra."

insights with the contents of communal festivals, the interpretation of key concepts, and God's graceful dealing with His followers. Nehemiah 8, that much is certain, has a special vision of unlimited access to the God who loves all his people thus causing exuberant joy which leads to very human and worldly eating, drinking, dancing and transpires into the general society. The needy and forlorn are to be provided with goods so that they feel included into the feasting congregation. What a wonderful sense of brother- and sisterhood among celebrating people under the auspices of the One God of all humankind and creation![6] Other difficulties with the conception and role of Torah in the Jewish community will come up later.

The Psalter: Fountainhead of Existential Joy of/in/over God

Sure, the OT Psalms do comprise very different genres of prayers and songs, meditations and other sacred poetry.[7] But there is a strong hymnic strand in the Psalter which motivated the Hebrew name *tehillim*, "praise songs," for the whole collection in Jewish tradition. Praise in most cases is connected to deeply felt joy, not with sadness and depression, the dark sides of life, although there are significant examples to the contrary. Hymns, in the ancient Near Eastern perspective, may turn the tide of suffering, alleviate distress[8] and are the proper present to a helpful, saving God. Most impressive examples are the Prayer of Azariah and the Song of the Three Men inside the burning furnace.[9] The Psalter gives witness to manifold situations in which praises to God are spontaneous or ritualized responses to various experiences of divine benevolence. Such experiences all in all provoke differently shaded excitement, eruptive joy, sometimes ecstatic motion. Varicoloured blissful emotions also seem to flow together in the longest Psalm (Ps 119) preserved in the OT. Martin Luther called it the "Golden ABC." We first look for concepts of delight/joy in some other psalm-genres.

---

6. Cf. Pope Francis' Encyclical *"Fratelli tutti"* (2020).

7. Cf. Gerstenberger, *Psalms, Part 1*; Gerstenberger, *Psalms, Part 2*; Miller, *They Cried unto the Lord*.

8. Cf. Gerstenberger, "Praise in the Realm of Death"; Gerstenberger, "The Power of Praise in the Psalter."

9. Additions to Daniel, cf. *HarperCollins Study Bible*, 1633–36. Very awful analogies, especially for a German reader, are the singing Jews walking into the crematories, cf. "Music of the Holocaust" in "United States Holocaust Memorial Museum" (internet).

Gratitude of Those Saved from Death

Many Psalms, about forty of them, originally had served as patient's prayers in casual ceremonies of healing, cleansing of false indictments, warding off evil spirits etc. They are called "Complaints (or: Laments) of the Individual."[10] Their "settings in life" originally were rituals administered by healers, conjurers, Levites or singers who had their patients recite those powerful implorations to the deities, as may be gleaned also from Babylonian and other related sacred poetry.[11] Psalms preserved in the OT Psalter were slightly worked over for use in synagogal offices retaining much of their older substance, cf. the archaic Pss 57; 59; 91, etc. with their demonic foes.

These supplications of individual persons suffering from imminent perils of death quite often end in a promise to God, to bring thankofferings and praise songs to the deity in case the patient would be cured, protected or saved. Sometimes such pledges seem to have been executed already before a salvation had taken place, cf. the anticipated thanksgiving of Hezekiah in Isa 38:10–20 ending in: "Yahweh has saved me and we will sing to stringed instruments all the days of our lives at the house of Yahweh" (v. 20; cf. Pss 31:20–25; 69:31–37). A vow to hail Yahweh's decisive help is included at the end of most individual complaints (cf. Pss 7:18; 42:6, 12; 43:5; 56:13–14; 57:6, 8–12; 59:17–18; 109:30 etc.). The expressions used, mostly on the basis of *ydh*, "offer thanks," do point to a "thanksgiving sacrifice" or a "thanksgiving song" or to both actions. The ensuing feast for a supplicant who was given a new chance to live brought forth a distinct genre of thanksgiving songs.[12] They tell us, that guests of the party indulged in adoration of Yahweh, the savior from dire needs, as well as in loud and opulent merrymaking:

> Sing praises to Yahweh, O God of the faithful ones
>> and give thanks to his holy name.
>
> For his anger is but for a moment;
>> his favor is for a lifetime.
>
> Weeping may linger for a night
>> but joy (*rinnah*) comes with the morning.
>
> (Ps 30:5–6 [ET 4–5])

---

10. Cf. Gerstenberger, *Psalms, Part 1*, 11–14.

11. Cf. Gerstenberger, "Navajo Chants, Babylonian Incantations, Old Testament Psalms" (Chap. 6 above).

12. Cf. Gerstenberger, *Psalms, Part I*, 14–16.

You have turned my mourning into dancing;
> you have taken off my sackcloth
> and clothed me with joy (śimḥah),
so that my soul may praise you and not be silent.
> O Yahweh, my God, I will give thanks to you forever.
> (Ps 30:12–13 [11–12])

From you comes my praise in the great congregation;
> my vows I will pay before those who fear him.
The poor shall eat and be satisfied,
> those who seek him shall praise Yahweh.
> May your hearts live forever! (Ps 22:26–27)

The contrast between life close to death, even engulfed by death and underworld (cf. Pss 69:2–3; 88:5–7; 130:1), and life in security makes all the difference. Supplicants who recited their cruel fate find themselves drawn out of hell (še'ol, "netherworld") and placed into the land of the living again.[13] What a profound change of destiny. There is a deep emotional rupture, the experience of darkness and forlorness with concomitant grief and mourning (to the point of wearing the funeral sackcloth!) abruptly changes into the opposite, immense joy and festive dancing, eating, drinking, shouting, laughing. Bleak suffering had touched upon the empathy of a few in the sufferer's environment, joy of life given back to the moribund involves a larger group. Joy inspires crowds and gives them new strength. Joy of life is a supreme divine gift keeping up the doings and happenings of our planet.

And yet there is a blemish in the "joy of life" just mentioned. It has been accomplished in a fierce struggle against opposing forces, often called the "enemies."[14] They loudly proclaim their delight in sufferings and death of the petitioner for God's help (cf. Pss 25:2; 35:15–16; 41:12, etc.). Distress which had befallen the supplicant at least partially had been their work. The consequence drawn in the Psalms seems to be: Since the adversaries are so adamant in their destructive actions and their hatred against the sufferer they must be fought off by all means, especially by God who "hates iniquity" (cf. Ps 5:5–7). They are, in consequence, condemned and cursed in individual complaints, the apex of such dubious behavior being Ps 109.

---

13. Cf. Barth, *Die Errettung vom Tode*.

14. Hebrew *'oyeb*, occuring 74 times in the Psalter, and there are numerous synonyms too in this book, cf. Keel, *Feinde und Gottesleugner*; Zenger, *Ein Gott der Rache?*

Their elimination is part of the prayer-ceremony and belongs to the cure or rehabilitation of the supplicant. But are we not back to the strange ambivalence of the delight in God if we accept the revenge-potential in supplication for divine help?

Joy over Jerusalem

The Psalter contains a special collection of pilgrim-songs (Pss 120–134) marked in the superscriptions by šir hamma'alot, "song of ascents," to be intoned on the way up to Jerusalem. After the exile David's city had assumed a central role in constituting the religious community of widely dispersed Judahites; three seasonal festivals gave opportunities to reunite there, offer sacrifices to Yahweh (Deut 12) and perform festive rites. The poems of "going up" are of very different origin; we cannot recognize a special genre of pilgrim-songs. But just as it does happen in our days: Popular songs used in religious congregations are, apparently at random, taken into the pilgrims' treasure to be used along the journey and for local ceremonies. A certain adaptation of texts and melodies is natural. Other psalms, outside the collection of Pss 120–134, may belong into the same or a related category of songs: Ps 84 is craving for the temple, considered the real dwelling of God. Verse 3b says: "my heart and my flesh sing for joy (*rnn*) to the living God" [ET 2b]; v. 5: "Happy are those who live in your house, ever singing your praise (*hll*)" [ET 4]. Furthermore, other Zion-hymns (Pss 46; 48; 76; 87; 132; 137) are closely related to the pilgrim songs whether or not they were used on the way up to Jerusalem. But they are abounding with expressions of beauty and joy: Ps 46:5: "There is a river whose streams make glad (*śmḥ*) the city of God, the holy habitation of the Most High" [ET 4]. Ps 48:2b–3: "His holy mountain, beautiful (*yepeh*) in elevation / is the joy (*meśoś* from *śuś*) of all the earth" [ET 1b–2]. Ps 48:12: "Let Mount Zion be glad (*śmḥ*) / let the towns of Judah rejoice because of your judgments" [ET 11]. Ps 87:3: "Glorious things (*nikbadot*, from *kbd*) are spoken of you, O city of God." Ps 87:7: "Singers and dancers all say: 'All my springs are in you.'" This means: Great public ceremonial performers communicate marvelous accomplishments, attributing them to the divine waters of God's abode. Ps 137:6: "Let my tongue cling to the roof of my mouth, / if I do not remember you, / if I do not set Jerusalem / above my highest joy (*r'oš śimḥati*)." The pilgrims songs referred to above, are permeated with fervent expectations to reach the Holy City; the pilgrimage itself is an escape from sorrows and distress, giving new hope for life's stress situations: Ps 121:1: "I lift up my eyes to the hills—/ from where will my help come?"—note the following personal blessings, vv. 3–8. Ps 122:1: "I was glad (*śmḥ*) when they said to me: / Let us go to the house of Yahweh." The most important cause for joy in this poem is peace for and in Jerusalem (vv. 6–9). The most outspoken song of joy is Ps 126:1–6:

> When Yahweh restored the fortunes of Zion
> > we were like those who dream.
> Then our mouth was filled with laughter,
> > and our tongue with shouts of joy (*rinnah*);
> Then it was said among the nations,
> > "Yahweh has done great things (*gdl* hiph.) for them."
> Yahweh has done great things (*gdl* hiph.) for us,
> > and we rejoiced (*śmḥ*).
> Restore our fortunes, O Yahweh,
> > like the watercourses in the Negeb.
> May those who sow in tears
> > reap with shouts of joy (*rinnah*).
> Those who go out weeping,
> > bearing the seed for sowing,
> shall come home with shouts of joy (*rinnah*),
> > carrying their sheaves.

Transformation of sorrow into explosive joy we already met in some complaint and thanksgiving songs. Here the memory of and liberation from captivity is part of Zion festivities; but also, perhaps in a more ancient layer, harvest celebration shines through. Important is the focus on Jerusalem. The singers of this hymn indulge in their fervor for the holy city and implicitly for the presence of Yahweh (cf. Ps 84). Ps 132 reflects the historical transfer of the ark, antique symbol of Yahweh's accompaniment of the tribes, to Jerusalem by David (cf. 2 Sam 6). Verses 9 and 16 give righteousness and salvation to the priests, and have the "faithful" (*ḥasidim*) be filled with joy, jubilating loudly (*rnn*). Thus the exuberant notion of happy excitement is not only tied to the festivities, especially the autumn celebration of Old Israel, but in a particular way also with that ominous physical presence of Yahweh in his holy temple and city (which is hard to stomach—especially for Protestants!).

What kind of joy is envisioned in those testimonies around Jerusalem, temple, and abode of Yahweh? Is it the pure, metaphysical, lofty spiritual feeling of the divine? We are certainly astonished to find substantial aggressiveness also in the Zion-related hymns. To give but a few examples: Ps 46 tells us that the enchantment of God's own city can be maintained only against cosmic and political powers by God's intervention (cf. vv. 2–7). Ps 48 refers to a war of unnamed kings against Jerusalem (vv. 5–7) to be frustrated by Yahweh. Ps 76 shows how terribly (vv. 8–9, 12–13) God acts to defend his abode on Mount Zion. Ps 74 and 79 lament conquest and desecration of the Jerusalem temple by "enemies." Ps 122 mentions the (final?) judgment over mankind (v. 5), Ps 124 the perils Israel has gone through, Ps 137 condemns Edom and Babylonia for their cruelties during the lost war (vv. 7–9; note the horrible visions of revenge in v. 9). Really, is joy and peace in God only attainable through violence, retaliation, and power?

Another deeply theological question arises when we consider the Psalmist's notion about the presence of God in his sanctuary.[15] There seems to be a trustful longing to get as close to Him as possible without any idea of how dangerous close distance to the divine being may be. Priestly accounts as well as narrators do warn everybody to draw too near to God. The Holy of Holies according to Lev 16 is accessible only to one person, the high priest, and only once a year under strong precautions. Moses, according to tradition, was the only human being admitted to see Yahweh and talk to Him face to face (Exod 33:11), or, according to a more cautious tradition, from behind (Exod 33:18–23). Also, the elders of Israel may "see Yahweh" at a banquet on Mount Sinai (Exod 24:9–10) and Micha ben Imla ascends to the heavenly counsel in a vision (1 Kgs 22:19–22), Ezekiel and Amos experience similar events. We recognize that human ideas about the visibility and closeness of God are different, also in the OT. The Psalter, at least in its Zion related songs, is quite negligent about the dangers of attending the temple grounds. On the contrary: It expects, e.g., that the supplicant may see God's face (cf. Pss 11:7; 42:3) while typically the ark narrative relates a deadly accident, when someone unwillingly touches the holy ark (2 Sam 6:4–11). Best intentions and faithful attitudes do not protect Usa from immediate death caused by the sheer energy residing in God's presence. Psalm 132 for its part does not mention the adverse incident at all. The beautiful image of swallows living even inside the altar (Ps 84:4) suggests save and blissful life in the immediate neighborhood of Yahweh himself: "Happy are those who live in your house, / ever singing your praise" (Ps 132:5 [ET 4]). "For a day in your courts is better / than thousands elsewhere" (Ps 132:11 [ET 10]). In consequence, the utter delight in God's holy presence and invincible sanctuary is somewhat tinged by uncertainties.

---

15. Cf. Hartenstein, *Die Unzugänglichkeit Gottes im Heiligtum*.

Victory Songs, Guidance through History, Yahweh Kingship

Some categories of psalms preserved in the Psalter with less numerous specimens show similar characteristics as the former examples. Psalm 68 is the only victory song extant in the collection, with some others embedded in diverse contexts outside the Psalter (cf. Exod 15:1–21; Judg 5:2–31; Isa 51:9–11; 59:17–20; 63:1–6). Mythical motifs of warfare around the Mountain of God enter the picture together with the battle against unnamed kings (Ps 68:13–22), and the end will be deep enchantment and jubilance of the faithful (Ps 68:4–5 [ET 3–4]): "Let the righteous be joyful (śmḥ), let them exult ('lṣ) before God, / let them be jubilant with joy (śiś beśimḥah). / Sing to God, sing praises to his name; / lift up a song to him who rides upon the clouds—/ his name is Yahweh—be exultant ('lṣ) before him." A very compact description of the state of mind in the festive congregation.—Historical psalms[16] we call a group of poems relating segments of Israel's past experiences with God (cf. Pss 78; 105; 114; 118; 135–136 on the positive side; Pss 44; 89; 106 on the negative). Ps 78:5–8 puts the giving of Torah as the decisive foundation of God's history with Israel. The people, however, disdained God's leniency and his chastisements (cf. Ps 78:32–39, esp. v. 38). Therefore he finally transferred his grace to the tribe of Judah, Mount Zion and David's dynasty (Ps 78:67–68). Ps 105 gives an account of ancient events from the Joseph story to the exodus, emphasizing the liberating joy ("So he brought his people out with joy [śaśon], / his chosen ones with singing [rinnah]." Ps 105:43; cf. vv. 2–3: "Sing to him ..., let the hearts of those who seek Yahweh rejoice [śmḥ]). Formally, in Ps 118, a thanksgiving of an individual, language and imagery used conjure up communal traits like battling multitudes (cf. vv. 10–11), feasting in a crowd (cf. v. 27). Two lines accentuate aspects of celebrating the defeat of dangerous foes: "There are glad songs of victory (rinnah wišuah) / in the tents of the righteous," v. 15), and: "This is the day that Yahweh has made; / let us rejoice and be glad (gil; śmḥ) in it" (v. 24). Powerful joy is the warrant of renewed life. Yahweh-kingship hymns (Pss 47; 93; 95; 96; 97; 98; 99), finally, for their part probably have come out of an annual festival celebrating the ascension of the supreme God to the throne, enacted by the human king. We do not find direct evidence for this event in the OT, but Babylonian sources testify to a similar ceremonial at New Year's day (akitu festival).[17] A festival of such dimensions and impact on yearly routines certainly offers ample opportunities for rejoicing: Ps 47:2 [ET 1]: "Clap your hands, all you peoples; / shout to God with loud songs of joy (ri' beqol rinnah). Ps 95:1–2: "O come let us

---

16. Cf. Gärtner, *Die Geschichtspsalmen*.
17. Cf. Pongratz-Leisten, "Akitu"; Sommer, "The Babylonian Akitu-Festival."

sing (*rnn*) to Yahweh; / let us make a joyful noise (*riʿ*) to the rock of our salvation! /Let us come into his presence with thanksgiving; / let us make a joyful noise (*riʿ*) to him with songs of praise!" The whole world is included into that surge of excitement: Ps 96:11–12: "Let the heavens be glad (*śmḥ*) and let the earth rejoice (*gil*), / let the sea roar, and all that fills it; / let the field exult (*ʿlṣ*), and everything in it. / Then shall the trees of the forest sing with joy (*rnn*)." Ps 97:1: "Yahweh is king! Let the earth rejoice (*gil*); let the many coastlands be glad!" (*śmḥ*). Ps 98:4: "Make a joyful noise (*riʿ*) to Yahweh, all the earth, / break forth into joyous song (*rnn*) and sing praises." Ps 98:8: "Let the floods clap their hands; let the hills sing together with joy (*rnn*)." Naturally, the people concerned and their habitat join in with the clamor of nature (cf. Ps 97:8, 11–12). Thanks and praise of Ps 100, from the festive congregation, close the sequence of kingship hymns: Ps 100:1–2: "Make a joyful noise (*riʿ*) to Yahweh all the earth. / Worship Yahweh with gladness (*śimḥah*); come into his presence with singing" (*renanah*). There is hardly any cluster of Psalms so much saturated with jubilant, impulsive, also musical motion. The festive joy exposed in these psalm-variations is overboarding and deeply rooted in their particular ceremonial contexts. Various destructive forces, however, do loom in the background of any of them.

Agricultural Blessings

We return for a moment to the more archaic, festive substructure of Israel's feasts. Since the Psalter was put together fairly late, presumably during the second and first centuries BCE, the old agrarian social structures were no longer so dominant. Israel's society by then had been reorganized more along urban patterns linked to synagogal routine. But we do notice still today basic structures of peasant life e.g., in the Passaḥ, Šabuoth, and Sukkoth festivals. Not many songs, however, are exclusively dedicated to agrarian lifestyle, rites and customs, cf. Pss 65:10–14; 104, and in later ritual contexts Lev 23:9–22, 40–43; Judg 21:19–21; 1 Sam 9:12. Psalm 65:10–14 is a peaceful portrait of a harvest thanksgiving in a village environment directed not to a God of storm and lightening, but a God of tender care:

> You visit the earth and water it,
> > you greatly enrich it,
> the river of God is full of water,
> > you provide the people with grain, for so you have prepared it.
> You water the furrows abundantly, settling its ridges,
> > softening it with showers, and blessing its growth.

> You crown the year with its bounty,
>> your wagon tracks overflow with richness.
> The pastures of the wilderness overflow,
>> the hills gird themselves with joy,
>
> The meadows clothe themselves with flocks,
>> the valleys deck themselves with grain,
>> they shout and sing together with joy.

The God of Creation provides fertility for soil and pastures (cf. Gen 1:11–13). Beautiful the picture of the countryside adorning itself with the products of a year's growth. Humans and other creatures are the beneficiaries and they respond to the bountiful gifts with jubilant songs. This is the way the ancients imagined a peaceful life "under one's own fig-tree" (cf. 1 Kgs 5:5; Mic 4:4), enjoying the fruits of rural abundance. A similar, but much larger picture is painted by Ps 104. Daily work certainly is necessary, yet the basis for all human effort are God's wise provisions of a natural habitat in the widest sense able to yield fruit (Ps 104:10–23). The Psalmist even includes creation of the cosmos among the preconditions of a well-provided, happy life (Ps 104:2–9). Everything has been put into being to make possible that bucolic life on the arable land. Even wild-life is included in the broad vision of abundance, happiness, gratitude (vv. 10–12, 16–18, 20–22). Verses 27–28 therefore state: "These all look to you, / to give them their food in due season; / when you open your hand, / they are filled with good things." And the proper response is the joy of God himself and in God (vv. 31: *jiśmaḥ yhwh*; v. 34: *'eśmaḥ beyhwh*). Is plain rural agitation at harvest festivals less dramatic than synagogal, urban emotion? We do not know. Evidence is too scarce to come to any conclusions. But we may imagine village communities which in peace-time were quite self-sufficient, even complacent in their seasonal ceremonies (cf. 1 Sam 9:12). Joy with all its cultic and frolic corollaries seems to have been very deep and peaceful, at times. It is consciousness of participation, thanks to the graciousness of God, in blissful life.

Thus the comprehensive notion of "joy in/of life" including spiritual and physical well-being, becomes a central concept of psalmic expression. Furthermore, it is very notable in e.g., Pss 26; 65; 126 that all explicit references to Torah or Covenant are missing. How is that possible? Confession to "Yahweh my Lord" (Ps 26:1) certainly implies the same theological and spiritual substance, we might say. But it may show a different mode of thinking. Is the direct affirmation of a personal belongingness an older way of discourse, and does "Torah" enter the scene because it reflects a later, more up-to-date vision of God's presence?

Meditations of/over Torah

Torah belongs into another conceptional category than delight, representing a stage or mode of divine-human communication.[18] When the total written "instruction (*torah*) of Yahweh"[19] in contrast to individual prescriptions (plural: *torot*) comes into focus we have to consider some basic questions. To highlight briefly the background of this discourse on "adhering to" and "enjoying in" torah viz. Yahweh himself: Old Israel in its spiritual history moved from early household and village cults to venerating the One and Universal God in the exilic and post-exilic periods, in constant implicit exchange with the political world-powers.[20] Affiliation to Yahweh implied a personal decision to enter into an exclusive relationship with God and the community which followed Him (cf. Josh 24:14–15; Jonah 1:9; much more evidence in the Psalms, see below). A prime example of this allegiance of individuals (plus their families) and their mode of communication with God is Ps 16:

> Protect me, O God,
>> for in you I take refuge,
>
> I say to Yahweh, "You are my Lord,
>> I have no good apart from you."
>
> As for the holy ones in the land,
>> they are the noble in whom is all my delight (*ḥepeṣ*).
>
> Those who choose another god multiply their sorrows,
>> their drink offerings of blood I will not pour out
>>
>> or take their names upon my lips. [footnote of NRSV: vv. 2–4 "very uncertain"]
>
> Yahweh is my chosen portion and my cup,
>> you hold my lot.

---

18. Cf. García López, "*torah*"; Oswald, "Tora"; Crouch, ed., *Mediation between Heaven and Earth*; Laato, ed., *The Challenge of the Mosaic Torah*.

19. Torah with reference to Yahweh's comprehensive will is frequent in Deuteronomy and Chronicles, late Old Testament writings, that is. For the psalms cf. Finsterbusch, *JHWH als Lehrer der Menschen*; Finsterbusch, "Yahweh's Torah."

20. Cf. Gerstenberger, *Theologies*; Gerstenberger, *Israel in the Persian Period*.

The boundary lines have fallen for me in pleasant places,
   I have a goodly heritage.
I bless Yahweh who gives me counsel,
   in the night also my heart instructs me.
I keep Yahweh always before me;
   because he is at my right hand, I shall not be moved.
Therefore my heart is glad (śmḥ) and my soul rejoices (gil),
   my body also rests secure.
For you do not give me up to Sheol,
   or let your faithful one see the Pit.
You show me the path of life.
   In your presence there is fullness of joy (śimḥah),
   in your right hand are pleasures (na'im) forevermore.

The confessional tone of this prayer is clear from the beginning: "you are my Lord" (v. 2), the use of the first person singular suffix with epithets of Yahweh being very common in individual complaints and thanksgivings (cf. Pss 3:4; 5:3; 7:2, 4, 11; 13:4; 18:2–3, 47; 22:2–3, 20; 23:1; 25:2; 27:1; 28:1, 7; 30:3, 13; 31:4, 15; 35:23–24, etc.).[21] All these prayers are extremely intimate, revealing, as it seems, close personal relationships to the Deity. There is direct address of God, and equally direct answer in Ps 16: by casting lots (v. 6), by receiving counsel (v. 7), by listening to one's own heart (v. 7), because of God's physical closeness (v. 8). Yet, the supplicant is not the author of the prayer-text because as a rule psalms are liturgical literature belonging to the leader of ceremony. He or she, for their part, set up the dialogical structure of the prayer. We may call this phenomenon a personal-liturgical-mood. Ceremonial masters let the worshiper use direct discourse, notwithstanding all free personal praying sometimes reported in narratives. Formalized, ceremonial exchange with God gradually became written down in collections or handbooks of diverse psalms.

Literary fixation of divine communications and consequent reliance on these fixed fonts came in slowly in those millennial centers of political power and literary culture of the Ancient Near East and Egypt, e.g., Babylonian collections of omina and their interpretation. It also led to written fixation of Israel's sacred tradition as a whole. The reconstruction of Judah's identity, socially, economically, spiritually, in the periods of exile and post-exile, under Babylonian and most of all under Old Persian rule provided

---

21. Cf. Vorländer, *Mein Gott*; Albertz, *Persönliche Frömmigkeit und offizielle Religion*.

the strongest motivations for "becoming a literate religion." Judeans in the diaspora and at home needed to know how to organize their lives as a community of faith, instead of a political organization under an independent dynasty. After the Babylonian victory in 587 BCE, with kingdom, temple, and national independence lost and after the deportations of thousands of upper class Judahites, a religious-societal regeneration, better: a completely new social organization, had to take place. People in the diaspora and in the homeland constituted synagogal societies on a civil basis without political ambitions. The Judahites formed a widely dispersed first "church"-like community, better, a Yahweh-followership. This new form of socio-religious organization, akin to the Zoroastrian community in Old Persia, brought forth, over several centuries, that canon of sacred writings, the Hebrew Scriptures, the most important part of them being the Torah of Moses.[22] More and more this Torah became the backbone of the scattered congregations,[23] along with the remote temple and city of Jerusalem. Torah, in actual spiritual life of the Judeans, was no longer a dialogical but a monologic discourse, mediated through Moses and prophets. God spoke to his representatives (cf. Exod 19-20; 32-34; Deut 5; 29-31; Jer 1-2; 25-26, etc.), and they handed down his message to the people.

In a very practical sense the newly emerging Jewish community thus became dependent on studying and interpreting the Torah, the source of all knowledge and the center of all authority coming from God replacing the direct, ritual relationship to him. Priests, Levites, scribes, wise men, later rabbis became the legitimate (or controversial) interpreters of Scripture. And literate members of faith community could study the will of God on their own or in school classes (Ps 1:2). While in former times people or leaders of the community had to turn to God personally when seeking counsel and orientation,[24] direct communication with God through mediums was widely shunned in postexilic times, cf. Deut 18:10-13; Lev 19:4; Isa 19:3; Ezek 21:26; Zech 10:2. This does not preclude, however, that the giving of oracles by a priest or Levite in official prayer-services survived for some time, cf. Pss 12:6; 35:3; 121:3-8, etc.

Small wonder that Torah, the preserved messages of Yahweh of past centuries, entered the stage in Second Temple times in Jewish communities, even in the Samaritan and Qumran branches of Judaism slightly differing from the Babylonian and Jerusalem factions. Only in the Jewish Elephantine

22. Cf. Garcia López, "*torah*"; Gerstenberger, *Theologies in the Old Testament*; Gerstenberger, *Israel in the Persian Period*.

23. Cf. Heschel, *Heavenly Torah*.

24. Cf., e,g., Exod 33:7-11; Lev 24:10-16; Num 15:32-36; Judg 18:5-6; 1 Sam 22:9-10; 23:1-4; 30:6-8; 1 Kgs 22:7-8, etc.

congregation of Upper Egypt does Torah seem to have been unknown. Torah for the Jewish mainstream now signified full orientation in all fields of new, emerging synagogal life. Expressions of joy, merriment, extreme satisfaction about the immense gift of God can be met across the board in all Jewish writings of the epoch. Questions arise, however, about the corollaries of pure and grateful excitement over against the divine scrolls. They remind us of the ambivalences of joy and Torah pointed out at the beginning. But what did this transfer in discourse really mean, from adhering to Yahweh, the living and liberating God, to his Torah, the written down tradition of old?

Joy in Torah

We have to examine a few psalms which directly refer to Torah as the object of study, meditation and joyful experience, in the first place Pss 1; 19; 119. Psalm 1 gives the profile of the righteous follower of Yahweh contrasting him with the apostate or godless person.[25] Typically, the literary form used is that of a "beatitude" frequently employed for this purpose:

> Blessed be the man
>> who does not follow the advice of the godless . . .
>
> but delights (*ḥepeṣ*) in Yahweh's instruction (*torah*)
>
> and meditates on his teaching (*torah*) day and night.
>
> (Ps 1:1–2, my trans.)

Similar sayings are to be found in Pss 106:3; 112:1; 119:1–3 and 2:12; 34:9; 40:5; 84:13; cf. Pss 32:1–2; 41:2; 84:5–6. The former group focuses on *torah* or equivalents: *mišpaṭ* (Ps 106:3); *torah* (Ps 119:1); *'edot* (Ps 119:2) and then God himself, which is obviously an equipotential expression: cf. Pss 2:12; 34:9; 40:5; 84:13; 112:1.

The ideal of a Yahweh-believer[26] portrayed in Ps 1 is the full-time study of Torah (v. 2), dedication and immersion in God's life-giving guidelines for existence, in words of old, to be sure, but destined to guide the contemporary exilic/post-exilic community. Psalm 19:8–11 and sporadically Ps 119:72, 93, 103, 105, 111, 120, 142, 144, 160, 172 give poetic descriptions of contents, qualities, and effects of Torah and what it means to the faithful.[27] To quote the compact passage from Ps 19:

25. Cf. Janowski, "Freude an der Tora"; Weber, "Meint die Tora JHWHs in Ps 1,2 (auch) den Psalter?"; Weber, "Von der Beherzigung der Tora JHWHs."

26. Designations for the adherent in the Psalter include: "righteous" (*ṣaddiq*), "pious" (*ḥasid*), "perfect" (*tamim*), "servant" (*'ebed*), cf. Fischer, "Frömmigkeit."

27. Psalm 119 is an acrostic poem in which each block of eight lines are begins with

> The law (*torah*) of Yahweh is perfect,
>> reviving the soul;
> the decrees (*'edut*) of Yahweh are sure,
>> making wise the simple;
> the precepts (*piqqud*) of Yahweh are right,
>> rejoicing the heart;
> the commandment (*miṣwah*) of Yahweh is clear,
>> enlightening the eyes;
> the fear (*yir'ah*) of Yahweh is pure,
>> enduring forever;
> the ordinances (*mišpaṭ*) of Yahweh are true
>> and righteous altogether.
> More to be desired are they than gold,
>> even much fine gold;
> sweeter also than honey,
>> and drippings of the honeycomb. (Ps 19:7–10 NRSV)

The full grandeur of Torah comes to the fore exhibiting its beauty, wholesomeness, life-giving power. Of course, it is the wonderful work and gift of Yahweh (cf. Ps 119:129), named by its main title Torah and five more synonyms (Ps 19:8–10; cf. Ps 119 and its alphabetical blocks).[28] The designations do have their specific meanings, but here they are used *pars pro toto* for the whole of God's declared and written down will collected through time. "To revive the soul" is to restore life which has been damaged or endangered; to "bestow wisdom" upon the ignorant is to give good quality to peoples life, similar to "enlighten the eyes." And, of course, the gift of joy must not be absent (vv. 8–9; ET 7–8). Joy, delight is one of the strongest reactions of grateful recipients of divine gifts, as we saw in the different categories of Psalms. It did imply physical and ceremonial reactions up to ecstasy.[29] "Fear of Yahweh" (v. 10; ET 9) in this context is only another synonym for Torah stressing its superhuman qualities, longevity.[30] And then the beautiful

---

the successive letter of the Hebrew alphabet (cf. the commentaries). In most blocks, each line contains a different synonym for Torah.

28. Grund-Wittenberg, *"Die Himmel erzählen die Ehre Gottes."*

29. Cf. Abart, *Lebensfreude und Gottesjubel*, 21–133; ritual reactions should be considered along with organic agitations.

30. Our concept of "eternity" has Greek philosophical roots; Hebrew *'olam* etc. signifies very long duration, cf. Preuß, "*'olam*," 1986; Fischer, "Ewigkeit."

summary of Torah's value: "more desirable than gold, sweeter than honey" (v. 11 [ET 10]; cf. Ps 119:108). Economic and culinary aspirations, among the highest of humankind, provide the metaphoric frame. Torah surpasses every imaginable fortune or pleasure. How? It replaces and fulfills human longings, not in an ascetic, other-worldly way, but within real life (cf. above Ps 16, and pp. 127–34). Confidence in Torah becomes tantamount to trust in God personally. Yet the relationship to a written tradition may be a different experience from living with God who "is at my right hand" (Ps 16:8), also changing spiritual behaviors and rites.

Dark Sides of Torah, Hampered Joy?

Several questions come up when we are looking at the specific Torah-Psalms: To choose a first one we may turn to Ps 19:12–14 [ET 11–13]:

> Moreover by them [i.e. the commandments] is your servant warned,
>> in keeping them there is great reward.
>
> But who can detect their errors?
>> Clear me from hidden faults.
>
> Keep back your servant also from the insolent (*zedim*);
>> do not let them have dominion over me.
>
> Then I shall be blameless,
>> and innocent of great transgressions.

Two experiences may threaten the pure delight, free of anxiety, in God's orientation: 1) One's own unrecognized transgressions of the rules set out by Torah. This is a serious problem for many ancient Israelites in special situations, cf. Pss 38:2–11; 51:3–14; 90:7–9, while other Psalms strongly insist on the innocence of the supplicant, cf. Pss 7; 17; 26; 44; 89 etc. What are these "hidden faults"? (Ps 19:13, *hapax legomenon*: *šegi'ot*; Ps 90:8: *'awon*; cf. Lev 4:2, 22, 27, etc.: *šegagah*). In general, all those possible transgressions which escape normal attention and categories, therefore being undetectable at first sight to the diagnostician of behavior, being a priest, or Levite. Torah does have the quality for the Yahweh believer to set up red lines almost in all fields of human life (economic; human relationships; political and civil; cultic, cf. the Decalogue and those 613 commandments in total which Jewish scholarship recognizes in the principal scrolls of veneration). Priestly, scribal and rabbinic experts have been busy to explain and define these borderlines over the centuries. And transgressions of Torah indeed have been threatening the conscience of the faithful all along (cf. 2 Kgs 22:10–11, 13;

Jer 36:14–26). Voices of defiance are rare in the Hebrew Scriptures, but they do occur: cf. Qoh 7:15–18; Ezek 20:10–26, in particular v. 25. How does Esra and his team, then, preach pure joy in Torah in the passage quoted above (Neh 8:9–12)? The only possible answer is: It is the exceptional privilege of that festive day after Sukkoth (which includes rites of atonement and general loosening of old burdens incurred by vows, e.g., a great prayer for all sinners and righteous, *kol nidre*).[31]

The second, at least for our western perspective of Torah, disquieting aspect of God's written word to his people is its intrinsic entanglement with antagonistic foes, enemies, adversaries of the divine orientations. How can we understand "Keep back your servant also from the insolent" in Ps 19:14, which equals the absolute renunciation of the "wicked," "sinners," and "scoffers" in Ps 1:1. And those numerous denunciations in Ps 119 of "insolent" (*zedim*; vv. 21, 51, 69, 78, 85, 122;[32] outside the Psalter only 5 occurrences), "wicked" (*reša'im*; vv. 53, 61, 110, 119, 155), "sinners" (*ḥaṭṭa'im*; only Pss 1:1; 25:8; 26:9; 51:15; 104:35), "scoffer" (*leṣim*; only Ps 1:1). What are these foes doing? In general, they despise Torah, oppose, denounce, and maltreat the supplicant. There is no indication in the Psalms that these opponents could be foreigners, adherents to another religion, or formal apostates from the Yahweh community. Rather, they seem to belong to the same congregation, disagreeing only with the interpretation of Torah by the supplicant (cf. Ps 119:21, 53, 139, 155, 158; they are really "tampering with" Torah in the opinion of the psalmist). Most outspoken in this regard is Ps 119:113: "I hate the waverers ("unsteady," "doubting" ones, NRSV "double-minded," *sa'apim, hapax legomenon*), but I love your Torah." This is a clear expression of internal strife and disruption, a statement of orthodoxy versus heterodoxy, as can be found so frequently in the history of Judaism, Christianity, and Islam in consequence of different interpretations of the written word of God. A very sad consequence of relying self-righteously on Holy Scriptures claiming it exclusively for one's own faction, without conceding liberty of interpretation to other "schools" of thought.

In spite of those cumbersome corollaries of accepting Torah as God's guidelines for human life and society we stick to the beautiful insights of especially the wisdom psalms mentioned. Psalm 19:8–11 may be the starting point. Torah in a comprehensive way makes life possible. As the divine will and provision it fosters and recreates wisdom, very necessary for human existence. On the other hand, absence of wisdom is responsible for all human failure to build up a wholesome existence for everyone and this whole

---

31. Cf. de Vries, *Jüdische Riten und Symbole*, 84–91.
32. Cf. Reynolds, "Torah as Teacher."

planet. These basic insights can be reached by the study of Torah. Exuberant joy is the outcome of such endeavour. Psalm 119, with 176 verses (22 blocks of 8 lines) is the most elaborate and artistic poem of the Hebrew Bible.[33] Its positive concerns are: Gratefulness and praise for divine orientation (e.g., vv. 7, 12, 62, 68, 103, 111, 129–130, 140, 151, 156, 171), expressions of longing for and enjoying to stay in good relationship with Torah (e.g., vv. 14, 16, 20, 24, 45, 47, 77, 81–82, 97, 123, 127, 131–135, 160, 162, 174), petitions to Yahweh for assistance in this endeavor (e.g., vv. 17–19, 25–28, 33–40, 66, 88, 116–117, 124–125, 145–147, 175), promises to keep close to Torah and Yahweh and tell the good news to others (e.g., vv. 13, 44, 46, 94, 106, 112). The whole meditation is an individual's confession of loyalty with no mention of congregation, people of Israel or Judah, nor covenant. Typical the commitment:

> I will never forget your precepts,
>> for by them you have given me life.
> I am yours, save me,
>> for I have sought your precepts." (vv. 93–94)

Communion with God, through Torah, sparks deepest delight, *Lebensfreude* or (vital) happiness.[34]

What exactly was "Torah" for the users of Ps 119? We do not have explicit indications of a sacred scroll containing the five books of Moses. There is an astonishing lack of references to "writing," "reading," "Moses," "Sinai," "covenant," "Israel," "congregation," etc. in this magnificent poem. But the great variety of synonyms for Torah, namely, e.g., "decrees" (*'edot*), "ways" (*derachim*; cr. "words," *debarim*), "precepts" (*piqqudim*), "statutes" (*ḥuqqim*), "commandments" (*miṣwot*), "righteous ordinances" (*mišpaṭim*) in Ps 119:2–7 to be repeated and modified in each block of eight lines throughout the composition strongly suggests that the psalmists did have in mind an authoritative document of the early Jewish community. Main concern of the adorants using this psalm is that everyone in the congregation including the orator might stay in the paths outlined by the diverse kinds of orientations which, taken as a whole, comprise the blissful gift of Torah. The adorant, for his or her part, ever so often emphasizes his "love" of and longing for Torah (*'hb*, vv. 97, 113, 127, 140, 159, 163; cf. vv. 20, 40, 47–48, 131; Deut 6:5–9),

---

33. Cf. Gerstenberger, *Psalms, Part 2*, 310–17; Reynolds, "Torah as Teacher."

34. Most interpreters agree on this point, cf. Janowski, "Freude an der Tora"; Abart, *Lebensfreude und Gottesjubel*; Zernecke, "Freude"; Staubli and Schroer, *Menschenbilder der Bibel*, 461–63; Grund-Wittenberg, *"Die Himmel erzählen die Ehre Gottes,"* 230–33; Vanoni, "*smḥ*."

his or her promises to keep the prescriptions (*nṣr*, 10 times in Ps 119; *šmr*, 23 times; cf. especially vv. 8, 22, 44, 55, 59–60, 67, 83, 87, 93, 101, 106 etc.), to ask for further instruction (vv. 12, 26, 33–40, 68, 73, etc.) and stress his or her determination to "study," "meditate on" the body of God's declared ordinances (*śiḥ*, "to ponder," "meditate"; Ps 119:15, 23, 27, 48, 78, 148). Torah this way becomes the "partner" of the supplicant to be "sought for" (cf. v. 45: *drš*). This term through various periods and constellations of Israel's history has been widely used for "to seek God" (cf. Pss 14:2; 34:5; 77:3). In Ps 119 it becomes equivalent to "look for Yahweh in his Torah" (cf. vv. 2, 4, 11, 30, 38, 55, 62, 94, 96, 125, 151–152, 164, 174, and all the personal pronouns of 2nd p. singular, subordinating Torah to Yahweh). Indeed, Torah itself turns an object of veneration, because it "personalizes" God? Or guarantees His presence? "I revere (*'aśa' kappay*, "raise my hands")[35] your commandments, which I love, and I will meditate on your statutes" (v. 48; cf. vv. 66, 86, 89, 92, 96–99, 111–112, 123, 131). Torah in Ps 119 becomes the outlet of divine benevolence, in the first place, it seems, for the individual believer in Yahweh. He or she does mention the solidarity with other "keepers of Torah" (cf. vv. 1–3, 63, 74, 79), and they also want to tell other members of congregation about their experiences with Torah (cf. vv. 13, 15, 27 etc.). On the whole, however, the I of the faithful is very dominant throughout.

Joy in Torah, strangely enough, also in Ps 119 is hampered by those ambivalences mentioned before. "My flesh trembles for fear of you, / and I am afraid of your judgments" (v. 120). "Judgments" (*mišpaṭim* can mean both punishment and "legal sentence"). In the background is consciousness of own misconduct (cf. vv. 67, 71, 75, etc.). Torah does have its promising and threatening sides. But joy apparently is stronger. The confessing believer in Yahweh (cf. v. 94: "I am yours") addressing God all the way directly indulges in highest excitement whenever he or she encounters his or her creator, savior, and permanent guide through Torah. Inherited Scripture (alone?) does offer the chance to find God, therefore it needs to be studied and searched, and even venerated with "uplifted hands" (v. 48; the expression abounds already in Sumerian prayer literature, antedating Israel's Torah by 2000 years).[36] "Delight in Yahweh," because of unbelievably benevolent gifts and deeds, now, in Israel's real times of birth during the Second Temple period is mediated by Torah. Eruptions of joy in Ps 119 are notable: cf. vv. 14, 16, 24, 47, 70, 74, 77, 117, 130, 143, 174. Eight of these eleven affirmations are formulated by a rare word derived from *š'*, "to enjoy," "relish," being hard to grasp in its meaning. It could be supplemented

---

35. Cf. Arnold, "Und ich will meine Hände erheben."
36. Cf. Gerstenberger, *Theologie des Lobens in sumerischen Hymnen*.

and explained by synonyms like "to revivify" (*ḥyh*, piel, cf. vv. 25, 37, 40, 50, 88, 93, 107, 149, 154, 156, 159). So we meet in Ps 119 that faithful believer in Yahweh who ardently clings to Torah, the precious orientation for his or her individual life. The encounter with his or her God happens within the written divine word through instruction, guidance, help from God.[37] Every meditation on Torah leads to deeper insight and closer realization of life, a true taste of happiness and joyful emotion.

To repeat a crucial point of our discussion and add some more aspects to it: Everything would seem to be all right, if the problem of ambivalence of Torah would not be present again, even in Ps 119 (cf. listings above) and in a very special way. What does it mean if the adversaries appear mockingly assailing the psalmist, trying to harm him or her? That they are despising Torah apparently following their own counsel? That the supplicant implores God to take these adversaries away, banish them from the scene? Who, after all, are these ominous *zedim*, "insolent"? They cannot be strangers, or plain, accidental evildoers of a chance neighborhood. Torah itself is the matter of strife between them.[38] Most likely, they have been members of the same community of Yahweh-believers who disagree on the importance and interpretation of Torah. A matter of early orthodoxy and heterodoxy, it seems. Rifts inside the new Jewish congregation of exilic times are already visible in the Hebrew Scriptures (cf. Lev 10; Num 12; Isa 65:1–16; Ezek 8 etc.). Different opinions and factions around emerging Torah come to the fore (cf. Deut 23:2–9 and Isa 56:1–8). Those who prevailed in the long run claiming the exclusive truth of their interpretation of Torah denounced opposing groups (*zedim!*) as aberrant and foes of God. "I hate the double-minded (*seʿapim*, "wavering," hapax legomenon), / but I love your torah" (Ps 119:113). "Go away from me, you evildoers (*mereʿim*), / that I may keep the commandments of my God" (v. 115). "You spurn all who go astray from your statutes; / for their cunning is in vain. / All the wicked of the earth you count as dross; / therefore I love your decrees" (vv. 118–119). Only the "orthodox" supplicant loves and keeps God's rules, the others are apostates worth to be thrown out. How does a self-righteous attitude like this come about? Is it generated by Torah itself, or inherent in human behavior? The opponents deviate from Torah (vv. 21, 53, 118, 139, 155, 158), they apparently "deride" and attack the faithful because of his or her rigid adherence to Torah (vv. 51, 61, 69, 85, 95, 110, 150), they are blocking better insight (v. 70), and deserve God's punishment (vv. 21, 118–119). Hate of the alleged disdainers of Torah and love of Torah viz. Yahweh stand in harsh opposition. This is

---

37. See Finsterbusch, *JHWH als Lehrer der Menschen*.
38. Cf. Erikson, "The Enemies in Psalm 119."

the attitude of absolute correctness over against God's will which underlies the long, cruel, bloody history of Jewish, Christian, and Islamic internal schisms through the ages.

Summarizing

Two Main Factors

The overall picture we have painted is heterogeneous. Two main factors play a decisive role in our investigation: One is the extension of time and subsequent changes also in theological conceptions we are witnessing in the manifold testimonies of the Hebrew Scriptures. The Old Testament itself took more than half a millennium to grow together, more or less from the tenth century BCE until the third century BCE. Changes in every respect, including modes of thinking, experiencing God and the world, cultural and economic customs did occur as everything in this world is prone to develop and mutate. Second, the Hebrew Scriptures are not a homogeneous work of just a few theological authors but contain voices of thousands of (mostly unknown, but thanks be to God!) witnesses of different social and historical contexts. Small wonder that they are so different to the extent of contradicting each other on important issues of faith and ethics.[39]

Communication with the Deity

Communication with deities developed in ancient Israel in a specific way as recognizable in the Scriptures themselves. In the beginning, with the art of writing not very much in use, people relied on cultic acts, e.g., sacrifices, personal prayer, and expert questioning of God and gods in order to receive divine guidance. Later in the monarchic period writing became more customary and first religious texts were fixed by script. Probably, the periods of exile and restoration (sixth through fifth centuries BCE) gave rise to conscious writing down and revising religious experiences in the fields of historical narration, prophetic proclamation, and poetic visions. The Torah finally was formed as the memorized Word of God in conjunction with the new construction of the synagogal community, that is, early second temple Judaism. Nehemiah 8 is the matrix of an early Jewish Torah service.

---

39. Basic lines of the growth of Hebrew Scriptures as I see it are to be found in Gerstenberger, *Theologies in the Old Testament*; and Gerstenberger, *Israel in the Persian Period*.

Joy as an Existential Emotion

Joy of being with God, if experienced as a positive, not destructive encounter, is a deep, existential emotion on all levels of spiritual development. It does embrace life as a whole. To delight in God is to realize oneness with existence, gratitude over the gift of breathing and the art of living, readiness to be useful in community, ability to laugh and praise and feast. And to follow safe guidelines in every sector of personal and congregational life. Presence and personal relationship with God are experienced differently over time: by divine words of comfort (oracles), dreams and visions, whisperings of own heart, teachings of parents and wise men, and, increasingly, after the exile, by the written Torah. It does acquire special importance, becoming a tangible, articulate, holy object. Beginning veneration is recognizable, e.g., Ps 119:48 later unfolding in ritual behavior over against the sacred scrolls in Sabbath services (cf. Neh 8:1–3, 6–8) and the Sukkoth festival until this day.

Torah grew out of desire and readiness to follow the lead of Israel's God. Originally, the verb *yrh* III, hiph, "to point out," signified individual instruction by father, priest, wise men and women or God himself (cf. Exod 24:12; Lev 14:57; Deut 17:9–11; Prov 4:4; Mic 3:11; etc.). To receive authentic instruction people had to ask God directly via various professionals that is, masters of diverse inquisitive techniques. More and more Yahweh followers, e.g., priests and Levites, took over the interrogative practice. They also started to collect divine answers. The noun derived from *yrh*, namely *torah*, "instruction," gradually came to mean the scroll of collected, written precepts from God received through a long tradition of spiritual existence (cf. Exod 4:12; Mic 4:2; Neh 8:1–3). Torah became the foundation of the faith community Israel in the exilic/postexilic period until hope, also part of the heritage of Christian churches as well as of the various branches of the Muslim community. In all three traditions the "Teachings of God" are a fundamental collection of written down experiences of the Divine which constantly need to be consulted and applied to present contexts and situations in the one world we live in together.

Ambivilance

All possible ways and means to communicate with God do have their ambivalences. For one: soliciting God's good counsel requires expertise, that is handling by learned, professional intermediaries. Torah-instruction is not an exception. The written testimonies of old come to us in different languages, from very different historical, cultural, social "life-settings." Already in exilic times laypeople allegedly could not stand the brute voice of Yahweh (Exod 19:23; 20:19; Deut 5:23–27). Only specially selected, educated and called persons received direct messages from God, normally to be handed down to others, not so privileged receivers. In case of Torah: Most parishioners at that time were illiterate. Professional scribes and teachers took over the task of interpreting the written Word. By and large this is true even in literate societies like ours. Furthermore: Precepts, commandments, ordinances of all types were double-edged. They heralded threats of punishment for offenders and promises of reward for fulfillers and loyal servants. Fear and joy, hope and doubts were closely packed together. Confessions of guilt and protestations of innocence both were possible reactions of the believers, depending on a given situation and its analysis viz. interpretation by some experts.

Torah and Covenant

How was Torah related to covenant (*berit*)? General opinion holds that there have been treaties every now and then between Yahweh and his people (cf. Gen 15:7–20; 17:1–14; Exod 24:3–8; Deut 29–30; Neh 10:1–40, etc.). Forms and contents of these alliances are quite different, depending on contextual conditions and conceptions. Most of the textual testimonies place great emphasis on the diverse commandments established in a given covenant ceremony. To keep these agreed upon ordinances or to break them makes all the difference, theologically speaking. In the Psalter we do find a good number of passages endorsing this concept of alliance with God (cf. Pss 25; 50; 78; 89; 105; 106; 111). Torah in this context is the sum-total of covenant conditions; some experts compare the pattern with ancient near eastern vassal treaties. Interestingly, though, the three particular Torah-Psalms (Pss 1; 19; 119) do not mention *berit* at all. They single out Torah as the body of Yahweh's written will for individual believers and the whole congregation. There is a flurry of synonyms for precepts and ordinances, while "covenant" does not appear. Apparently, the legal pressure on the partners of an alliance was lighter whenever the frame of treaty obligations was left aside.

Despisers and Enemies of Torah

The problem of "despisers" or "enemies" of Torah poses serious problems for our understanding. Why did our ancient witnesses not simply express their extreme content and jubilant exultation over the gift of God's instruction without, almost at the same breath, denounce others, as contenders or false competitors? In the case of complaint psalms and the experience of joy we still find some plausibility in their discrimination. The foes were, in their mind, directly responsible for the evil they had suffered. Therefore evil-mongers must be shunned and, if possible, annihilated. In the Zion songs there is equally reason to fight usurpers who battle for the Mount of God. But what about the good gift of Torah, how can it cause strife and division? Only by claiming exclusive rights to the will of God and denouncing others as trespassers. Psalm 119:51, 61, 69, 78, 84–87, 95, 110, 122, 150, 157, 161 accuse the "insolent" of violence. And the psalmist judges on his own that their relationship to Torah is wrong and that God takes action against them (cf. Ps 119:118–119, 126, 139, 158, etc.). Thus the correct ("orthodox"?) interpretation of Torah becomes a matter of internal dissents in Judaism, distorting or marring pure delight in God's orientation.

Pure joy of Torah, without anxiety or animosities, is visible, though, in the Hebrew Scriptures and its tradition from Neh 8 to the medieval feast of śimḥat torah. In fact, the cultic history of Sukkoth, the autumn festival of ancient Israel in the seventh month (cf. Lev 23:33–43) does contain the nucleus of that deeply grounded sentiment in commemorating the liberation from Egyptian slavery taking in elements of the harvest festival: "You shall rejoice before Yahweh" (Lev 23:40) is the overarching motto. No other festival in Lev 23 receives this connotation (but cf. Deut 16:11 for the "feast of weeks," Pentecost). Nehemiah 8:7–12 very clearly proclaims the message of "do not fear" punishments: The Levites "helped the people to understand" Torah (v. 7). "They read from the book, from the Torah of God, with interpretation. They gave the sense, so that the people understood the reading" (v. 8). In spite of the clarity of the reading, people show signs of shock (v. 9b). Ezra and the Levites have to speak more directly to the point: The supreme goal of Torah is liberation and joy, not oppression and sanction. They explain: "This day is holy to Yahweh your God, do not mourn or weep" (v. 9a). "Go your way, eat the fat and drink sweet wine and send portions of them to those for whom nothing is prepared, for this day is holy to our Lord, and do not be grieved, for the joy (ḥedwah) of Yahweh is your strength" (v. 10). These are radical theological statements. Holiness is fully benign, not harmful; the joy over the presence of Yahweh (corresponding to the joy of Torah!) may be deeply tasted with all human senses, and without fears or threats over against deviant brothers and sisters of the congregation. Divine delight, found in Torah, goes far beyond religious precautions, confessional dogmatics, claims of exclusive truths. It is pure excitement and gratitude to be, notwithstanding all personal and human deficiencies, somehow on the line of life enshrined in the presence of the One and Universal God of the universe (or at least of our solar system?).

10

Psalms in the Book of the Twelve

How Misplaced Are They?

Paradigm Switches within the Study of the Hebrew Scriptures

LIKE OTHER LAYERS OF the Old Testament tradition, the prophetic writings in the Hebrew Scriptures are undergoing new investigations because the modern exegete's style of living, thinking, and questioning has dramatically changed over the past decades.[1] Alterations in the reader's perspective and living conditions, according to any self-critical hermeneutical theory, necessarily result in fresh reconstructions of our own concepts of past history and theology. The Hebrew canon of three "large" and twelve "minor" prophets, being an important part of the TaNaK (Torah; Nebi'im; Ketubim) consequently needs to be scrutinized almost from scratch in regard to composition, form and tradition history, the profile of possible authors and transmitters, possible life-situations, and many other points of view. The results of such endeavors are amazing. They confront us with unfamiliar visions of the growth and use of prophetic literature within the social texture of exilic/post-exilic communities in Judah and perhaps other regions. They also reveal a characteristic remolding of prophetic images by later tradition, a result that calls into question our traditional concepts of "classical prophecy."

---

1. To cite but one effort of a fundamental re-evaluation of the prophets and prophecy: Deist, "The Prophets: Are We Heading for a Paradigm Switch?"

Liturgical Genres within the Prophetic Corpus

As a case in point, we focus on the abundance of liturgical genres within the prophetic writings. It seems strange, indeed, that most of the fifteen prophetic books in the Hebrew Bible contain examples of what we may call psalmic genres, be they more on the side of purely "liturgical" and "hymnic" or else of "homiletical"[2] categories of text. Setting aside the latter for the time being, we notice a wealth of passages which seem to belong to worship agendas, both in the form of unilateral prayers (i.e. prayers oriented from people to God) and of hymns sung in praise of Yahweh, both polyphonic and antiphonic (in a strictly "liturgical" shape), as a proclamation to and response of the community at hand. Thus we find almost full-scale communal complaints in Jer 14:2–14; Isa 63:7—64:10; Joel 1–2, while, e.g., Hos 6:1–3; 14:3–4 apparently are fragments of more extensive collective prayers. The so-called "individual complaints" are at least mirrored in the "Confessions of Jeremiah" (Jer 11:18–22; 12:1–6; 15:10–21; 17:12–18; 18:18–23; 20:7–18). A full individual thanksgiving song is placed into narrative contexts (Isa 38; Jonah 2), while a communal variety comes up in the "Isaiah Apocalypse" (Isa 26:1–6). Regular hymns or passages reminiscent of praise show up here and there, sometimes marking the end of collected sayings (cf. Isa 42:10–12; Hab 3; Zeph 3:14–20).[3] All in all, this phenomenon calls for fresh attention and explanation: Have these psalmic elements been placed in the context of prophetic utterances and discourses by mistake? Or imagining the opposite extreme: Do the liturgical components constitute the original matrix of communal interaction out of which have grown prophetic sayings and speeches?

---

2. Note this truly Protestant distinction between altar and pulpit, so to speak, or between fixed agendaric and more spontaneous parts of worship. Some scholars have already investigated prophetic texts under liturgical and homiletical perspectives; cf. von Waldow, "Anlass und Hintergrund der Verkündigung des Deuterojesaja"; Nicholson, *Preaching to the Exiles*; Reventlow, *Liturgie und prophetisches Ich bei Jeremia*; Bellinger, *Psalmody and Prophecy*. Also Gerstenberger, "Höre, mein Volk."

3. Gunkel and Begrich (*Einleitung*, 32–33 [ET *Introduction*, 22–23]) list a whole sequence of mostly brief prophetic passages classified as "hymns": Isa 6:3; 12:1–2, 3–6; 25:1, 5, 9; 30:18d; 40:12–17, 22–24, 26, 28–29; 41:13; 42:5, 10–12; 43:1, 14, 15, 16–17; 44:2, 6, 23, 24–28; 45:6–7, 11, 15, 18; 46:10–11; 47:4; 48:12, 17, 20; 49:5, 7, 13; 51:15, 22; 52:9–10; 57:15; 61:10–11; 63:7; Jer 2:6; 5:22, 24; 10:6–7, 10, 12–16; 31:7, 35; 33:2; 51:10, 15–16; Joel 2:21, 23; Amos 4:13; 5:8; 9:5–6; Nah 1; Hab 1:12–13; 3:18–19; Zeph 3:14–15; Zech 2:14; 9:9; 12:1.

History of Research on Liturgical Components in Prophetic Corpora

The question just posed runs counter, of course, to everything we had been led to believe about prophets and prophetic utterances in biblical contexts. In contrast with anonymous, liturgical beginnings, we traditionally prefer a different anchoring of prophetic speech. One of the firmly entrenched and most influential views of prophetic activity through the nineteenth and twentieth centuries has been that of personal identity and authorship of each individual messenger of God. Bernhard Duhm, for example, based his interpretation of prophetic writings exclusively on the authenticity of prophetic personality.[4] His lead has been followed by many Old Testament scholars. The historical figures named in superscriptions of prophetic books (and sometimes nowhere else!) were widely considered the authors of at least a nucleus of the respective writings. Disciples may have functioned as secretaries to these "men of God," but all later additions to their authentic "minutes" of divinely inspired kerygma were regarded as inferior or worthless, because they could not possibly match the genius of the prophetic mind and spirit, surpassing, as it were, by far the normal frame of contemporary conscience, experience, and ethical standards.

This traditional, personalistic view by and large has been replaced by subsequent research with its changing hermeneutical parameters. One important moment in the shift certainly was the discovery of form criticism by Hermann Gunkel and Sigmund Mowinckel. The authors of biblical texts, especially of individual psalms, recede into the background. Instead, communicative situations are credited with the production of texts serving collective, i.e. communal, ends. Mowinckel in particular emphasized the thoroughly cultic character of the psalms. To his mind, temple servants and cultic singers composed the larger part of the psalms in the service of the temple community and for collective use in worship.[5]

A second impetus for changing the traditional paradigm came from tradition-historical studies which reevaluated the formative forces shaping and inventing the inherited texts, be they orally transmitted or handed down in written form. Many exegetes today agree that considerably large parts of prophetic books have been molded (composed and formulated) by transmitters and scribes in a long process of scriptural development. By the same token scholars today recognize that the image of prophets and prophecy

---

4. Cf. Duhm, *Die Theologie der Propheten*; Duhm, *Israels Propheten*.

5. Cf. Mowinckel, *Psalmenstudien III* [ET "Cultic Prophecy and Prophetic Psalms"]. He believed that the prophets were cultic functionaries, yet theoretically free to communicate the word of God to the congregation using the first person of the deity.

has been at least partially if not completely formed by later interpretation.⁶ Setting aside, therefore, the idea of personal authorship of prophetic sayings, discourses, narratives—which certainly has had and further has its merits at some point—more and more interpreters are discovering the real depth dimensions of the prophetic traditions and the changes which went on through the centuries of Israelite and Judean history. Other parameters are also necessary in tracing this development. The growth of prophetic books and the understanding of their remote, "classical" eponyms cannot be pictured in terms of biographical, personalistic, historical factors, but has to be grasped within the whole context of group processes affecting the community of believers and worshippers that treasured and modulated that sacred heritage.⁷

Taking into account, furthermore, anthropological and sociological research on prophetic phenomena around the world, considering in this light more intensively and less dogmatically biblical evidence itself, we may conclude, that the agents of later communal organization were indeed paramount in forming the prophetic messages as well as the concepts of prophecy in general, as they now are extant in the Scriptures. This means that it has been principally the needs, aspirations, sufferings of the early Jewish community that have brought forth the prophetic books, using, as it were, rather faint memories of "classical" prophecy in Israel. Further, very few, if any, "authentic" words coming from the eighth and seventh centuries BCE have been preserved.

Psalms in the Twelve

Applying these new visions of prophecy to the Book of the Twelve and seeking psalm-like materials within the relevant writings, we will venture a rough purview and evaluation of the 82 printed pages in the Hebrew Bible according to Rudolf Kittel's edition, as well as the 96 pages of the Biblia

---

6. To give but a few examples: Joseph Blenkinsopp freely admits the creative role of tradition in forming the biblical concepts of prophecy, e.g.: "It will now be apparent that those who edited and transmitted the book of Jeremiah over a period of several centuries have been at pains to present him as fulfilling the paradigm of the prophetic role in Israel." Blenkinsopp, *A History of Prophecy in Israel*, 135; cf. my own epilogue ("Ausblick") to the German translation titled *Geschichte der Prophetie in Israel*, 266–89. The research done by scholars like A. Graeme Auld, Robert P. Carroll, David L. Petersen, Ernest W. Nicholson, Robert R. Wilson, Ehud Ben Zvi, Bernhard Lang, Karl Friedrich Pohlmann, and many others has paved the way for this kind of reassessment.

7. The literature in regard to biblical prophecy is too extensive to be recited at this point, cf. instead Hayes, "Prophecy and Prophets, Hebrew Bible"; K. Koch, "Propheten/ Prophetie II."

Hebraica Stuttgartensia, provided by Karl Elliger. There is no claim, however, of being exhaustive at this time.

Psalms with an Opening Formula

From the outset it is clear that psalmic passages in the Book of the Twelve do belong to different genres, and they have been placed—if that is what happened to them—into their context in various ways. Some of them are highlighted by some kind of opening formula. Jonah 2:2 [ET 1], on account of its context, is a narrative introduction: "Then Jonah prayed to Yahweh, his God, from the belly of the fish." It is followed by the formulaic expression "he said" (cf. Isa 38:9 ["I said"]; 1 Sam 2:1; Exod 15:1; Judg 5:1 etc.). Clearly, this is a case of inserting a narrative (oral or written, literary) psalm,[8] a thanksgiving song, to serve the plot of the story. Regardless of whether there are any liturgical implications in the position of such psalms, each inset text is entirely dependent on the use of the surrounding narrative. There are, in any case, no hints of the participation of worshippers intoning a song like tills. The book of Jonah is the only true narrative text among the Twelve. Hence, it may be worthwhile to investigate more fully the rationale of its being there in the midst of so much prophetic proclaiming and preaching.

A second, and quite different, example of formal citation of a psalm is offered by Hab 3:1: "A prayer (*tephillah*) of the prophet Habakkuk according to *šigyonot*." This phrase is strongly reminiscent of redactional superscriptions, attributing a poem to some traditional singer, like Asaph, Korah, or David. In this case Habakkuk, the *nabi'*, is named the author or performer of the psalm, two details unknown in the Psalter.[9] The term *šigyonot*, on the other hand, appears in a similar form in the headline of Psalm 7 (*šiggayôn leDavid*), while the designation "prayer" is part of five psalmic superscriptions (Pss 17; 86; 90; 1 02; 142). Furthermore, psalmic annotations do conclude the Habakkuk text. The last two words are *lamnaṣṣeaḥ binginôtay* ("To the leader, with my stringed instruments"; cf. Pss 4:1; 6:1; 54:1; 55:1; 61:1; 67:1; 76:1). Thus, the psalm in Habakkuk is framed by elements which we know from superscriptions to Psalms. But how do we interpret this fact? Apart from the basic issue of how the superscriptions in the psalms may have worked, we ask: Have parts of prophetic books been used in worship contexts, have they acquired a liturgical frame and then been inserted again

---

8. Cf. Watts, *Psalm and Story*.

9. The only occurrences of the name Habakkuk are in Hab 1:1; 3:1. The designation *nabi'* appears three times in the Psalter, but never as an author: Ps 51:2 refers to the prophet Nathan, and Pss 74:9; 105:15 mention prophets of Yahweh in general.

into the original collection of prophetic sayings? Or has the psalm Hab 3, a kind of theophanic victory song, attracted the discourses of Hab 1–2?

From the beginning the liturgical frame featured an author's name, even specifying that the poet was a "prophet." So the psalm may have provided the prophetic identity for the whole book. Be it as it may, modern interpretations vary greatly. Some experts follow the track that later readers of the prophetic writings may have extracted opportune texts, i.e. psalm-like prophetic sayings, from that tradition and remodeled them for use in worship service.[10] The Qumran Psalm tradition may be cited in support of this theory, but any relocation of the amended (liturgized!) version into the prophetic book remains enigmatic. Another hypothesis fully recognizes the liturgical provenance of Hab 3 and makes the author a cultic prophet firmly anchored in the temple in situation.[11] If the prophet really had been a liturgical leader of a temple community, then his message as a whole would have featured cultic traits and contents. For some scholars, consequently, the book of Habakkuk reveals a perfectly liturgical structure of prophetic complaint being answered by God. The text of Habakkuk itself this way becomes proof of the much-conjured institution of cult prophecy.[12]

The crux of this theory, however, is that it has to leave behind the conception of the prophets as free-lance divine messengers, so dear to the mainstream of relevant research. If prophets are held responsible for cult liturgies in the prophetic writings as well as the Psalter, they hardly can remain spontaneous critics of social, political and religious conditions in Israel. They in fact become cult officials and functionaries. More serious, to my mind, and instrumental to that erroneous interpretation is the fact that this representation of prophecy (although recognizing correctly the liturgical character of some texts) still clings to outmoded views of an objective, author-to-audience relationship with textual creativity belonging to the author-speaker alone. The creative stimulus of communal action, in this case of corporate worship, does not enter into consideration at all. If, on the contrary, scholars would admit diverse forms of free mediation between people and God and perhaps some institutionalized ways of communication with the divine, and if scholars learned to consider all systematizing concepts of prophecy to belong to later periods of Israel's spiritual history, then the diverse phenomena might fall into place.

---

10. Thus, e.g., Rudolph, *Micha, Nahum, Habakkuk, Zephanja*, 239–43.

11. Cf., e.g., Horst and Robinson, *Die Zwölf kleinen Propheten*, 183–86; Jeremias, *Kultprophetie und Gerichtsverkündigung*, 85–100.

12. Besides Jeremias, *Kultprophetie und Gerichtsverkündigung*, 99–100 n.11, cf. Johnson, *The Cultic Prophet and Israel's Psalmody*; Gerstenberger, "Psalm 12."

The smallest of all prophetic writings within the Twelve is Obadiah, comprising only 21 verses, which partly coincide with Jer 49:9, 14–16. Biblical tradition does qualify these divine "threats against Edom" as typically prophetic utterances, namely, as a "vision" (*ḥazôn*) of the spokesman of Yahweh.[13] Seemingly, therefore, the genre "oracle against foreign nations" does not belong into the liturgical fold. Nevertheless, we may still surmise that such oracles have been used in worship situations as a means of Israel's self-defense against foreign domination.[14] Furthermore, communal complaints in the Psalter do incorporate threats and curses against enemy nations and the oppressive rule of foreign powers (cf. Pss 60; 83; 137). Interestingly enough, all three psalms just referred to mention the neighboring rival Edom, besides other nationalities. We have good reason, therefore, to include oracles against foreign nations into the repertoire of liturgical texts. The little book of Obadiah, consequently, constitutes a prime example of agendaric material being placed between (or cutout from) Amos and Jonah, emphasizing salvation for Israel through destruction of Edom. Obadiah gained book status by a special superscription, extremely short as it may be (v. 1, the first six Hebrew words). Nevertheless, it seems that the booklet acquired an important liturgical function in the context of the Twelve.

Psalms with no Opening Formula

There are, by contrast, psalm-like passages in the Book of the Twelve that stand out without being formally separated from their contexts by formulaic introductions or subscriptions. One example is Joel 1:2—2:27.[15] Some

---

13. "Vision" as a typical communication to messengers of Yahweh is used widely, especially in exilic/post-exilic prophetic texts; cf. Isa 1:1; Jer 14:14; 23:16; Ezek 7:26; 12:22–27; Hos 12:11; Mic 3:6; Nah 1:1; Hab 2:2–3, and heavily concentrated in Dan 8.

14. The genre and *Sitz im Leben* of these particular "oracles" have not been sufficiently studied so far. Cf. Höffken, "Untersuchungen zu den Begründungselementen der Völkerorakel des Alten Testaments"; Gosse, *Isaie 13,1—14,23 dans la tradition litteraire du livre d'Isaie*; Blenkinsopp, *History Prophecy in Israel*, 131–32; 175–76 et passim. Scholars in general agree on the exilic/post-exilic dates for the inclusion of these passages into the *corpus propheticum*.

15. Other divisions of the book are under discussion, e.g., between Joel 1:2—2:17 and 2:18—4:21 [ET 3:21]. Cf. Zenger, *Einleitung in das Alte Testament*, 381–85. More important is Zenger's evaluation of the booklet as mere "literary prophecy and prophetic interpretation of prophetic writings . . . probably written to be placed into its present position in the Book of the Twelve" (383). Cf. Nogalski, *Redactional Processes in the Book of the Twelve*, 3–57. Determining the literary origin, however, does not solve the question of the Sitz, because literary texts may have been used in worship. "The liturgical character of these texts indicates that the prophetic books of which they are a part were read as part of the temple liturgy." Cf. Sweeney, *Isaiah 1–39*, 17.

scholars consider this part of the book its authentic nucleus, declaring the subsequent passages as later accretions. The first two chapters of Joel contain elements of communal complaint[16] and responses by Yahweh. Many exegetes regard Joel 1–2 a full-fledged worship liturgy motivated by a locust plague or some other public calamity.[17] In fact, most interpreters think of some liturgical provenance for the text. The question remains, however, how such a special genre could possibly enter the prophetic canon to begin with. According to traditional presuppositions the prophet must enter the temple sphere and become a cultic functionary in order to make plausible the existence of a whole duster of liturgical-agendaric genres in the prophetic collections, presumably consisting of freely communicated messages of Yahweh. The opposite view may be closer to ancient Israel's reality, but still misses the point by a wide margin. It claims that the prophet did not need to enter the cultic realm. Rather, the ideal figure of a communicator of Yahweh's word and will to the early Jewish congregation emerged from cultic practice, because that word had been synthesized right in the midst of the community's anxieties and hopes.

In Joel 1–2 we have an agendaric block of material to which, in the course of worship, other liturgical passages (Joel 3–4) have been added. (A similar relationship seems to prevail regarding Mic 7 and the preceding chapters of the book). At first glance it appears as if a liturgical block has been placed at the end of a collection of prophetic sayings.[18] For what purpose? Why would the composers of the book choose liturgical forms to conclude a written composition? And why, for that matter, did they occasionally use prayer language when shaping the body of the text (cf. Mic 1:8–16; 4:5; 5:4–5; 5:8; 6:6–8)? Would it not be more reasonable to image the reverse of this procedure, namely that prophetic sayings, in oral or written transmission, had been drawn into and molded by community services of exiled congregations.[19] Had these Yahwists fashioned prophetic sayings,

16. As to the terms used here for genres—especially "complaint," "lament," "divine response," etc., cf. Gerstenberger, *Psalms, Part 1*, esp. 10–14; and Gerstenberger, *Psalms, Part 2*, 506–43 (Glossary of genre terms).

17. Cf. Ahlström, *Joel and the Temple Cult of Jerusalem*; Loretz, *Regenritual und Jahwetag im Joelbuch*.

18. Ever since Gunkel ("Der Micha-Schluss" [ET "The Close of Micah"]) exposed the liturgical character of this final chapter of Micah, scholars have speculated about the genre and function of these verses (Mic 7:8–20). There is a certain agreement on the basic forms being "agendaric," but many colleagues shun away from calling them "real liturgical texts." They think rather of literary imitations (cf. Kessler, *Micha*, 296–312).

19. Ehud Ben Zvi in his commentary (*Micah*, 3–11, 171–72, 181–82), emphasizes individual and communitarian reading of the written text. The "bearers" of this communicative office was a "circle of literati . . . of high literacy in their society, and who

just as early Christians incorporated and developed the words of Jesus in their texts?

Another example of sorts, again slightly different from the preceding two, is Nah 1:1–11. Clearly, there once was an alphabetical acrostic somewhere within or without the book of Nahum, parts of which have been preserved in Nah 1:2–8. Its lines successively begin, with some errors and omissions, with the letters *aleph* to *kaph* of the Hebrew alphabet. Equally clear is the fact that the text of an acrostic poem has been severely remodeled, perhaps to fit into the congregational philosophy and the liturgical practice of the ancient assembly. The enemies directly addressed (Nah 2–3) will suffer defeat from Yahweh's retaliating onslaught, and implicitly Israel will be liberated from her foes. This in all likelihood is the subject of liturgical celebrations, and the vividness of language and metaphors contributes to create this very impression.[20]

Psalms Reacting to Prophetic Speeches

A larger number of psalmic passages have been tightly interwoven with the regular "prophetic" contexts.[21] Apparently, they react to messenger speeches or prophetic denunciations of Judah or Israel. A good example is Hos 6:1–6. The preceding lines (Hos 5:8–14) are a terrible invective against the cities and tribes of northern Israel, conjuring—in military and accusatory terminology—an enemy invasion. The diatribe culminates in a divine pronouncement of destruction and deportation (Hos 5:14b–15):[22]

---

took the role of brokers of the knowledge imparted by the book of Micah . . ." (181 and often). I do not see a reading culture in ancient Judah as early as the late Persian period. Rather, the texts in their dramatic orientation, preserved in the written sources, testify to authentic liturgical proceedings.

20. Floyd (*Minor Prophets*, 10–20) decidedly rejects the idea of Nahum's being "an extended eschatological hymn" or "a prophetic liturgy," but he faces serious difficulties in explaining the vivid direct address discourse throughout the book as "resembling those [i.e. rhetorical conventions] that are home in some kind of ritual or ceremonial context . . ." (12, cf. 15–18). "Although the conventions of direct address used in Nahum are somewhat similar to ones that might also be used in a ritual setting, they neither entail ritual acts nor reflect a cultic tableau" (17). His solution, then, is to locate the literary prophet in groups of scribes and wise men who "wrote books like Nahum to be studied among themselves, and to be used for the instruction of public officials and others . . ." (19). For the book of Habakkuk, however, he partially admits cultic use (85, 87; etc.).

21. Cf. Schart, *Die Entstehung des Zwölfprophetenbuches*.

22. Analytical details can be found in Wolff, *Hosea*, 131–67 [German ed.]; Jeremias, *Der Prophet Hosea*, 78–83.

I myself will tear and go away;
> I will carry off, and no one shall rescue.

I will return again to my place
> until they acknowledge their guilt and seek my face.

In their distress they will beg my favor.

Thus the severe announcement of divine castigation ends up in giving the catchword for the following communal confession of guilt and declaration of confidence,[23] forms well known from collective complaints (to Hos 6:1-6 compare, e.g., Pss 95:6-7; 100; 106:6; Neh 9:16-31; Ezra 9:9-15; Dan 9:5-16, etc.). The communal complaint of Hos 6:1-6, therefore, is an integral part of the prophetic text, and it makes the unit Hos 5:8—6:6 a true reflection of communal worship.

The same holds true or else may be reasonably claimed, e.g., for Zeph 3:14-15;[24] Hab 1:2-4, 12-14; Mic 4:1-5 (parallel to Isa 2:1-5); 6:6-8; and other passages. Even dirge-like poems, e.g., in Mic 1:8-16;[25] Amos 5:1-3, may have to be reevaluated under the hypothetical perspective of being an authentic witness of some sort of communal or perhaps individual (i.e. small group[26]) worship. This kind of intimate relationship between psalm-like passages and "prophetic" pronouncements can hardly be explained by any theories about cultic prophecy. Hans Walter Wolff may have come pretty close to the truth when summing up his observations as to the liturgical qualities of Mic 7:8-20:

> Relevant worship services comprised in the first place readings of old prophetic sayings announcing the evil . . . , secondly contemporary prophetic utterances highlighting the actual situation by biting critiques or comforting words . . . , and finally the psalm-like response of the congregation, referring to the preceding kerygma.[27]

---

23. Wolff (*Hosea*, 48-49) calls it a "song of penitence" (*Bußlied*).

24. Cf. Gerstenberger, "Der Hymnus der Befreiung im Zefanjabuch."

25. Cf. Kessler, *Micha*, 90-111.

26. We should resolutely move away from the unilateral idea that worship in exilic/postexilic times had consisted only in temple ceremonies, animal sacrifice and occasional pilgrimages to Jerusalem. There were manifold rites and rituals even under the influence of exclusivistic thinking in terms of monotheism. Cf. Gerstenberger, *Der bittende Mensch*; Gerstenberger, *Yahweh the Patriarch*, 55-66; and Gerstenberger, *Theologien im Alten Testament* [ET *Theologies in the Old Testament*].

27. Wolff, *Micha*, 194 [ET *Micah*].

Psalms with no Apparent Connection to Their Context

Only a very few relevant psalm-like texts seem to have been included in prophetic books, like erratic pieces of non-prophetic origin, or meteor-like material witnesses of another world. Closer investigation still may yield contextual ligatures, though. The items most frequently discussed over an extended period of time are those fragmented parts (?) of Yahweh hymns found in the book of Amos (4:13; 5:8–9; 9:5–6; [Amos 8:8?]), the so-called doxological intrusions. They indeed have long puzzled exegetes, precisely for being so disconnected from their context.[28] Be that as it may, the inclusion of seemingly disconnected hymnic elements may constitute more evidence for the possible cultic origin and use of "prophetic" books. In an orderly written theological treatise, sudden hymnic exclamations hardly seem to fit.

Conclusions

The Role and Setting of Psalmic Texts in the Prophets

Psalmic texts are integrated into the Book of the Twelve in a variety of ways. We have to describe the modalities and functions these passages or literary units are performing in their respective contexts. A frame of introductory and/or concluding formulas in the fashion of Psalm superscriptions suggests the availability of the text for liturgical ends. Such redactional superscriptions are no mere literary dressing without meaning for the reader. Instead, they contain real information about the use of the text in communal ceremonies, about which we may understand little from our historical distance. Unframed, semi-autonomous psalmic texts may be equally convenient pieces for worship services of the community. For a psalm-like text marked as in Hab 3 and for most poems of the Psalter, one is hard pressed to imagine another than a liturgical purpose. Superscriptions consisting of

---

28. Perhaps Karl Budde ("Zur Geschichte des Buches Amos") was the first to focus on this phenomenon. Friedrich Horst ("Die Doxologien im Amosbuch") gave the first comprehensive treatment of the form. To him doxologies are customary responses of those accused of crimes. They have to admit their guilt, so that they may be sentenced. Cf. also Schmidt, "Die deuteronomistische Redaktion des Amosbuches"; Berg, *Die sogenannten Hymnenfragmente im Amosbuch*; K. Koch, "Die Rolle der hymnischen Abschnitte in der Komposition des Amos Buches." Koch rejects Horst's interpretation, arguing instead for each hymnic fragment's being a marker of a book division, which actually points back to some liturgical use of the texts (536). Crenshaw (*Hymnic Affirmation of Divine Justice*) develops Horst's position further.

personal ascriptions and technical terms hardly serve the interests of individual readers.[29]

Communicative and interactive uses of psalmic texts in "prophetic" writings may hint at the possibility that it was not the prophetic texts that attracted liturgical elements. Instead, cultic situations may have produced prophetic pronouncements and literature. At least, it seems to me, all the traditional theories of (a) the authentic, historical men of God in the name of Yahweh creating collections of oracles and proclamations, and (b) such collections migrating into the cultic memory are much less plausible. How and why would the voices of autonomous communicators of Yahweh's will, addressing themselves to very concrete and transient contemporary problems, be preserved over the centuries? It is much easier to imagine communities which—experiencing the pressures of the exilic/post-exilic age—looked backwards to find some explanation and orientation for their daily lives under the rule of Yahweh. They wanted to understand their destiny at the hands of Babylonians and Persians. They knew or invented prophetic figures in the past that should have known beforehand the plans of God for his people, the fate of the monarchy, and the spiritual uncertainties in a very pluralistic and hostile world. So whatever little information still was available of Isaiah, Jeremiah, Ezekiel, and the Twelve would be brought into the assemblies, discussed and actualized there. The processes of collecting traditions of the past, of joining their bits of the "prophetic" heritage together, of actualizing the older sayings and exhortations by creating new "prophetic" proclamation were all interwoven as part and parcel of the same gradual compilation of the prophetic canon.

Only the erratic variety of willfully interspersed psalms or fragments of psalms in an apparently psalm resistant context could cause problems for our present tentative of interpretation. Why should later redactors place such texts into an alien context like "prophetic" discourse? The best explanation, it seems to me, is the real worship situation in exilic and post-exilic Judah (or Diaspora, for that matter). Perhaps congregations would respond to brutal announcements of doom by intoning hymns or staging complaint services. Hymn singing, in fact, can be a weapon against destruction and misery. Eulogizing the supreme power of God, the mighty benevolence of the Creator and Protector, all by itself may defeat the hateful powers or evil potencies. Thus, the Chronicler tells of military victory on account of hymn

---

29. To regard the Psalter (and the Prophets?) as private reading material has come into vogue in the past years. It seems to me, however, that "the underlying concepts of writing and reading presuppose a modern literary society, which does not even exist in all countries of our world today. Investigations, e.g., in Latin America, show that less than 10% of the population read regularly.

singing (2 Chr 20:21–22). And the legendary witnesses of Yahweh in Dan 3, according to the Greek apocryphal tradition sing hymns in the midst of the "fire oven." Furthermore, hymnic passages may constitute part of complaint songs.[30] For these reasons the fragmented hymn of Amos should not seem too strange to us. On the contrary, it could be another piece of evidence for the origin and transmission of prophetic preaching, which solicits from the beginning communal response and participation.

Reading Texts in Post-exilic Judah

Textual analysis alone will not solve the enigmas in regard to prophetic tradition and prophetic office. Readers of ancient texts will always bring with them culturally acquired paradigms of ancient reality, which serve as background and matrix for the interpretation of individual texts. Thus our general ideas of what prophecy and prophetic tradition was like will determine to a large extent the results of our exegetical endeavors. As indicated at the beginning of this paper there are numerous basic issues to be critically evaluated before we come to grips with the psalmic passages in the Book of the Twelve. Here are some of the underlying questions. What has been the significance of putting prophetic proclamation into writing? Millions of words of different mediators between God and humans certainly have not been preserved in any kind of document. Why and to which end were some of them frozen into letters? How have the emerging written collections been used? Has there been already in Persian times a culture of reading books for private edification? If so, which parts of society were able to indulge in the luxury of buying and reading written documents? On the other hand, how can we visualize communities cultivating their own traditions in written form? The era of public libraries evidently began only in the Hellenistic period.[31] What kind of experts did they need to handle the written records? Quite naturally, learned scribes were highly important, but also theologians and spiritual leaders of sorts who determined the quality and authenticity of the written words.[32]

Of these the most critical issue is this: What was the purpose of the written tradition, on the one hand for the Torah of Moses, and on the other hand for the emerging prophetic canon? Can we claim the written word was destined principally for public recitation as in Neh 8:2–3 and—reduced to the royal court—Jer 36:4–26? If that has been the case, how much influence

---

30. Cf. Gerstenberger, *Psalms, Part 1*, 11–14.
31. Cf. Davies, *Scribes and Schools*, 74–88, 107–25.
32. Cf. Blenkinsopp, *Sage, Priest, Prophet*.

is to be attributed to the community of recipients of the words of God? In analogy to the *Gemeindebildung* (formulation of kerygma by the congregation) in New Testament times, the authorship of "prophetic" words to a large extent may be located in that living process of communal expectation and the shaping of contemporary (early Jewish) liturgical agendas promoted by the scribal and theological elite. Thus, considerable parts of the prophetic "books" prove to be retro-projected compositions of the late community, rather than the "classical" prophetic authors mentioned in the superscriptions.[33]

If this assumption is plausible, we have to investigate primarily the living conditions, theological outlooks and communitarian practices of the early Jewish community of the Persian epoch in order to understand correctly prophetic "books" and "writings." The life setting of prophetic words and psalms would not be "the book" as is sometimes erroneously claimed. Rather, written records of the congregations of believers in Yahweh in Persian times (beginning, as it were, under the dominance of the Babylonians) point to various worshipping rites in which written words were used, recited either from memory or by open and public reading. The people "told the scribe Ezra to bring the book of the law of Moses . . . he read from it . . . from early morning until midday . . ." (Neh 8:1, 3). "Baruch wrote on a scroll at Jeremiah's dictation . . . ," "you shall read the words of the Lord from the scroll that you have written at my dictation" (Jer 36:4, 6). "When Hilkiah gave the book to Shaphan he read it . . . Shaphan then read it aloud to the King" (2 Kgs 22:8, 10). Moses "took the book of the covenant and read it in the hearing of the people" (Exod 24:7). He "commanded them: Every seventh year . . . you shall read this torah before Israel in their hearing" (Deut 31:10-11). Joshua "read all the words of the torah, blessings and curses, according to all that is written in the book of the torah" (Josh 8:34). There are a good number of Deuteronomistic passages hinting at the written precepts of Yahweh put down by Moses and communicated by him. All of these references may be understood as reflections of exilic/post-exilic habits

---

33. The facts are quite obvious in case of the book of Isaiah. Cf., e.g., Kaiser, *Das Buch des Propheten Jesaja Kapitel 1-12* [ET *Isaiah 1-12*]; Becker, *Jesaja*. The facts are also clear for Jeremiah. Cf., e.g., Carroll, *Jeremiah*; Thiel, *Die deuteronomistische Redaktion von Jer 1-25: von Jer 26-45*; Pohlmann, *Die Ferne Gottes*. On Ezekiel, cf., e.g., Lust, ed., *Ezekiel and His Book*; Lang, *Ezechiel*. For Amos, cf. Schmidt, "Die deuteronomistische Redaktion des Amosbuches"; and Rottzoll, *Studien zur Redaktion und Komposition des Amosbuches*. On Hosea, cf. Wolff, *Hosea*; Jeremias, *Der Prophet Hosea*. On Micah, compare, e.g., Ben Zvi, *Micah*; Kessler, *Micha*. It is strange, indeed, that many exegetes still ignore the facts and start their investigations from the alleged fountainhead, the historical prophet himself, instead of working backwards from the most productive, later communities towards earlier layers of tradition.

of reading aloud the words of Yahweh to the assembled congregation. This also implies that where we hear of "reading the Word" in Hebrew Scriptures it is public recitation, not private musing (except in Deut 17:18; Ps 1:2?).[34]

The recitation of Scripture by itself becomes a liturgical act, a scenario with the essential ingredients of authorized reader, scroll of Torah, listening and responding community (which, by the way orders the scroll to be brought into the assembly; cf. Neh 8:1).

Post-exilic Worship as the *Sitz im Leben* of Prophetic Literature

Returning to the issue of psalms in the Twelve we may say that most scholars probably agree that the bulk of "psalmic" passages in the prophetic canon (and particularly in the Book of the Twelve) does have some affinity to liturgical texts and outlooks. Few, however, will accept the idea that these cultic elements may be the *Leitfossil* of the whole prophetic literature and especially the Book of the Twelve. I should like to argue that way. The psalm-like parts may betray the formative matrix at least for the compilation of the Book of the Twelve, and beyond this general frame they may hint at the enormously creative *Sitz im Leben* that brought forth a considerable part of retrospective "prophetic" proclamation and other divinely inspired discourse. Unfortunately, we do not have much direct, authentic information about the early Jewish communities and their leadership as being active in writing prophecies under the disguise of Isaiah, Jeremiah, Ezekiel and the Twelve. But all the Hebrew prophetic writings in their formative phases have been, as pointed out above, quite susceptible of becoming carriers of contemporary theology and preaching. It is only from this perspective that prophetic books as a whole become really understandable.

Prophetic speech in this regard becomes solidly grounded in community worship without the "classical" prophets becoming cultic functionaries. An additional, thorough investigation of speech forms (i.e. taking seriously congregational involvement in the production of prophetic books) in the Twelve and the bigger Three—I am thinking in particular of the frequent genres of "admonition" or "exhortation," "call for repentance," "ethical reflection," etc.—would without doubt greatly enhance the quest for a primarily cultic origin of "prophetic" compositions and discourses. There are some indications in the Hebrew canon itself that such a model of "prophecy" comes close to ancient reality.

---

34. Cf. Hossfeld and Lamberty-Zielinski, "*qr'*": "The meaning 'to read' for *qr'* is attested only from the exilic period onward . . ." (134). "[P]ublic reading as part of covenant-making acquired a cultic character . . ." (135); Hossfeld and Reuter, "*seper.*"

We should, for example, reconsider the famous relationship of Jeremiah to his personal scribe Baruch under this angle. Ancient "prophetic" words and figures in fact need to be transmitted to posterity by mediation of "scribes." Classical prophets did not write down their messages. Nor were they called *nabi'* for that matter (cf. 1 Sam 9:9). Baruch wrote down the words of God communicated to Jeremiah and read them to the congregation, like court officials read the "prophetic" work to the king (cf. Jer 36). This beautiful and theologically most meaningful story, made up in Deuteronomistic circles, clearly depicts the mediation of the Word through written documentation. The "words of Jeremiah" are put down faithfully to be recited to the people, so that it can "amend its ways and its doings" (cf. Jer 7:3). Mediation through letters and literature is important. Therefore, the prophet is seen barred from the temple, in order that his (later) representative may communicate with the congregation. The destruction of the written Word is the imminent danger, not the possible demise of the prophet himself. Even the mediators of the Word of Jeremiah step into the background. The victorious writings prevail; they are victorious. The king may burn the first scroll, a new, enlarged edition will appear immediately at Jeremiah's dictation, containing all the speeches destroyed before, "and many similar words were added to them" (Jer 36:32). Of course, there is no explicit admission that the mediators themselves enlarged some original collection of prophetic sayings. But everyone understanding the human genesis of sacred writings, and everyone who thoughtfully and attentatively reads our "prophetic" books in the Hebrew Bible should be able to recognize the growth of prophetic traditions. And the psalmic components indeed may lead us to the sources of prophecy and *nabi'*-hood: the proper community of faith struggling with its own past and for its identity and survival in turbulent times.

Hymns as Indicators of the Communal Authorship of the Prophets

With good evidence at hand of (a) the growth and shaping of "prophetic" traditions to have taken place in exilic/post-exilic times and (b) the unifying concept of Yahweh having sent in vain a whole series of prophets for the sake of his people to be a late systematization, we may finally compare the two approaches to prophetic literature, bearing in mind the lead of the psalmic passages in the Book of the Twelve.

The interpretation of prophetic texts in the past tried to start out from the historical person who communicated the will and verdict of Yahweh to his people in concrete historical moments of the life of Israel. Mentally starting from this point zero, the point of origin of individual texts, normally short sayings, modern exegetes tried to identify authentic messages and later, consecutive additions or modifications of these more or less divine words. Eventually, the main interpretative effort having cleared the very fountainhead of prophetic activity, the various layers of subsequent interpretations and comments had to be analyzed and explained, down to the Masoretic fixation of the Hebrew writings and the ancient versions as well as on through posterior theological debates in Jewish and Christian history of interpretation. A complete exegesis of a given text would include, therefore, a painstaking scrutiny of its first utterance as well as of its subsequent reworkings, alterations in diction and meaning. If later additions, corrections, etc. had overgrown the original "prophetic" word, the modern interpreter would have to muster his or her sharp tools of historical-critical and form and social-critical research and cut back through the jungle of later interpretations in order to get to the fountainhead of that overarchingly significant first saying and its author.

The presence of psalm-like texts in the prophetic canon, which may point to the late, community-bound matrix of all "prophetic" texts, alerts us to the possibility of a very different approach. What we do have in the Hebrew prophetic books, especially in the Twelve, are pieces of literature probably going back to the fifth and fourth centuries BCE. We would have to take seriously the final shape and the late origin of these "prophetic" writings. First, the final literary product would have to be analyzed, including a probe into the social, cultural, theological conditions under which the book or writing came about. The creative interests prevalent in the group which used a given prophetic book or compilation have to be investigated. No human being and no group of people can avoid, while designing for him- or itself relevant pictures of the past, to impose his/its own, contemporary experiences on the older witnesses or interweave the bygone testimony with actual patterns of thinking and acting. This insight of everyone constructing the world in his or her own likeness is valid for biblical writers as well as for modern exegetes. In the case of the biblical tradition, the images of prophets and their messages as preserved in the Book of the Twelve to a very large extent are condensations of prophetic types and roles, known and/or invented exactly in the period under discussion. Having established the profiles of the youngest layer of tradition in the final written "prophetic" document, we would go upstream in order to recognize more clearly the historical depths of "prophetic" transmissions. Who knows whether one day we may come to discover or reconstruct one or two authentic words of some historical prophetic figure? In the case of the Twelve it seems obvious that we hardly encounter any trustworthy information about the eponyms of those booklets that carry their names.

Are the psalmic passages, then, misplaced in the Book of the Twelve? I trust that this is not the case. On the contrary, the psalm-like parts are not inserts at all in the fourth collection of "prophetic" words. They are treasures of prayers and hymns all testifying to a vivid Israelite community life in Persian times; and they open our eyes as to the wondrous world of preaching, teaching, debating theology, which must have gone on in many congregations of Yahwists within the small province of Judah as well as in Diaspora situations abroad.

Bibliography

Abart, Christine. *Lebensfreude und Gottesjubel. Studien zu physisch erlebter Freude in den Psalmen.* WMANT 142. Neukirchen-Vluyn: Neukirchener Verlag, 2015.

Abusch, Tzvi I. *Corpus of Mesopotamian Anti-Witchcraft Rituals.* Ancient Magic and Divination 8. Leiden: Brill, 2010.

———. *The Magical Ceremony Maqlû: A Critical Edition.* Ancient Magic and Divination 10. Leiden: Brill, 2016.

Abros, Claus, et al., eds. *Die Welt der Rituale: Von der Antike bis heute.* Darmstadt: Wissenschaftliche Buchgesellschaft, 2005.

Ahlström, Gösta W. *Joel and the Temple Cult of Jerusalem.* Vetus Testamentum Supplements 21. Leiden: Brill, 1971.

Ahn, Gregor. *Religiöse Herrscherlegitimation im achamenidischen Iran.* Acta Iranica 31. Leiden: Brill, 1992.

Aitken, James K. *The Semantics of Blessing and Cursing in Ancient Hebrew.* Ancient Near Eastern Studies Supplements 223. Leuven: Peeters, 2007.

Albertz, Rainer. *Persönliche Frömmigkeit und offizielle Religion.* Calwer Theologische Monographien A9, Stuttgart: Calwer, 1978.

Alonso Schökel, Luis. *A Manual of Hebrew Poetics.* Subsidia Biblica 11. Rome: Pontificio Istituto Biblico, 1988.

Alster, Bendt. "Edin-na ú-sag-gá: Reconstruction, History, and Interpretation of a Sumerian Cultic Lament." In *Keilschriftliche Literaturen: Ausgewählte Vorträge der XXXII. Rencontre assyriologique internationale, Münster, 8.–12.7.1985,* edited by Karl Hecker and Walter Sommerfeld, 19–31. Berliner Beiträge zum Vorderen Orient 6. Berlin: Reimer, 1986.

———. "Inanna Repenting: The Conclusion of 'Inanna's Descent.'" *Acta Sumerologica* 18 (1996) 1–18.

———. "The Mythology of Mourning." *Acta Sumerologica* 5 (1983) 1–16.

Apffel-Marglin, Frédérique. *Subversive Spiritualities: How Rituals Enactced the World.* Oxford: Oxford University Press, 2011.

Arendt, Hannah. *Eichmann in Jerusalem: A Report on the Banality of Evil.* 1963. Reprint, New York: Penguin, 2006.

Arnold, Tina. "'Und ich will meine Hände erheben zu deinen Geboten' (Ps 119,48): Ungewöhnliche Aspekte eines Gebetsgestus." In *Ich will dir danken unter den Völkern: Studien zur israelitischen und altorientalischen Gebetsliteratur: Festschrift für Bernd Janowski zum 70. Geburtstag*, edited by Alexandra Grund-Wittenberg, 253–64. Gütersloh: Gütersloher Verlag, 2013.

Assmann, Jan. *Ägypten: Eine Sinngeschichte*. Darmstadt: Wissenschaftliche Buchgesellschaft, 1996.

Attinger, Pascal. *Éléments de linguistique sumeriénne: La construction de du11/e/di "dire."* OBO Sonderband. Göttingen: Vandenhoeck & Ruprecht, 1993.

Barney, Gerald O., ed. *Global 2000: The Report to the President—Entering the Twenty-first Century*. Rev. ed. Arlington, VA: Seven Locks, 1988.

Barth, Christoph. *Die Errettung vom Tode in den individuellen Klage- und Dankliedern des Alten Testaments*. 2nd ed. Edited by Bernd Janowski. Neukirchen-Vluyn: Neukirchener Verlag, 1997.

Becker, Uwe. *Jesaja: von der Botschaft zum Buch*. FRLANT 178. Göttingen: Vandenhoeck & Ruprecht, 1997

Bell, Catherine. *Ritual: Perspectives and Dimensions*. Oxford: Oxford University Press, 1997.

Bellinger, William H. *Psalmody and Prophecy*. JSOTSup 27. Sheffield: JSOT Press, 1984.

Ben Zvi, Ehud. *Micah*. FOTL 21B. Grand Rapids: Eerdmans, 2000.

Berg, Werner. *Die sogenannten Hymnenfragmente im Amosbuch*. Europäische Hochschulschriften, Reihe 23, Theologie 45. Frankfurt: Lang, 1974.

Berlin, Adele. "Poetry, Hebrew Bible." In *Dictionary of Biblical Interpretation*, edited by John H. Hayes, 2:290–96. 2 vols. Nashville: Abingdon, 1999.

Black, Jeremy. "A-se-er Gi$_6$-ta, a Balag of Inana." *Acta Sumerologica* 7 (1985) 11—87.

———. "Poesie/Poetry." In *Reallexikon der Assyriologie* 10:196. Berlin: de Gruyter, 2003–2005.

———. *Reading Sumerian Poetry*. Ithaca, NY: Cornell University Press, 1998.

Black, Jeremy, et al. *The Literature of Ancient Sumer*. New York: Oxford University Press, 2004.

Blenkinsopp, Joseph. *Geschichte der Prophetie in Israel: Von den Anfängen bis zum hellenistischen Zeitalter*. Translated by Erhard S. Gerstenberger. Stuttgart: Kohlhammer, 1998.

———. *A History of Prophecy in Israel*. 2nd ed. Louisville: Westminster John Knox, 1996.

———. *Sage, Priest, Prophet: Religious and Intellectual Leadership in Ancient Israel*. Library of Ancient Israel. Louisville: Westminster John Knox, 1995.

Botterweck, G. Johannes, Helmer Ringgren, and Heinz-Josef Fabray, eds. *Theological Dictionary of the Old Testament*. 17 vols. Grand Rapids: Eerdmans, 1974–2001.

———. *Theologisches Wörterbuch zum Alten Testament*. 8 vols. Stuttgart: Kohlhammer, 1973–1995.

Bowra, Maurice C. *Primitive Song*. Cleveland: World, 1962.

Boyce, Mary. *Under the Achaemenians*. History of Zorastrianism 2. Handbuch der Orientalistik. Leiden: Brill, 1982.

Brosius, Christiane et al., eds. *Ritual und Ritualdynamik: Schlüsselbegriffe, Theorien, Diskussionen*. Uni-Taschenbucher 3854. Göttingen: Vandenhoeck & Ruprecht, 2013.

Brueggemann, Walter. *Israel's Praise: Doxology against Idolatry and Ideology*. Philadelphia: Fortress, 1988.

Budde, Karl. "Zur Geschichte des Buches Amos." In *Studien zur semitischen Philologie und Religionsgeschichte: Julius Wellhausen zum 70. Geburtstag am 17. Mai 1914 gewidmet von Freunden und Schülern*, edited by Karl Marti, 63–77. BZAW 27. Gießen: Töpelmann, 1914.

Burkert, Walter, and Fritz Stolz, eds. *Hymnen der Alten Welt im Kulturvergleich*. OBO 131. Göttingen: Vandenhoeck & Ruprecht, 1991.

Câmara, Hélder. *Mach aus mir einen Regenbogen*. Zurich: Pendo, 1981.

Cambridge Ancient History. London: Cambridge University Press.

Cantos dos lavradores de Goiás. Goiânia: Centro de Reflexão e Documentação, 1979.

Cardenal, Ernesto. *Psalms*. Translated by Thomas Blackburn. New York: Crossroad, 1981.

———. *Salmos*. Buenos Aires: Lohle, 1969.

Carroll, Robert P. *Jeremiah: A Commentary*. OTL. Louisville: Westminster John Knox, 1989.

Casaldáliga, Pedro. *Creio na Justiça e na Esperança*. Rio de Janeiro: Civilização Brasileira, 1978.

Cohen, Mark E. *The Canonical Lamentations of Ancient Mesopotamia*. 2 vols. Potomac, MD: Capital Decisions, 1988.

———. *Sumerian Hymnology: The Ersemma*. Hebrew Union College Annual Supplements 2. Cincinnati: Hebrew Union College, 1981.

Conrad, Joachim. *TWAT* 5 (1987) 237–45. [*TDOT* 9 (1998).]

Crenshaw, James L. *Hymnic Affirmation of Divine Justice*. SBL Dissertation Series 24. Missoula, MT: Scholars, 1985.

Cross, Frank Moore, Jr., and David Noel Freedman. *Studies in Ancient Yahwistic Poetry*. SBL Dissertation Series 21. Missoula, MT: Scholars, 1975.

Crouch, Carly L. et al., eds. *Mediating Between Heaven and Earth*. Library of Hebrew Bible/Old Testament Studies 566. London: T. & T. Clark, 2012.

Crüsemann, Frank. *Studien zur Formgeschichte von Hymnus und Danklied in Israel*. WMANT 32. Neukirchen-Vluyn: Neukirchener Verlag, 1969.

Cunningham, Graham. *Deliver Me from Evil: Mesopotamian Incantations 2500–1500 B.C.* Studia Pohl: Series maior 17. Rome: Pontificium Institutum Biblicum, 1997.

Danby, Herbert. *The Mishnah*. Oxford: Clarendon, 1958.

Davies, Philip R. *Scribes and Schools: The Canonization of Hebrew Scriptures*. Library of Ancient Israel. Louisville: Westminster John Knox, 1998.

Deist, Ferdinand E. "The Prophets: Are We Heading for a Paradigm Switch?" In *Prophet und Prophetenbuch: Festschrift für Otto Kaiser zum 65. Geburtstag*, edited by Volkmar Fritz et al., 1–18. BZAW 185. Berlin: de Gruyter, 1989.

Dreves, Guido Maria, and Clemens Blume. *Analecta hymnica medii aevi*. 55 vols. Leipzig: Reisland, 1886–1922.

Droogers, André. *Play and Power in Religion: Collected Essays*. Religion and Reason. Berlin: de Gruyter, 2012.

Duhm, Bernhard. *Israels Propheten*. 2nd ed. Lebensfrage 26. Tübingen: Mohr Siebeck, 1922.

———. *Die Theologie der Propheten als Grundlage für die innere Entwicklungsgeschichte der israelitischen Religion*. Bonn: Marcus, 1875.

Ebeling, Erich et al., eds. *Reallexikon der Assyriologie und Vorderasiatischen Archäologie*. 15 vols. Berlin: de Gruyter, 1928–2018.

Edzard, Dietz O. "Königslisten und Chroniken. A. Sumerisch." *Reallexikon der Assyriologie und Vorderasiatischen Archäologie*, edited by Erich Ebeling et al., 6:77–86. Berlin: de Gruyter, 1980.

Elbogen, Ismar. *Der jüdische Gottesdienst in seiner geschichtlichen Entwicklung*. 1931. Reprint, Hildesheim: Olms, 1967.

The Electronic Text Corpus of Sumerian Literature. www.etcsl.orinst.ox.ac.uk.

Eisen, Ute E., and Erhard S. Gerstenberger, eds. *Hermann Gunkel Revisited: Literatur- und religionsgeschichtliche Studien*. Münster: Lit, 2010.

Eliade, Mircea. *Shamanism: Archaic Techniques of Ecstasy*. 1951. Reprint, Princeton: Princeton University Press, 2004.

Elliott, Dale E. "Toward a Grammar of Exclamatives." *Foundations of Language* 11 (1974) 231–46.

Eriksson, Lars Olov. "The Enemies in Psalm 119." In *Encountering Violence in the Bible*, edited by Markus Zehnder and Hagelia Hallvard, 68–78. Bible in the Modern World 55. Sheffield: Sheffield Phoenix, 2013.

Fabry, H.-J., and N. van Meeteren. *TWAT* 8 (1995) 547–54. [*TDOT* 15 (2006).]

Falkenstein, Adam. *Sumerische Götterlieder*. Abhandlungen der Heidelberger Akademie der Wissenschaften, Philosophisch-Historische Klasse; Jahrg. 1959, 1. Abhandlung. Heidelberg: Winter, 1959.

Farber-Flügge, Gertrud. *Der Mythos Inanna und Enki unter besonderer Berücksichtigung der Liste der me*. Studia Pohl 10. Rome: Biblical Institute Press, 1973.

Faris, James C. *The Nightway: A History and a History of Documentation of a Navajo Ceremonial*. Albuquerque: University of New Mexico Press, 1990.

Finsterbusch, Karin. *JHWH als Lehrer der Menschen: Ein Beitrag zur Gottesvorstellung der Hebräischen Bibel*. Biblisch-Theologische Studien 90. Neukirchen-Vluyn: Neukirchener Verlag, 2007.

———. "Yahweh's Torah and the Praying 'I' in Ps 119." In *Wisdom and Torah: The Reception of Torah in the Wisdom Literature of the Second Temple Period*, edited by Bernd U. Schipper and D. Andrew Teeter, 119–35. Journal for the Study of Judaism Supplements 163. Leiden: Brill, 2013.

Fischer, Stefan. "Ewigkeit." wibilex Bibelwissenschaft, 2014.

———. "Frömmigkeit." wibilex Bibelwissenschaft, 2018.

Floyd, Michael H. *Minor Prophets*. FOTL 22. Grand Rapids: Eerdmans, 2000.

Flückiger-Hawker, Esther. *Urnamma of Ur in Sumerian Literary Tradition*. OBO 166. Göttingen: Vandenhoeck & Ruprecht, 1999.

Fohrer, Georg. *Glaube und Leben im Judentum*. Uni-Taschenbücher 885. Heidelberg: Quelle & Meyer, 1979.

Fortune, Richard F. *Sorcerers of Dobu: The Social Anthropology of the Dobu Islanders of the Western Pacific*. 1932. Reprint, New York: Dutton, 1963.

Foster, Benjamin R. *Before the Muses. An Anthology of Akkadian Literature*. 2 vols., Bethesda: CDL Press, 2nd ed. 1996; 3rd enlarged ed. in 1 vol., 2005.

Franciscan Fathers. *An Ethnologic Dictionary of the Navaho Language*. 1910. Reprint, Leipzig: Breslauer, 1929.

Frechette, Christopher. *Mesopotamian Ritual Prayers (Šuillas): A Case Study Investigating Idiom, Rubric, Form, and Function*. AOAT 379. Ugarit-Verlag, 2012.

Freire, Paulo. *Pedagogia do oprimido*. Rio de Janeiro: Paz e Terra, 1976.

———. *Pedagogy of the Oppressed*. Translated by Myra Bergman Ramos. New York: Herder & Herder, 1970.

Fritz, Volkmar. "Tempel II: Alter Orient und Altes Testament." In *Theologische Realenzyklopädie*, edited by Gerhard Krause and Gerhard Müller, 33:46–54. Berlin: de Gruyter, 2002.

Futterknecht, Veronika, et al., eds. *Heilung in den Religionen: Religiöse, spirituelle und leibliche Dimensionen*. Schriftenreihe der Österreichischen Gesellschaft für Religionswissenschaft 5. Vienna: Lit, 2013.

García López, Félix. "torah." In *TWAT* 8 (1995) 597–637. [*TDOT* 15 (2006)].

Gärtner, Judith. *Die Geschichtspsalmen: Eine Studie zu den Psalmen 78, 105, 106, 135 und 136 als hermeneutische Schlüsseltexte im Psalter*. Forschungen zum Alten Testament 84. Tübingen: Mohr Siebeck, 2012.

George, Andrew R. "'Bond of the Lands': Babylon, the Cosmic Capital." In *Die Orientalische Stadt*, edited by Gernot Wilhelm, 125–45. Colloquien der Deutschen Orient-Gesellschaft 1. Saarbrücken: SDV, 1997.

Gerstenberger, Erhard S. *Der bittende Mensch. Bittritual und Klagelied des Einzelnen im Alten Testament*. WMANT 51. Neukirchen-Vluyn: Neukirchener Verlag, 1980. Reprint, Eugene, OR: Wipf and Stock, 2009.

———. *Charting the Course of Psalms Research: Essays on the Psalms*, vol. 1. Edited by K. C. Hanson. Eugene, OR: Cascade Books, 2022.

———. "Enemies and Evildoers in the Psalms." *Horizons in Biblical Theology* 4/5 (1982–83) 61–77. [Chapter 8 in this volume.]

———. "Höre, mein Volk, laß mich reden! (Ps 50,7)." *Bibel und Kirche* 56 (2001) 21–25.

———. "Der Hymnus der Befreiung im Zefanjabuch." In *Der Tag wird kommen*, edited by Walter Dietrich et al., 102–12. Stuttgart Biblische Studien 170. Stuttgart: Katholisches Bibelwerk, 1996.

———. *Israel in the Persian Period: The Fifth and Fourth Centuries B.C.E.* Translated by Siegfried S. Schatzmann. Biblical Encyclopedia 8. Atlanta: Society of Biblical Literature, 2011.

———. *Leviticus: A Commentary*. OTL. Louisville: Westminster John Knox, 1996.

———. "Navajo Chants, Babylonian Incantations, Old Testament Psalms: A Comparative Study of Healing Rituals." *Intégrité* 17.1 (2018) 16–35. [Chapter 6 in this volume.]

———. "The Power of Praise in the Psalter." In *Between Israelite Religion and Old Testament Theology*, edited by Robert D. Miller II. Leuven: Peeters, 2016. [Chapter 2 in this volume.]

———. *Praise and Petition in the Old Testament: Essays on the Psalms*, vol. 2. Edited by K. C. Hanson. Eugene, OR: Cascade Books, 2024.

———. "Praise in the Realm of Death: The Dynamics of Hymn-Singing in Ancient Near Eastern Lament Ceremony." In *Lamentations in Ancient and Contemporary Cultural Contexts*, edited by Nancy C. Lee et al., 115–24. SBL Symposium 43. Atlanta: Society of Biblical Literature, 2008. [Chapter 3 in this volume.]

———. "Psalm 12: Gott hilft den Unterdrückten: Zum Thema Kultprophetie und soziale Gerechtigkeit in Israel." In *Anwalt des Menschen: Beiträge aus Theologie und Religionspädagogik: Zum Gedenken an Prof. Dr. Friedrich Hahn*, edited by Bernhard Jendorff und Gerhard Schmalenberg, 83–104. Gießener Schriften zur Theologie und Religionspädagogik des Fachbereichs Religionswissenschaften der

Justus-Liebig Universität 2. Gießen: Religionswissenschaften der Justus-Liebig Universität, 1983.

———. *Psalms, Part 1: With an Introduction to Cultic Poetry*. Forms of the Old Testament Literature 14. Grand Rapids: Eerdmans, 1988.

———. *Psalms, Part 2, and Lamentations*. Forms of the Old Testament Literature 15. Grand Rapids: Eerdmans, 2001.

———. *Theologie des Lobens in sumerischen Hymnen*. Orientalische Religionen in der Antike 28. Tübingen: Mohr Siebeck, 2018.

———. *Theologien im Alten Testament: Pluralität und Synkretismus alttestamentlichen Gottesglaubens*. Stuttgart: Kohlhammer, 2001.

———. *Theologies in the Old Testament*. Translated by John Bowden. Minneapolis: Fortress, 2002.

———. *Yahweh the Patriarch: Ancient Images of God and Feminist Theology*. Translated by Frederick J. Gaiser. 1996. Reprint, Eugene, OR: Wipf & Stock, 2021.

Gerstenberger, Erhard S., and Wolfgang Schrage. *Suffering*. Translated by John E. Steely. Biblical Encounter Series. Nashville: Abingdon, 1986.

Goetze, Albrecht. *Kleinasien*. Handbuch der Altertumswissenschaft. Munich: Beck, 1957.

Gosse, Bernhard. *Isaie 13,1—14,23 dans la tradition littéraire du livre d' Isaïe et dans la tradition des oracles contre les nations*. OBO 78. Göttingen: Vandenhoeck & Ruprecht, 1988.

Grayson, A. Kirk. *Assyrian Rulers of the Third and Second Millenia (to 1115 B.C.) and the Early First Millenium (1114-859 B.C.)*. Royal Inscriptions of Mesopotamia: Assyrian Periods vol. 2, 13. Toronto: University of Toronto Press, 1991.

Greenberg, Henry, and Georgia Greenberg. *Power of a Navajo—Carl Gorman: The Man and His Life*. Santa Fe, NM: Clear Light, 1996.

Grimes, Ronald L. *The Craft of Ritual Studies*. New York: Oxford University Press, 2014.

Groneberg, Brigitte R. M. *Syntax, Morphologie, und Stil der jungbabylonischen "hymnischen" Literatur*. 2 vols. Freiburger altorientalische Studien 14. Stuttgart: Steiner, 1987.

Grund-Wittenberg, Alexandra. *"Die Himmel erzählen die Ehre Gottes": Psalm 19 im Kontext der nachexilischen Torahweisheit*. WMANT 103. Göttingen: Vandenhoeck & Ruprecht, 2004.

Gunkel, Hermann. "The Close of Micah." In *What Remains of the Old Testament: And Other Essays*, 115–50. Translated by A. K. Dallas. New York: Macmillan, 1928.

———. "Der Micha-Schluss: Zur Einführung in die literaturgeschichtliche Arbeit am Alten Testament." *Zeitschrift für Semitistik* 2 (1924) 145–78.

Gunkel, Hermann, and Joachim Begrich. *Einleitung in die Psalmen: Die Gattungen der religiösen Lyrik Israels*. Handkommentar zum Alten Testament Supplements. Göttingen: Vandenhoeck & Ruprecht, 1933.

———. *Introduction to Psalms: The Genres of the Religious Lyric of Israel*. Translated by James D. Nogalski. 1998. Reprint, Eugene, OR: Wipf & Stock, 2020.

Haile, Berard. *Waterway: A Navajo Ceremonial Myth*. 1932. Reprint, American Tribal Religions 5. Flagstaff, NM: Museum of Northern Arizona Press, 1979.

Hallo, William W., ed. *The Context of Scripture*. Vol. 1: *Canonical Compositions from the Biblical World*. Leiden: Brill, 1997.

———. *The Context of Scripture*. Vol. 2: *Monumental Inscriptions from the Biblical World*. Leiden: Brill, 2001.

———. *The Context of Scripture.* Vol. 3: *Archival Documents from the Biblical World.* Leiden: Brill, 2002.

———. *Early Mesopotamian Royal Titles.* American Oriental Series 43. New Haven: Yale University Press, 1953.

———. *Origins: The Ancient Near Eastern Background of Some Modern Western Institutions.* Studies in the History of the Ancient Near East 6. Leiden: Brill, 1996.

Hallo, William W., and Johannes J. A. van Dijk. *The Exaltation of Inanna.* Yale Near Eastern Researches 3. New Haven: Yale University Press, 1968.

HarperCollins Study Bible: New Revised Standard Version, with the Apocryphal/ Deuterocanonical Books. New York: Harper, 1993.

Hartenstein, Friedhelm. *Die Unzugänglichkeit Gottes* im *Heiligtum: Jesaja 6 und der Wohnort JHWHs in der Jerusalemer Kulttradition.* WMANT 75. Neukirchen-Vluyn: Neukirchener Verlag, 1997.

Hayes, John H. "Prophecy and Prophets, Hebrew Bible." In *Dictionary of Biblical Interpretation,* edited by John H. Hayes, 2:310–17. 2 vols. Nashville: Abingdon, 1999.

Heeßel, Nils. *Babylonisch-assyrische Diagnostik.* AOAT 43. Münster: Ugarit-Verlag, 2000.

Heiler, Friedrich. *Das Gebet: Eine religionsgeschichtliche und religionspsychologische Untersuchung.* 1919. Reprint, Munich: Reinhart, 1969.

Heschel, Abraham Joshua. *Heavenly Torah: As Refracted Through the Generations.* Translated and edited with commentary by Gordon Tucker with Leonard Levin. New York: Continuum, 2005.

Hieke, Thomas. "Esra." In wibilex Bibelwissenschaft, 2005.

Höffken, Peter. "Untersuchungen zu den Begründungselementen der Völkerorakel des Alten Testaments." PhD diss., University of Bonn, 1977.

Hoffman, Rodolfo. "Desigualdade e Pobreza no Brasil no Período de 1979–1990." *Revista Brasileira de Economia* 49.2 (1995) 277–94.

Horst, Friedrich. "Die Doxologien im Amosbuch." *ZAW* 47 (1929) 45–54.

Horst, Friedrich, and Theodor H. Robinson. *Die Zwölf kleinen Propheten: Hosea bis Maleachi.* Handbuch zum Alten Testament 1/14. Tübingen: Mohr Siebeck, 1954.

Hossfeld, Frank-Lothar, and H. Lamberty-Zielinski. "*qr*." In *TWAT* 7 (1993) 133–36. [*TDOT* 12 (2004).]

Hossfeld, Frank-Lothar, and E. Reuter. "*seper*." In *TWAT* 5 (1987) 932–44. [*TDOT* 8 (1996).]

Hossfeld, Frank-Lothar, and Erich Zenger. *Psalmen 51–100.* Herders Theologischer Kommentar zum Alten Testament. Freiburg: Herder, 2000.

———. *Psalms 2: A Commentary on Psalms 51–100.* Translated by Linda M. Maloney. Hermeneia. Minneapolis: Fortress,

Hultkrantz, Åke. *Shamanic Healing and Ritual Drama: Health and Medicine in Native North American Religious Traditions.* Health/Medicine and the Faith Traditions. New York: Crossroad, 1992.

Insoll, Timothy, ed. *Oxford Handbook of the Archaeology of Ritual and Religion.* Oxford University Press, 2011.

Jacobsen, Thorkild. *The Harps that Once . . . : Sumerian Poetry in Translation.* New Haven: Yale University Press, 1997.

———. *The Sumerian King List.* Assyriological Studies 11. Chicago: University of Chicago Press, 1939.

Janowski, Bernd. "Freude an der Tora. Psalm 1 als Tor zum Psalter." *Evangelische Theologie* 67 (2007) 18–31.
Jeremias, Jörg. *Kultprophetie und Gerichtsverkündigung*. WMANT 35. Neukirchen-Vluyn: Neukirchener Verlag, 1970.
———. *Der Prophet Hosea*. Das Alte Testament Deutsch 24/1. Göttingen: Vandenhoeck & Ruprecht, 1983.
Johnson, A. R. *The Cultic Prophet and Israel's Psalmody*. Cardiff: University of Wales Press, 1979.
Kaiser, Otto. *Das Buch des Propheten Jesaja Kapitel 1–12*. Alte Testament Deutsch 17. Göttingen: Vandenhoeck & Ruprecht, 1963.
———. *Isaiah 1–12: A Commentary*. 2nd ed. Translated by John Bowden. Old Testament Library. Philadelphia: Westminster, 1983.
Kamlah, Jens, Rolf Schäfer, and Markus Witte. *Zauber und Magie im Alten Palästinas und in seiner Umwelt: Kolloquium des Deutschen Vereins zur Erforschung Palästinas vom 14. bis 16. November 2014 in Mainz*. Abhandlungen des Deutschen Palästina-Vereins 46. Wiesbaden: Harrassowitz, 2017.
Keel, Othmar. *Feinde und Gottesleugner: Studien zum Image der Widersacher in den Individualpsalmen*. Stuttgarter biblische Monographien 7. Stuttgart: Katholisches Bibelwerk, 1969.
Kehoe, Alice B. *Shamans and Religion: An Anthropological Exploration in Critical Thinking*. Prospect Heights, IL: Waveland, 2000.
Kessler, Rainer. *Micha*. Herders Theologischer Kommentar zum Alten Testament. Freiburg: Herder, 1999.
Klein, Jacob. *Three Šulgi Hymns: Sumerian Royal Hymns Glorifying King Šulgi of Ur*. Bar-Ilan Studies in Near Eastern Languages and Culture. Ramat-Gan: Bar-Ilan University Press, 1981.
Kluckhohn, Clyde, and Leland Wyman. *Introduction to Navajo Chant Practice*. 1940. Memoirs of the American Anthropological Association 53. Iola, WI: Kraus, 1969.
Koch, Edward Emil. *Geschichte des Kirchenleids und Kirchengesangs*. 8 vols. 3rd ed. Stuttgart: Belser, 1866–76.
Koch, Heidemarie. *Es kündet Dareios der König . . . : Vom Leben im persischen Großreich*. Kulturgeschichte der Antiken Welt 55. Mainz: von Zabern, 1992.
Koch, Klaus. "Gibt es ein Vergeltungsdogma im Alten Testament?" *Zeitschrift für Theologie und Kirche* 52 (1955) 1–42.
———. "Is There a Doctrine of Retribution in the Old Testament?" In *Theodicy in the Old Testament*, edited by James L. Crenshaw, 57–87. Issues in Religion and Theology. Philadelphia: Fortress, 1983.
———. "Propheten/Prophetie II. In Israel und seiner Umwelt." In *Theologische Realenzyklopädie*, edited by Gerhard Krause and Gerhard Müller, 27:477–99. Berlin: de Gruyter, 1997.
———. "Die Rolle der hymnischen Abschnitte in der Komposition des Amosbuches." *ZAW* 86 (1974) 504–37.
Kramer, Samuel N. "Lamentation over the Destruction of Nipur." *Acta Sumerologica* 13 (1991) 1–26.
———. *Two Elegies on a Pushkin Museum Tablet: A New Sumerian Literary Genre*. Moscow: Izd-vo vostochnoi lit-ry, 1960.
Laato, Antti, ed. *The Challenge of the Mosaic Torah in Judaism, Christianity and Islam*. Studies on the Children of Abraham 7. Leiden: Brill, 2020.

Lang, Bernhard. *Ezechiel: Der Prophet und das Buch*. Darmstadt: Wissenschaftliche Buchgesellschaft, 1981.
Larsen, Mogens Trolle. "The Tradition of Empire in Mesopotamia." In *Power and Propaganda*, edited by Mogens Trolle Larsen, 75–103. Mesopotamia 7. Copenhagen: Akademisk Forlag, 1979.
Lenzi, Alan, ed. *Reading Akkadian Hymns and Prayers*. Ancient Near East Monographs 3. Atlanta: Society of Biblical Literature, 2011.
Leuenberger, Martin. *Segen und Segenstheologien im alten Israel*. Abhandlungen zur Theologie des Alten und Neuen Testaments 90. Zurich: Theologischer Verlag Zurich, 2008.
Loretz, Oswald. *Regenritual und Jahwetag im Joelbuch*. Ugaritisch-biblische Literatur 4. Altenberge: CIS-Verlag, 1986.
Luckert, Karl W. *Navajo Mountain and Rainbow Bridge Religion*. American Tribal Religions 1. Flagstaff: Museum of Northern Arizona Press, 1977.
Ludwig, Marie-Christine. *Untersuchungen zu den Hymnen des Išme-Dagan von Isin*. Santag 2. Wiesbaden: Harrassowitz, 1990.
Lust, Johan, ed. *Ezekiel and His Book: Textual and Literary Criticism and Their Interrelation*. Bibliotheca Ephemeridum theologicarum Lovaniensium 74. Leuven: Peeters, 1986.
MacDonald, Nathan, ed. *Ritual Innovation in the Hebrew Bible and Early Judaism*. BZAW 468. Berlin: de Gruyter, 2016.
Maier, Johann. "Zur Verwendung der Psalmen in der synagogalen Liturgie (Wochentag und Sabbat)." In *Liturgie und Dichtung: Ein interdisziplinäres Kompendium*, edited by H. Becker and R. Kaczynski, 55–90. Pietas Liturgica. St. Ottilien: Eos, 1983.
Matthews, Washington. *The Night Chant: A Navaho Ceremony*. Memoirs of the American Museum of Natural History 6. Anthropology 5. 1902. Reprint, edited by John Farella. Salt Lake City: University of Utah Press, 1995.
Maul, Stefan. "Die altorientalische Hauptstadt—Abbild und Nabel der Welt." In *Die Orientalische Stadt*, edited by Gernot Wilhelm, 109–24. Colloquien der Deutschen Orient-Gesellschaft 1. Saarbrücken: SDV, 1997.
———. *"Herzberuhigungsklagen": Die sumerisch-akkadischen Eršaḫunga-Gebete*. Wiesbaden: Harrassowitz, 1988.
———. *Zukunftsbewältigung: Eine Untersuchung altorientalischen Denkens anhand der babylonisch-assyrischen Löserituale (Namburbi)*. Baghdader Forschungen 18. Mainz: Zabern, 1994.
Meinhold, Wiebke. *Ritualbeschreibungen und Gebete*. 2 vols. Wissenschaftliche Veröffentlichungen der Deutschen Orient-Gesellschaft. Wiesbaden: Harrassowitz, 2017.
Michalowski, Piotr. "Ancient Poetics." In *Mesopotamian Poetic Language*, edited by Marianna E. Vogelzang and Herman L. J. Vanstiphout, 141–53. Groningen: Styx, 1996.
———. *The Lamentation over the Destruction of Sumer and Ur*. Winona Lake, IN: Eisenbrauns, 1989.
Miller, Patrick D. "The Theological Significance of Poetry." In *Language, Theology, and the Bible: Essays in Honor of James Barr*, edited by Samuel B. Balentine and John Barton, 225–30. Oxford: Clarendon, 1994.
———. *They Cried to the Lord. The Form and Theology of Biblical Prayer*. Minneapolis: Fortress, 1994.

Miller, Robert D. "Iron Age Medicine Men and Old Testament Theology." In *Between Israelite Religion and Old Testament Theology: Essays on Archaeology, History, and Hermeneutics*, edited by Robert D. Miller II, 87–128. Contributions to Biblical Exegesis and Theology 80. Leuven: Peeters, 2016.

Mowinckel, Sigmund. "Cultic Prophecy and Prophetic Psalms." In *Psalm Studies*, 2:495–598. 2 vols. Translated by Mark Biddle. History of Biblical Studies 2–3. Atlanta: Society of Biblical Literature, 2014.

———. *He That Cometh: The Messiah Concept in the Old Testament and Later Judaism*. Translated by G. W. Anderson. 1955. Reprint, Grand Rapids: Eerdmans, 2005.

———. *Psalm Studies*. 2 vols. Translated by Mark Biddle. History of Biblical Studies 2–3. Atlanta: Society of Biblical Literature Press, 2014.

———. *Psalmenstudien III: Kultprophetie und prophetische Psalmen*. Oslo: Kristiania, 1923. Reprint, Amsterdam: Schippers, 1961.

———. *The Psalms in Israel's Worship*. Translated by D. R. Ap-Thomas. 2 vols in 1. 1962. Reprint, Grand Rapids: Eerdmans, 2004.

Näser-Lather, Marion. *Beten, Büßen, Befreien: Das Zwangspotenzial religiöser Rituale*. Wissenschaftliche Beiträge aus dem Tectum Verlag: Religionswissenschaften. Baden-Baden: Tectum Wissenschaftsverlag, 2011.

Nicholson, Ernest W. *Preaching to the Exiles: A Study of the Prose Tradition in the Book of Jeremiah*. Oxford: Blackwell, 1970.

Nicholson, Shirley, ed. *Shamanism: An Expanded View of Reality*. Wheaton, IL: Theosophical Society, 1987.

Niebuhr, Reinhold. *Moral Man and Immoral Society*. New York: Scribner, 1932.

Nogalski, James D. *Redactional Processes in the Book of the Twelve*. BZAW 218. Berlin: de Gruyter, 1993.

North, Robert. *TWAT*, 2:775.

Nos lavradores unidos, Senhor. São Paulo: Loyola, 1980.

Oswald, Wolfgang. "Tora." In wibilex Bibelwissenschaft 2016.

Otto, Eckart, and Tim Schramm. *Fest und Freude*. Kohlhammer-Taschenbücher 1003. Stuttgart: Kohlhammer, 1977.

Podella, Thomas. *Das Lichtkleid JHWHs: Untersuchungen zur Gestalthaftigkeit Gottes im Alten Testament und seiner altorientalischen Umwelt*. Forschungen zum Alten Testament 15. Tübingen: Mohr Siebeck, 1996.

Pohlmann, Karl-Friedrich. *Die Ferne Gottes*. BZAW 179. Berlin: de Gruyter, 1989.

Pongratz-Leisten, Beate. "Akitu." In *The Encyclopedia of Ancient History*. Edited by Roger S. Bagnall et al. 13 vols. Oxford: Oxford University Press, 2012.

Postgate, J. N. *Early Mesopotamia: Society and Economy at the Dawn of History*. Rev. ed. London: Routledge, 1994.

Preuß, Horst-Dieter. "le'im." *TWAT* 4 (1984) 412–13. [*TDOT* 8 (1996).]

———. "'olam." In *TWAT* 6 (1989) 1144–59. [*TDOT* 10 (2000).]

Rad, Gerhard von. *Old Testament Theology*. Vol. 1: *Theology of the Historical Traditions*. Translated by D. M. G. Stalker. New York: Harper, 1962.

———. *Theologie des Alten Testaments*. Vol. 1: *Die Theologie der geschichtlichen Überlieferungen Israels*. Munich: Kaiser, 1957.

Rambach, August J. *Anthologie christlicher Gesänge*, 6 vols. Leipzig: Hammerich, 1817–1833.

Reichard, Gladys A. *Prayer: The Compulsive Word*. Monographs of the American Ethnological Society 7. New York: Augustin, 1944.

———. *Navajo Religion: A Study of Symbolism*. 1950. Princeton: Princeton University Press, 1990.
Reiner, Erica. *Šurpu: A Collection of Sumerian and Akkadian Incantations*. Archiv für Orientforschung Beiheft 11. 1958. Reprint, Bissendorf: Biblio-Verlag, 1970.
Reiser, Antonio, and Paul G. Schoenborn. *Sehnsucht nach dem Fest der freien Menschen: Gebete aus Lateinamerika*. Wuppertal: Jugenddienst, 1982.
Renner, Erich. *Navajo: Der Pfad der Harmonie und Schönheit*. Hamburg: Persimplex, 2011.
Reventlow, Hennig Graf. *Liturgie und prophetisches Ich bei Jeremia*. Gütersloh: Gütersloher Verlag, 1963.
Reynolds, Kent A. "Torah as Teacher." In *The Exemplary Torah Student in Psalm 119*, 126–28. Vetus Testamentum Supplements 137. Leiden: Brill, 2010.
Richter, Horst-Eberhard. *Der Gotteskomplex: Die Geburt und die Krise des Glaubens an die Allmacht des Menschen*. Hamburg: Rowolt, 1979.
Ringgren, Helmer. "*hll* I und II." In *TWAT* 2 (1977) 433–41. [*TDOT* 4 (1980).]
Robinson, H. Wheeler. "The Hebrew Concept of Corporate Personality." In *Werden und Wesen des Alten Testaments: Vorträge gehalten auf der Internationalen Tagung Alttestamentlicher Forscher zu Göttingen vom 4.-10. September 1935*, edited by Paul Volz et al., 49–62. BZAW 66. Berlin: Töpelmann, 1936.
Römer, Willem H. Ph. *Hymnen und Klagelieder in sumerischer Sprache*. AOAT 276. Münster: Ugarit-Verlag, 2001.
———. *Die Klage über die Zerstörung von Ur*. AOAT 309. Münster: Ugarit-Verlag, 2004.
Root, Margaret E. *The King and Kingship* in *Achaemenid Art*. Acta Iranica 19. Leiden: Brill, 1979.
Rosengren, Inger. "Zur Grammatik und Pragmatik der Exklamation." In *Satz und Illokution*, edited by Inger Rosengren, 1:263–306. Linguistische Arbeiten 278. Tübingen: Niemeyer, 1992.
Rottzoll, Dirk U. *Studien zur Redaktion und Komposition des Amosbuches*. BZAW 243. Berlin: de Gruyter, 1996.
Rudolph, Wilhelm. *Micha, Nahum, Habakkuk, Zephanja*. Kommentar zum Alten Testament XIII/3. Gütersloh: Gütersloher Verlag, 1975.
Ruffing, Andreas. *Jahwekrieg als Weltmetapher*. Stuttgarter biblische Beiträge 24. Stuttgart: Katholisches Bibelwerk, 1992.
Sallaberger, Walter. "Ur III-Zeit." In *Mesopotamien*, edited by Pascal Attinger and Markus Wafler, 119–390. OBO 160/3. Göttingen: Vandenhoeck & Ruprecht, 1998.
Sasson, Jack M., ed. *Civilizations of the Ancient Near East*. 4 vols. 1995. Reprint, Peabody, MA: Hendrickson, 2000.
Scharbert, Joseph. "Das 'Wir' der Psalmen auf dem Hintergrund altorientalischen Betens." In *Freude an der Weisung des Herrn*, edited by Ernst Haag and Frank-Lothar Hossfeld, 297–324. Stuttgarter biblische Beiträge 13. Stuttgart: Katholisches Bibelwerk, 1986.
Schart, Aaron. *Die Entstehung des Zwölfprophetenbuches*. BZAW 260. Berlin: de Gruyter, 1998.
Schmidt, Werner H. "Die deuteronomistische Redaktion des Amosbuches." *ZAW* 77 (1965) 168–93.
Schottroff, Luisa, and Wolfgang Stegemann. *Jesus von Nazareth: Hoffnung der Armen*. Stuttgart: Kohlhammer, 1978.

---. *Jesus and the Hope of the Poor*. Translated by Matthew J. O'Connell. Maryknoll, NY: Orbis, 1986.
Schwemer, Daniel. *The Anti-Witchcraft Ritual Maqlû: Cuneiform Sources of a Magic Ceremony from Ancient Mesopotamia*. Wiesbaden: Harassowitz, 2017.
Seybold, Klaus. *Das Gebet des Kranken im Alten Testament*. Beiträge zur Wissenschaft vom Alten und Neuen Testament 99. Stuttgart: Kohlhammer, 1973.
---. *Krankheit und Heilung*. Kohlhammer-Taschenbücher 1008. Stuttgart: Kohlhammer, 1978.
---. "Das 'Wir' in den Asaph-Psalmen." In *Neue Wege in der Psalmenforschung: Für Walter Beyerlin*, edited by Klaus Seybold et al., 143–55. Freiburg: Herder, 1994.
Sladek, William R. "Inanna's Descent to the Netherworld." PhD diss., Johns Hopkins University, 1974.
Sommer, Benjamin D. "The Babylonian Akitu-Festival: Rectifying the King or Renewing the Cosmos?" *Journal of the Ancient Near Eastern Society* 27 (2000) 81–96.
Spencer, Katherine. *Mythology and Values: An Analysis of Navaho Chantway Myths*. 1957. American Folklore Society, 1971.
Spickard, James V. "Experiencing Religious Rituals: A Schutzian Analysis of Navajo Ceremonies." *Sociological Analysis* 52 (1991) 191–204. www.inspire.redlands.edu.
Staubli, Thomas, and Silvia Schroer. *Menschenbilder der Bibel*. Ostfildern: Patmos, 2014.
Steck, Odil Hannes. *Friedensvorstellungen im Alten Jerusalem: Psalmen, Jesaja, Deuterojesaja*. Theologische Studien 111. Zurich: Theologischer Verlag, 1972
Steiner, Gerd. "Altorientalische Reichvorstellungen im 3. Jahrtausend." In *Power and Propaganda: A Symposium on Ancient Empires*, edited by Mogens Trolle Larsen. Mesopotamia 7. Copenhagen: Akademisk Forlag, 1979.
Stemberger, Günter. "Talmud." In wibilex, Bibelwissenschaft, 2015.
Stewart, Pamela J., and Andrew J. Strathern, eds. "The Efficacy of Rituals." *Journal of Ritual Studies* (Special Issues) 24.1 and 2 (2010).
Stolz, Fritz. *Strukturen und Figuren im Kult von Jerusalem: Studien zur altorientalischen, vor- und frühisraelitischen Religion*. BZAW 118. Berlin: de Gruyter, 1970.
Strack, Hermann L. *Einleitung in Talmud und Midrasch*. 1920. Reprint, Munich: Beck, 1961.
Strack, Hermann L., and Günter Stemberger. *Introduction to the Talmud and Midrash*. Translated by Marcus Bockmuehl. Minneapolis: Fortress, 1992.
Sweeney, Marvin A. *Isaiah 1–39*. FOTL 16. Grand Rapids: Eerdmans, 1996.
Sznaider, Natan. "Das moralische Gefühl." *Frankfurter Rundschau* 262 (November 10, 2010) 32.
Tătăran, Alexandra. *Contemporary Life and Witchcraft: Magic, Divination and Religious Ritual in Europe*. Stuttgart: Ibidem-Verlag, 2016.
Thiel, Winfried. *Die deuteronomistische Redaktion von Jer 1–25: von Jer 26–45*. WMANT 41 and 51. Neukirchen-Vluyn: Neukirchener Verlag, 1973, 1981.
Thureau-Dangin, F. *Die sumerischen und akkadischen Königsinschriften*. Vorderasiatische Bibliothek 1. Leipzig: Hinrichs, 1907.
Tinney, Steve. *The Nippur Lament*. Occasional Publications of the S. N. Kramer Fund 16. Philadelphia: University of Pennsylvania Museum, 1996.
Tomášková, Silvia. *Wayward Shamans: The Prehistory of an Idea*. San Francisco: University of California Press, 2013.
Toorn, Karel van der, et al., eds. *Dictionary of Deities and Demons in the Bible*. 2nd ed. Leiden: Brill, 1999.

Turner, Edith. *The Hands Feel It: Healing and Spirit Presence among the Northern Alaskan People*. DeKalb: Northern Illinois University Press, 1996.
Underhill, Ruth M. *Red Man's Religion: Beliefs and Practices of the Indians North of Mexico*. Chicago: University of Chicago Press, 1965.
Vanoni, Gottfried. "*smḥ*." In *TWAT* 7 (1993) 808–22. [*TDOT* 14 (2004).]
Vogelzang, Marianna E., and Herman L. J. Vanstiphout, eds. *Mesopotamian Poetic Language: Sumerian and Akkadian: Proceedings of the Groningen Group for the Study of Mesopotamian Literature*, vol. 2. CM 6. Groningen: Styx, 1996.
Volk, Konrad. *Die Balag-Komposition Uru Am-ma-ir-ra-bi*. Freiburger altorientalistische Studien 18. Stuttgart: Steiner, 1989.
Vorpahl, Jenny. "Sukkot." In wibilex Bibelwissenschaft, 2015.
Vries, Simon Philip de. *Jüdische Riten und Symbole*. Wiesbaden: Fourier, 1982.
Wackernagel, Philipp. *Das deutsche Kirchenlied von der ältesten Zeit bis zu Anfang des 17. Jahrhunderts*. 5 vols. Leipzig: Teubner, 1864–1877.
Wagner, Andreas. *Emotionen, Gefühle und Sprache im Alten Testament*. Kleine Untersuchungen zur Sprache des Alten Testaments und seiner Umwelt 7. Waltrop: Spenner, 2006.
Waldow, Eberhard von. "Anlass und Hintergrund der Verkündigung des Deuterojesaja." PhD diss., University of Bonn 1953.
Watts, John W. *Psalm and Story*. JSOTSup 139. Sheffield: Sheffield Academic, 1992.
Weber, Beat. "Meint *die Tora JHWHs* in Ps 1,2 (auch) den Psalter?" *Biblische Notizen* 178 (2018) 75–102.
———. "Von der Beherzigung der Tora JHWHs (Ps 1,2) zur Darbringung der Tehilla JHWHs (Ps 145,21)." In *Zur Theologie des Psalters und der Psalmen: Beiträge in Memoriam Frank-Lothar Hossfeld*, edited by Ulrich Berges, et al., 16–43. Bonner Biblische Beiträge 189. Göttingen: V&R Unipress, 2019.
Webster, Anthony K. "Keeping the Word: On Orality and Literacy (With a Sideways Glance at Navajo)." *Oral Tradition* 21 (2006) 295–324.
Weippert, Manfred. "'Heiliger Krieg' in Israel und Assyrien." *ZAW* 84 (1972) 460–93.
Wendt, Herbert, and Norbert Loacker, eds. *Kindlers Enzyklopädie: Der Mensch*. 10 vols. Zurich: Kindler, 1981–1985.
Westermann, Claus. *Praise and Lament in the Psalms*. Translated by Keith R. Crim and Richard N. Soulen. Atlanta: John Knox, 1981.
———. *The Praise of God in the Psalms*. Translated by Keith R. Crim. Richmond, VA: John Knox, 1965.
Wick, John W. "An Analysis of the Shamanistic Healing Practices of the Navajo through Mircea Eliade's Theories of Time, Space and Ritual." BA thesis, Trinity College, 2013. https://www.jstor.org/stable/community.34030904.
Widengren, Geo. *Die Religionen Irans*. Die Religionen der Menshheit 14. Stuttgart: Kohlhammer, 1965.
Wilcke, Claus. "Formale Gesichtspunkte in der sumerischen Literatur." In *Sumerological Studies in Honour of Thorkild Jacobsen*, edited by Stephen J. Lieberman, 205–316. Acta Sumerologica 20. Chicago: University of Chicago Press, 1974.
Wolff, Hans Walter. *Hosea*. 2nd ed. Biblischer Kommentar XIV/I. Neukirchen-Vluyn: Neukirchener Verlag, 1965.
———. *Hosea: A Commentary on the Book of Hosea*. Translated by Gary Stansell. Hermeneia. Philadelphia: Fortress, 1974.

———. *Micah: A Commentary*. Translated by Gary Stansell. Continental Commentaries. Minneapolis: Augsburg, 1990.

———. *Micha*. Biblischer Kommentar XIV/4. Neukirchen-Vluyn: Neukirchener Verlag, 1982.

Wyman, Leland C. *Blessingway*. Tucson: University of Arizona Press, 1970.

———. *The Mountainway of the Navajo*. Tucson: University of Arizona Press, 1975.

Wyman, Leland C., and Bernard L. Fontana, eds. *Beautyway: A Navaho Ceremonial*. Bollingen Series 53. New York: Pantheon, 1957.

Wyman, Leland C., and Clyde Kluckhohn. *Navajo Classification of Their Song Ceremonials*. Memoirs of the American Anthropological Association 50. Manasha, WI: American Anthropological Association, 1938.

Zenger, Erich. *Ein Gott der Rache? Feindpsalmen Verstehen*. Freiburg: Herder, 1994.

———. *Einleitung in das Alte Testament*. Studienbücher Theologie 1/1. Stuttgart: Kohlhammer, 1995.

Zernecke, Anna Elise. "Freude." wibilex Bibelwissenschaft, 2015.

Zgoll, Annette. *Die Kunst des Betens: Form und Funktion, Theologie und Psychagogik in babylonisch-assyrischen Handerhebungsgebeten zu Ištar*. AOAT 308. Münster: Ugarit-Verlag, 2003.

———. *Der Rechtsfall der En-ḫedu-Ana im Lied nin me šara*. AOAT 246. Münster: Ugarit-Verlag, 1997.

Zwickel, Wolfgang. "Tempel." In *Neues Bibel-Lexikon*, edited by Manfred Görg and Bernhard Lang, 3:799–810. Zurich: Benziger, 1988–.

———. *Der Tempelkult in Kanaan und Israel*. Forschungen zum Alten Testament 10. Tübingen: Mohr Siebeck, 1994.

Index of Authors

Abart, Christine, 169
Abusch, Tzvi I., 81n77, 169
Abros, Claus, 169
Ahlström, Gösta W., 169
Ahn, Gregor, 52n31
Aitken, James K., 7n24, 8, 8n28
Albertz, Rainer, 137n21
Alonso Schökel, Luis, 4n10–12, 5, 5nn15, 19
Alster, Bendt, 34n14
Ambrose of Milan, 95
Apffel-Marglin, Frédérique, 169
Arendt, Hannah, 119n12
Arnold, Tina, 144n35
Assmann, Jan, 49n24
Attinger, Pascal, 14n8
Auld, A. Graeme, 153n6

Barney, Gerald O., 121n14
Barth, Christoph, 88n87, 129n13
Becker, Uwe, 163n33
Begrich, Joachim, 2n3, 3n8, 4nn9, 13, 14, 6n22, 57n2, 61n13, 88n86, 151n3
Bell, Catherine, 67nn2, 3
Bellinger, William H., 151n2
Ben Zvi, Ehud, 153n6, 158n19, 163n33
Bentzen, Aage, 67
Berg, Werner, 160n28
Berlin, Adele, 2n2

Black, Jeremy, 3n7, 5nn16, 17, 18, 34n14, 58, 59nn9, 10, 60nn11, 12, 61n14
Blenkinsopp, Joseph, 153n6, 156n14, 162n32
Blume, Clemens, 94n2
Botterweck, G. Johannes, 16n12, 18n13, 20n18
Bowra, Maurice C., 2nn3, 6, 93n1
Boyce, Mary, 51n29
Brosius, Christiane, 170
Brueggemann, Walter, 4n9
Budde, Karl, 160n28
Burkert, Walter, 57n3, 65n20

Câmara, Hélder, 102, 102n11,
Cardenal, Ernesto, 99, 99n6, 115n7
Carroll, Robert P., 153n6, 163n33
Casaldáliga, Pedro, 103, 107n21
Cohen, Mark E., 34nn11, 12, 13, 35n17, 36n18
Conrad, Joachim, 42n10,
Crenshaw, James L., 160n28
Cross, Frank Moore, Jr., 94n3
Crouch, Carly L., 136n18
Crüsemann, Frank, 32n3, 62n17
Cunningham, Graham, 36n17, 78n55, 81n76, 77
Danby, Herbert, 171
Davies, Philip R., 162n31

Deist, Ferdinand E., 150n1
Dijk, J. J. A. van, 34n14
Dreves, Guido Maria, 94n2
Droogers, André, 171
Duhm, Bernhard, 152, 152n4

Edzard, Dietz O., 46n15
Elbogen, Ismar, 95n4
Eisen, Ute E., 57
Eliade, Mircea, 172
Elliot, Dale E., 2
Ephrem of Syria, 95
Eriksson, Lars Olov, 172

Fabry, H.-J., 41n5
Falkenstein, Adam, 37n25
Farber-Flügge, Gertrud, 34n14
Faris, James C., 69n11, 15, 70n16, 75n39, 86n80, 91n90, 92n93
Finsterbusch, Karin, 136n19, 145n37
Fischer, Stefan, 139n26, 140n30
Floyd, Michael H., 158n20
Flückiger-Hawker, Esther, 35n15
Fohrer, Georg, 123n2, 124n4
Fontana, Bernard L., 77n53
Fortune, Richard F., 87n83
Foster, Benjamin R., 57n5
Franciscan Fathers, 74n36, 75n39
Frechette, Christopher, 78n55, 81nn76, 77
Freedman, David Noel, 94n3
Freire, Paulo, 102, 102n10, 116n8, 120, 120n13
Fritz, Volkmar, 32n4
Futterknecht, Veronika, 67n3, 86n80

García López, Félix, 136n18, 138n22
Gärtner, Judith, 133n16
George, Andrew R., 47n18
Gerstenberger, Erhard S., vii, 10n30, 13n6, 14n8, 15n9, 16n11, 19n16, 20n17, 29n1, 31n3, 39n1, 57nn2, 4, 86n79, 81, 82, 89n89, 102n12, 103n14, 108n22, 114nn5, 6, 127nn7, 8, 128nn10, 11, 12, 136n20, 138n22, 143n33, 144n36,

146n39, 151n2, 155n12, 157n16, 159nn24, 26, 162n30
Goetze, Albrecht, 49n24
Gosse, Bernhard, 156n14
Grayson, A. Kirk, 49n26, 50n27
Greenberg, Georgia, 75n40
Greenberg, Henry, 75n40
Grimes, Ronald L., 67n2
Groneberg, Brigitte R. M., 4n15, 5n17, 8n26
Grund-Wittenberg, Alexandra, 140n28, 143n34
Gunkel, Hermann, 2n3, 3, 3n8, 4, 4nn9, 13, 14, 6n22, 57, 57n2, 61n13, 88n86, 151n3, 152, 157n18
Gutiérrez, Gustavo, 105

Haile, Berard, 69n14, 70, 70nn18, 19, 71nn20, 21, 74n37, 76
Hallo, William W., 34n14, 46n16, 48n19, 56n1
Hartenstein, Friedhelm, 4820, 132n15
Hayes, John H., 153n7
Heeßel, Nils, 20n19, 78nn55, 58, 81n77
Heiler, Friedrich, 93n1
Heschel, Abraham Joshua, 138n23
Hieke, Thomas, 126n5
Höffken, Peter, 156n14
Hoffmann, Rodolfo, 98
Hooke, S. H., 67
Horst, Friedrich, 155n11, 160n28
Hossfeld, Frank-Lothar, 6n22, 39n1, 164n34
Hultkrantz, Åke, 175

Insoll, Timothy, 175

Jacobsen, Thorkild, 46n15, 57n5
Janowski, Bernd, 139n25, 143n34
Jeremias, Jörg, 155nn11, 12, 159n22, 163n33
Johnson, A. R., 67, 155n12

Kaiser, Otto, 163n33
Kamlah, Jens, 176
Keel, Othmar, 87n83, 88n84, 109n1, 129n14
Kehoe, Alice B., 176

Kessler, Rainer, 157n18, 159n25, 163n33
Klein, Jacob, 62n16
Kluckhohn, Clyde, 68, 68nn4, 6–10, 69n11
Koch, E. Emil, 94n2
Koch, Heidemarie, 52n32
Koch, Klaus, 112n4, 153n7, 160n28
Kramer, Samuel N., 33nn5, 8, 35n16

Laato, Antti, 136n18
Lang, Bernhard, 153n6, 163n33
Larsen, Mogens Trolle, 53n33
Lenzi, Alan, 78nn55, 56, 81nn76, 77, 83n78, 86n80
Leuenberger, Martin, 7n24
Loacker, Norbert, 1n1
Loretz, Oswald, 157n17
Luckert, Karl W., 69n14, 70n18
Ludwig, Marie-Christine, 60n12
Lust, Johan, 163n33

MacDonald, Nathan, 177
Maier, Johann, 95n4
Matthews, Washington, 69, 69nn12–13, 74nn35–36, 75n39
Maul, Stefan, 36n17, 36nn19, 21, 47n18, 78–79, 78nn55, 57, 79, 79nn59–69, 80, 80nn70–75, 81n77, 86nn79–80, 92n94
Meeteren, N. van, 41n5
Meinhold, Wiebke, 177
Meißner, Bruno, 177
Michalowski, Piotr, 5, 5n16–18, 20, 33nn5, 7, 9
Miller, Patrick D., 2n2, 4n9, 8n27, 64, 64n19, 127n7
Miller, Robert D., 177
Mowinckel, Sigmund, 3, 3n8, 28, 57, 57n2, 65n20, 67, 118n11, 152, 152n5

Näser-Lather, Marion, 178
Nicholson, Ernest W., 151n2, 153n6
Nicholson, Shirley, 178
Niebuhr, Reinhold, 117n10
Nogalski, James D., 156n15
North, Robert, 97

Oswald, Wolfgang, 136n18
Otto, Eckart, 123n2
Petersen, David L., 153n6
Podella, Thomas, 48n20
Pohlmann, Karl-Friedrich, 153n6, 163n33
Pongratz-Leisten, Beate, 133n17
Postgate, J. N., 46n17
Preuß, Horst-Dieter, 41n7, 44n13, 140n30

Rad, Gerhard von, 9, 9n29, 11, 11n1–2, 27, 64
Rambach, August J., 94n2
Reichard, Gladys A., 66, 66n1, 69n11, 70n17, 71, 71nn22–25, 72nn26–30, 73, 73nn31–34, 74, 74n36, 75, 75nn38–39, 41, 76nn45–50, 77n53, 78n54, 91n91–92, 106n19
Reiner, Erica, 178
Reiser, Antonio, 104n15, 105n16
Renner, Erich, 178
Reuter, E., 164
Reventlow, Hennig Graf, 151n2
Reynolds, Kent A., 142n32, 143n33
Richter, Horst-Eberhard, 48n21
Ringgren, Helmer, 2n5
Robinson, H. Wheeler, 117n9
Robinson, Theodor H., 155n11
Römer, Willem H. Ph., 33n5–6
Root, Margaret E., 52n32
Rosengren, Inger, 2n6
Rottzoll, Dirk U., 163n33
Rudolph, Wilhelm, 155n10
Ruffing, Andreas, 50n28

Sallaberger, Walter, 48nn19, 22
Sasson, Jack M., 56n1
Schäfer, Rolf, 176
Scharbert, Joseph, 7n24, 43n12
Schart, Aaron, 158n21
Schmidt, Werner H., 160n28, 163n33,
Schoenborn, Paul G., 104n15, 105n16, 106n19
Schottroff, Luisa, 110n2
Schrage, Wolfgang, 103n14, 114n6
Schramm, Tim, 123n2

Schroer, Silvia, 123n1, 143n34
Schwemer, Daniel, 179
Seybold, Klaus, 43n12, 88n85, 112n3
Sladek, William R., 34n14
Sommer, Benjamin D., 133n17
Spencer, Katherine, 75–76, 76nn42–44
Spickard, James V., 180
Staubli, Thomas, 123n1, 143n34
Stegemann, Wolfgang, 110n2
Steck, Odil Hannes, 118n11
Steiner, Gerd, 48n19
Stemberger, Günter, 180
Stewart, Pamela J., 180
Stolz, Fritz, 57n3, 65n20, 118n11
Strack, Hermann L., 180
Strathern, Andrew J., 180
Sweeney, Marvin A., 157n15
Sznaider, Natan, 10, 10n30

Tătăran, Alexandra, 180
Thiel, Winfried, 163n33
Thureau-Dangin, François, 48n22
Tinney, Steve, 33nn5, 8, 34n10
Tomášková, Silvia, 180
Toorn, Karel van der, 15n10
Turner, Edith, 180

Underhill, Ruth M., 77nn51–52

Vanoni, Gottfried, 143n34
Vanstiphout, Herman L. J., 3n7, 5n17

Vogelzang, Marianna E., 3n7, 5n17
Volk, Konrad, 34n11
Vorpahl, Jenny, 123n2
Vries, Simon Philip de, 124n3, 142n31

Wackernagel, Philipp, 94n2
Wagner, Andreas, 12n4, 123n1
Waldow, Eberhard von, 151n2
Watts, John W., 154n8
Weber, Beat, 139n25
Webster, Anthony K., 181
Weippert, Manfred, 50n28
Wendt, Herbert, 1n1
Westermann, Claus, 4n9, 31n3
Wick, John W., 181
Widengren, Geo, 52n31, 67
Wilcke, Claus, 5n17, 58n8, 61, 61n14
Wilson, Robert R., 153n6
Witte, Markus, 176
Wolff, Hans Walter, 159, 159nn22–23, 160n27, 163n33
Wyman, Leland, 68, 68nn4–10, 69nn11, 14, 77n53, 93n1

Zenger, Erich, 6n22, 39n1, 129n14, 156n15
Zernecke, Anna Elise, 123n1, 143n34
Zgoll, Annette, 14n7, 36nn17, 20, 37, 37nn23–25, 57n4, 61n15
Zwickel, Wolfgang, 32n4

Index of Ancient Documents

SUMERIAN

ETCSL[1]

1.1.3 Enki and the World Order
61–80	63
81–83	63

1.3.1 Inana and Enki
	8

1.3.4 Inana and Gudam
	15
Segm. C, l. 37	15

1.3.5 Inana and An
Segm. D, l. 62	15

2.4.2.03 Praise Poem of Šulgi
Segm. A, l. 20	15

2.4.2.05 Praise Poem of Šulgi
	8
14–39	81
240–257	62

1. ED: While Gerstenberger generally uses the ETCSL document numbers only, I have supplied here the titles found on the ETCSL website.

2.5.3.1 A *šir-namursaĝa* to Ninsiana for Iddin-Dagan
1–16	60

2.5.4.01 Praise Poem of Išme-Dagan
403	15

2.5.4.03 Hymn to Nibru and Išme-Dagan
13	15

2.5.6.2 A *tigi* to Enki for Ur-Ninurta
1–7	60
47	15

2.6.9.2 Hymn to Ḫaia for Rīm-Sîn
56	15

4.05.1 Enlil in the E-kur
100–108	63
171	15

4.07.2 Exaltation of Inana
60–65	8
63–65	14

4.07.2 Exaltation of Inana (continued)

63	61
65	61
139–141	14
150–152	14
153–154	14
154	14

4.12.1 A *šir-gida* to Martu

59	15

4.19.1 A *balbale* to Ninĝišzida

34–36	13

4.80.2 A Keš Temple Hymn

9	8
14–20	59
28–30	59
38–39	14

5.5.4 The Song of the Hoe

94–97	59
99–100	59

BABYLONIAN

Codex Hammurapi

1,1–41	49

Namburbi ritual

	80

ASSYRIAN

RIMA

I.58 (Šamši-Adad I)	50
I.131 (Adad-narari I)	50

Tiglath-Pileser I

1, I

1–14	49
29–30	49

PERSIAN

Behistun Inscription

	51–51

OLD TESTAMENT

Genesis

1	24
1:3–27	20
1:11–13	135
1:26	63
3	116
3:16	115
9:26	27
11:1–9	116
14:20	27
15:7–20	148
17:1–14	148
20:13	18
20:17–18	84
21:23	18
24:27	27
24:49	18
27ff	110
28:20–22	19
29:21	12
30:1	12
32:23–32	89
34	18
47:15–16	12
47:29	18

Exodus

2:9–11	148
4:12	147

INDEX OF ANCIENT DOCUMENTS

15	62	19	18
15:1–21	133	19:4	138
15:1	154	23	123, 149
15:3	17	23:5–6	124
15:21	94, 113	23:9–22	134
15:26	84	23:33–43	124, 149
17:1–7	45	23:34	123
18:10	27	23:40–43	134
19–20	138	23:40	124, 149
19	21	23:42–43	124
19:9–22	12	24:10–16	138
19:19	18	26:14–33	125
19:23	148		
20:5	19	**Numbers**	
20:12	18	5:11–28	85
20:19	148	12	145
23	123	15:32–36	138
23:1–13	18	22–24	84
23:15	124	23:23	84
23:16b	123	24:3–4	84
23:17	123	24:15–16	84
24:3–8	148	29:12–39	124
24:7	163	36	21
24:9–11	92		
24:9–10	132	**Deuteronomy**	
24:12	147		21, 44, 136
24:15–17	12	3:24	12
32–34	138	5	138
32:20	86	5:23–27	148
33:7–11	138	5:24	12
33:11	132	5:25–27	19
33:18–23	12, 132	6:5–9	143
34	123	6:5	25
34:6	12	9:26	12
34:10–16	110	12	130
40:34–35	12	16	123
		16:11	149
Leviticus		17:9–11	147
4:2	141	17:18	164
4:22	141	18	84
4:27	141	18:10–13	138
10	145	18:10–11	84
13:7–8	87	18:15–18	21
14:3–7	85	20	110
14:57	147	23:2–9	145
16	132	24:6–21	18
16:5–22	80		

Deuteronomy (continued)

27:14–26	125
28:15–68	125
28:54–57	125
29–31	138
29–30	148s
29:9–14	44
30:11	44
30:15–20	44
31:10–11	164
32	62
32:3	12
34:10	21

Joshua

	125
2:12	18
8:34	164
9	110
24:14–15	136

Judges

1	110
5	62, 94, 105, 113, 115
5:1	154
5:2–31	133
18:5–6	138
21:19–21	134

1 Samuel

1:9–18	89
2:1–10	116
2:1	154
9:9	165
9:12	134, 135
13ff	110
14:41	12
15:32–33	110
18ff	110
18:7	113
22:9–10	138
23:1–4	138
25:32	27
25:39	27
28:6	20
30:6–8	138

2 Samuel

2:5–6	18
6	131
6:4–11	132
7	54
8:1–2	110
9:1–3	18
9:7	18
10:1ff	117
16:17	18
21:1–9	117

1 Kings

1:48	27
5:5	135
5:21	27
8:31–53	89
14:1–18	85
14:3	85
14:6–16	85
15:3	85
17:8–24	84, 85
17:24	85
19	54
20:31–34	18
22	63
22:7–8	138
22:19–28	20
22:19–22	132

2 Kings

	125
1:2	85
2:19–22	85, 86
4:13	18
4:18–37	85
4:38–41	85
4:42–44	85
5	85
5:1–19	85
5:11	85
8:29	86
9:13	40
20:1	85
20:4–5	85
20:12	85

22–23	20	8:9a	149
22:8–20	125	8:9b	149
22:8	163	8:10	126, 149
22:10–11	141	9:16–31	159
22:10	163	10:1–40	148
22:13	142	13	103
23:1–20	125		
23:25	17	## Job	
23:26–27	125		
23:26	17		24, 39, 89
24–25	110	1–2	63
		2:1–6	20
		19:11	110
## 1 Chronicles		33:23–26	85
15	87	37:23	17
16	87, 95	38–41	39
16:27	126		
16:28–29	11	## Psalms	
25	87, 95	1	90, 148
		1:1–2	139
## 2 Chronicles		1:1	142
20:22	6	1:2	138, 139
21:15	85	2	54, 55, 113, 116
21:18–19	85	2:1	41, 44
22:5–6	85	2:5	12
		2:8–9	113
## Ezra		2:8	41
7:6	126	2:12	139
9	64	3:1	89
9:9–15	159	3:4	137
		3:7	111
## Nehemiah		4:1	89, 154
8	126, 127, 149	4:3–5	79
8:1–8	21	4:7–9	92
8:1–3	147	5	12
8:1	163, 164	5:1	89
8:2–3	163	5:2–4	86
8:2	126	5:3	137
8:3	21, 163	5:4–6	112
8:5	21	5:4	79
8:6–8	147	5:5–7	12, 129
8:7–12	149	5:8	12
8:7–8	22	5:9–10	111
8:7	149	:12–13	92
8:8	149	6:1	89, 154
8:9–12	126, 142	6:5	12
		6:6	12

Psalms (continued)

Reference	Page
6:9	79
7	112, 141
7:2	137
7:4	137
7:8	41
7:11	137
7:18	128
8	6
8:1	89
8:3	6, 12
8:7ff	115
9:1	89
9:9	41, 44
10	103, 120
11:7	92, 132
12	103
12:5	120
12:6	138
13:4	137
13:6	12, 92
14	99
14:2	144
16	136–37, 141
16:2–11	92
16:2	137
16:6	137
16:7	137
16:8	137, 141
17	112, 141
17:15	92
18	105
18:1–2	42
18:2–3	137
18:3	42
18:31	42
18:47	27, 137
19	90, 139, 148
19A	11
19:2–5	93
19:2	6, 12
19:7–10	140
19:8–11	22, 139, 142
19:8–10	140
19:8–9	140
19:10	140
19:11	141
19:12–14	141
19:13	141
19:14	142
21:8	12
21:10	12
22	31, 72, 97, 100
22:2–3	86, 137
22:2	88
22:4	6, 27, 31
22:6–8	111, 114
22:6–7	31
22:12–18	114
22:13–14	88
22:17	88
22:20	137
22:23	31
22:25	92
22:26–27	129
22:32	17
23:1	137
24:1	40
24:8	4
25	148
25:2	129, 137
25:5–7	12
25:28	142
26	112, 135
26:1	135
26:9	142
26:11–12	92
27:1	137
27:10	18
27:13	92
28:1	137
28:6	27
28:7	137
28:8	12
29	40, 63
29:1–2	6, 11, 26, 38
29:1	63, 93
29:9	93
29:11	12
30:3	137
30:5–6	128
30:12–13	92, 129
30:13	137
31:4	137
31:6	19

INDEX OF ANCIENT DOCUMENTS

31:15	137	39:13	86
31:20–25	92, 128	38:19	87
31:20–22	30	40	103
31:22	7, 27, 30	40:4	96, 97
32:1–2	139	40:5	139
32:10	92	40:6	4
33:3	7, 96	40:11	17
33:4–5	20	40:17–18	92
33:5	17	40:17	31
33:6	20	41:2	139
33:8	41	41:5	84
33:9	20	41:12	129
33:20	42	41:13	92
34:1	89	41:14	7
34:2	7	42–83	90
34:4	7	42:3	132
34:5	144	42:6	128
34:9	139	42:12	128
34:15	12	43:3	8
35	103	43:5	128
35:1–8	111	44	29, 89, 133, 141
35:3	138	44:2–9	29
35:9–10	30	44:6	29
35:11–16	111	44:9–22	112
35:13–14	118	44:9–16	114
35:15–16	129	44:9	29
35:18	31	44:15	41, 44
35:19–26	111	45:3–7	113
35:23–24	137	45:5	63
35:27	31, 92	46	132
36:6–11	92	46:5	130
36:6–7	8	46:8–11	118
36:8	31	47	39, 133
37	103	46	62, 94, 130
38	86–87, 97, 112	46:2–7	132
38:2–11	141	47:2–3	42
38:2–4	87	47:2	40, 133
38:2–3	87	47:3	40, 41, 44
38:3–8	114	47:4–5	43
38:4–6	87	47:4	41, 44
38:4–5	86	47:5–9	44
38:6	86	47:5	44
38:4b	87	47:7	43
38:10	87	47:8	40
38:12–13	87	47:9–10	42
38:16–17	87	47:9	40
38:17	87	47:10	42, 44
38:22–23	87	48	62, 94, 130

Psalms (continued)

48:2	4
48:2b–3	130
48:5–7	132
49	103
50	148
50:2	92
50:12	41
51:1–2	89
51:2	154
51:3–14	141
51:15	142
51:16	17
51:17–18	94
52:1–2	89
52:3–7	79
52:10	92
54:1	89, 154
54:3–4	86
55	87–88, 103
55:1	154
55:5–6	88
55:10	88
55:11	88
55:13–15	88
55:16	88
55:24	88
56:13–14	92, 128
57	128
57:2–3	86
57:3	19
57:6	128
57:8–12	128
57:10	41, 44
58	63
58:2–3	79
59	128
59:6	31
59:7	88
59:10	31
59:12	42
59:14	41
59:15–16	88
59:17–18	92, 128
59:18	31
60	156
60:13	12
61:1	154
61:2–3	86
61:4	12
62:4	79
62:6–9	92
62:8	12
62:11	79
62:12	4
65	135
65:6	12
65:8	41, 44
65:10–14	134
66:20	7
67:1	154
67:5	41, 44
68	113
68:4–5	133
68:13–22	133
68:20	7
68:35	12
68:36	7
69	97
69:2–3	102, 129
69:25	12
69:31–37	128
71:15–18	17
72:8	41
72:9–11	113
72:18	7
72:19	7, 12
73	103
74	112, 132
74:4–8	112
74:9	154
74:13–15	4
74:13	12
74:18–23	112
76	62, 94, 130
76:1	154
76:8–9	132
76:12–13	132
77:3	144
77:14	4
77:15	4
78	62, 133, 148
78:5–8	133
78:32–39	133
79	132

INDEX OF ANCIENT DOCUMENTS 195

79:11	12	93:5	44
81	62	94	39, 103
82	63	94:1	12, 19
82:1–4	20	95	43, 44, 54, 133
83	112, 156	95:1–2	133
83:13	112	95:3	40
83:15	112	95:6–7	44, 159
84	130, 131	95:7c–11	44
84:3b	130	95:10–12	44
84:4	132	96	93, 133
84:5–6	139	96:1–3	40
84:5	130	96:1	7, 96, 97
84:13	139	96:3	40
85:11–12	8, 12, 63	96:4	40
86:15	12	96:5–6	44
87	130	96:6	40
87:3	130	96:7–9	44
87:7	130	96:7–8	11, 26
88	88–89, 103	96:7	6
88:5–7	102, 129	96:10–13	41
88:8	88	96:10	40
88:9	88	96:11–12	134
88:11–13	31	96:13	40, 44
88:13	17	97	133
88:15	88	97:1	40, 41, 134
88:19	88	97:4	40
89	29, 54, 133, 141, 148	97:5	40
89:2–38	29	97:6–7	44
89:12	41	97:7	44
89:13	29	97:8	134
89:14–15	29	97:9	40
89:15	8	97:11–12	134
89:11	8	98	93, 133
89:15	18–19, 63	98:1	7, 96, 97
89:38–45	112, 114	98:2	40
89:53	7	98:3	41, 43
90	64	98:4	134
90:7–9	141	98:7–9	41
90:7	12	98:7	40
90:8	141	98:8	6, 134
90:11	12	98:9	40, 44
91	88, 128	99	133
92:6	4, 31	99:1	40
93—100	39	99:2	40
93	44, 133	99:5	43
93:1	40	99:8	43
93:3–4	6	99:9	43
93:3	42	100	134, 159

Psalms (continued)

Reference	Pages
100:1–2	134
100:3	44
102:1	89
102:11	12
103:3	84
103:8	12
103:11	12
103:17	12
104	134, 135
104:1–2	92
104:1	4
104:2–9	135
104:10–23	135
104:10–12	135
104:16–18	135
104:20–22	135
104:27–28	135
104:31	135
104:34	135
104:35	142
105	62, 133, 148
105:2–3	133
105:15	154
105:43	133
105:44	41, 44
106	133, 148
106:3	139
106:6	159
107	31, 97
107:4–6	86
107:10–13	86
107:17–19	86
107:23–28	86
108:4	41, 44
108:13	12
109	129
109:6–20	88
109:8–13	111
109:9–20	111
109:17–18	112
109:30	128
110	55, 113, 116
110:1	114, 115
110:5–6	114
111	148
112:1	139
113:4–5	12
114	133
115:1	12
117:1	44
117:2	8
118	133
118:10–11	133
118:15	133
118:24	133
118:27	133
119	22, 54, 90, 127, 140, 142, 143, 144, 148
119:1–3	139, 144
119:1	139
119:2–7	143
119:2	139, 144
119:4	144
119:7	143
119:8	144
119:11	22, 144
119:12	143, 144
119:13	143, 144
119:14	143, 144
119:15	144
119:16	143, 144
119:17–19	143
119:20	143, 144
119:21	142, 145
119:22	144
119:23	144
119:24	143, 144
119:25–28	143
119:25	145
119:26	144
119:27	144
119:30	144
119:33–40	143, 144
119:37	145
119:38	144
119:40	143, 145
119:44	143, 144
119:45	143, 144
119:46	143
119:47–48	143
119:47	143, 144
119:48	144
119:50	145
119:51	142, 145, 149

INDEX OF ANCIENT DOCUMENTS

119:53	142, 145	119:117	144
119:55	144	119:118–119	145, 149
119:59–60	144	119:118	145
119:61	142, 145, 149	119:119	142
119:62	143, 144	119:120	139, 144
119:63	144	119:122	142, 149
119:66	143, 144	119:123	143, 144
119:67	144	119:124–25	143
119:68	143, 144	119:125	144
119:69	142, 145, 149	119:126	149
119:70	144, 145	119:127	143, 144
119:71	144	119:129–130	143
119:72	139	119:129	140
119:73	144	119:130	144
119:74	144	119:131–135	143
119:75	144	119:131	143
119:77	143, 144	119:139	142, 145, 149
119:78	142, 144, 149	119:140	143, 144
119:79	144	119:142	139
119:81–82	143	119:143	144
119:83	144	119:144	139
119:84–87	149	119:145–147	143
119:85	142, 145	119:148	144
119:86	144	119:149	145
119:87	144	119:150	145, 149
119:88	143, 145	119:151–152	144
119:89	144	119:151	143
119:92	144	119:154	145
119:93–94	143	119:155	142, 145
119:93	139, 144, 145	119:156	143, 145
119:94	143, 144	119:157	149
119:95	145, 149	119:158	142, 145, 149
119:96–99	144	119:159	143, 145
119:96	144	119:160	139, 143
119:97	143, 144	119:161	149
119:101	144	119:162	143
119:103	139, 143	119:163	143
119:105	139	119:164	144
119:106	143, 144	119:171	143
119:107	145	119:172	139
119:108	141	119:174	143, 144
119:110	142, 143, 145, 149	119:175	143
119:111–112	144	120–134	130
119:111	139	121:1	130
119:112	143	121:3–8	130, 138
119:113	142, 143, 145	122:1	130–31
119:115	145	122:5	132
119:116–117	143	122:6–9	131

Psalms (continued)

124	132
126	135
126:1–6	131
126:2–3	4
130:1–2	86
130:1	102, 112, 129
132	54, 62, 94, 130, 131
132:5	132
132:9	131
132:11	132
132:16	131
133	18
135–136	133
135	62
136	62
137	94, 130, 156
137:6	130
137:7–9	132
137:8–9	112
137:9	132
138:5–6	4
139	64
143:11	12
144:1–2	42
144:9	7, 96, 97
145:6–7	17
145:7	18
145:8	12
145:11–12	12
147:3	86
148	6, 16, 26
148:1–4	27
148:7–12	27
148:11	41, 44
149:1	7, 96
149:7	41
150:2	12

Proverbs

3:3–4	18
4:4	147
8	17
19:22	18
21:21	18

Qoheleth/Ecclesiastes

	125
7:15–18	142

Isaiah

	24, 85, 161, 164
1:1	156
1:6	86
2:1–5	159
5	102
6:3	93, 151
9:1–6	55
9:5	19
10:5	49
10:21	19
12:1–2	151
12:3–6	151
13–23	45
19:3	138
25:1	151
25:5	151
25:9	151
26:1–6	151
26:12	12
30:18d	151
34:1	44
38	38, 151
38:1	85
38:4–5	85
38:9	154
38:10–20	29, 128
38:17–20	29
38:21	85
38:31	86
40:12–17	151
40:22–24	151
40:26	151
40:28–29	151
41:1	41, 44
41:5	41
41:13	151
42:4	41
42:5	151
42:10–12	42, 151
42:10	7, 41, 96, 97
42:12	41
42:15	41

43:1	151	56:7	89
43:4	41, 44	57:15	151
43:9–10	41	59:16	7
43:9	44	59:17–20	133
43:14	151	59:17	17
43:15	151	59:18	12
43:16–17	151	60:1–3	92
44:2	151	61:10–11	151
44:6–8	39	63:1–6	17, 110, 133
44:6–7	24	63:5	7
44:6	151	63:7—64:10	151
44:23	151	63:7	151
44:24–28	39, 151	63:10	110
44:28	53	65:1–16	145
45:1–7	53	65:17–25	97
45:6–7	24, 151		
45:11	151	**Jeremiah**	
45:15	151		153, 161, 163, 164
45:18	151	1–2	138
45:22	41	2:6	151
45:24	17	5:22	151
46:10–11	151	5:24	151
47:4	151	7:1–10	18
48:12–13	24	7:1	21
48:12	151	7:3	165
48:17	151	10:6–7	151
48:20	151	10:10	151
49:1–6	39	10:12–16	151
49:1	41, 44	11:1	21
49:5	151	11:18–22	151
49:7	151	12:1–6	151
49:13	151	12:1–4	89
49:15	18	14:2–14	151
49:22–26	39	14:14	156
51:4	41	15:10–21	151
51:5	41	15:10–18	89
51:8	16	16:19	41
51:9–11	133	17:12–18	151
51:15	151	18:18–23	151
51:17	17	18:19–23	89
51:22	151	20:7–18	89, 151
52:7–12	39	22	102
52:9–10	151	23:9–40	21
52:10	41	23:16	156
54:10	12	23:29	21
55:4	41, 44	25–26	138
55:10–11	21	26	21
56:1–8	145		

Jeremiah (continued)

30:1	21
31:7	151
31:35	151
33:2	151
34:1	21
35:1	21
36	20, 21, 165
36:4–26	163
36:4	163
36:6	163
36:14–26	142
36:32	165
46–51	45
49:9	156
49:14–16	156
50:28	12
51:8	86
51:10	151
51:15–16	151

Lamentations

1–5	94

Ezekiel

	161, 164
1:26–28	12, 92
3:12	27
7:26	156
8	145
10:4	12
12:22–27	156
20:10–26	142
20:25	142
21:26	138
34:23–24	55
43:2	12

Daniel

2	38
3	6, 162
3:1–25	29
3:24	29
3:26–45	29
7	117
8	156

8:7	85
9:5–16	159
9:7	17

Hosea

5:8—6:6	159
5:8–14	158
5:14b–15	159
6:1–6	158, 159
6:1–3	151
6:3	92
12:11	156
14:3–4	151

Joel

1–2	151, 157
1:2—2:27	156
1:2—2:17	156
2:13	12
2:16	6
2:18—4:21	156
2:21	151
2:23	151
3–4	157

Amos

1–6	101
1:2	19
1:3—2:3	110
4:13	151, 160
5:1–3	159
5:8–9	160
5:8	151
5:23	94
6:5	94
8:8	160
9:5–6	151, 160

Obadiah

	156
1	156

Jonah

	31, 38, 154
1:9	136

2	29, 151	Zechariah	
2:2	154	2:14	151
		7:9–10	18
Micah		9:9–10	55
	158, 163	9:9	151
1:8–16	157, 159	9:10	41
3:6	156	10:2	138
3:11	147	12:1	151
4:1–5	159		
4:2	147		
4:4	135	✹	
4:5	157		
5:1–5	55	## APOCRYPHA	
5:4–5	157		
5:4	12	**Sirach**	
5:8	157	27:23	86
5:14	12		
6:6–8	157, 159	**Prayer of Azariah**	
7	157		127
7:1–6	18		
7:8–20	157, 159	**Song of the Three Men**	
7:18	19		127
Nahum			
	158	✹	
1	151		
1:1–11	158	## NEW TESTAMENT	
1:1	156		
1:2–8	158	**Matthew**	
2–3	158	4:17	55
		5:30–42	110
Habakkuk		5:43–48	120
	154–55, 158	9:15	107
1–2	155	13:24–30	110, 119
1:1	154	19:24	120
1:2–4	159	23	102
1:12–14	159	23:13–32	110
1:12–13	151	25	102
2:2–3	156	25:31–46	119
3	151, 155, 161		
3:1	154	**Mark**	
3:18–19	151	1:15	55
		11:17	89
Zephaniah		13	117
3:14–15	151, 159	14:26	95

Luke

1:46–55	94
1:68–79	94
2:29–32	94
10:9	55
18:18–27	102
23:43	107

John

6:35	107
8:7	119
8:36	107
11:25	107

Romans

3:9–20	99
13:1–7	110

1 Corinthians

14:15	95

Ephesians

5:19	94, 95

Philippians

2:5–11	94

Colossians

3:16	94

1 Timothy

3:16	94

James

5:1–6	110
5:13	94, 95

Revelation

	117
1–12	94
5:9	94, 95
6:10	94
7:10	94
7:12	94
11:17–18	94
12:10–12	94
14:3	94, 95
15:3–4	94
15:3	94
19:1–8	94

www.ingramcontent.com/pod-product-compliance
Lightning Source LLC
Chambersburg PA
CBHW020340240426
43662CB00048B/720